Also available at all good book stores

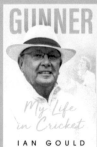

9781785316302

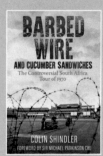

9781785316340

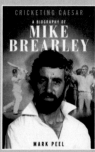

9781785316623

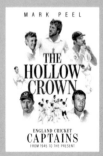

9781785316630

9781785316395

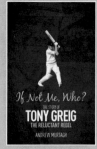

9781785316418

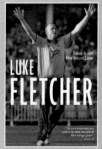

9781785316876

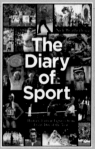

9781785316289

9781785316197

THE
THIN WHITE LINE

THE
THIN WHITE LINE

The Inside Story of
Cricket's Greatest Scandal

NICK GREENSLADE

First published by Pitch Publishing, 2020

Pitch Publishing
A2 Yeoman Gate
Yeoman Way
Worthing
Sussex
BN13 3QZ
www.pitchpublishing.co.uk
info@pitchpublishing.co.uk

A CIP catalogue record is available for this book
from the British Library.

ISBN 978 1 78531 733 0

Typesetting and origination by Pitch Publishing

Printed and bound by TJ International, Padstow, UK

CONTENTS

FOREWORD

ON THE evening of Saturday, 28 August 2010, I sat on the sports desk of the *Sunday Times* waiting for the first editions of our rivals to be brought to the editorial floor. The arrival of the early copies of the Sunday papers, usually shortly before 10pm, always livened up our Saturday nights. Here was a chance to compare oneself against the competition. In the instances where one of them had an eye-catching exclusive, there was the opportunity to, in the best traditions of journalism, rip it off and include it in our later editions.

Word had got around that day that the *News of the World* had something big in the offing because the *Sunday Times* shared a parent company, News International, and offices with the tabloid. Both titles were printed on the presses a few floors below us at Wapping. This meant that the production staff who worked across both papers would receive advance warning if a larger print run – the tell-tale sign of a juicy scoop and expected spike in sales – was needed. 'They must have something good tonight,' were the words one of them would invariably utter with a cheeky grin as they walked through the *Sunday Times* floor around Saturday teatime.

When it arrived that evening, the *News of the World* did not disappoint. The front page said it all: *CAUGHT! Match-fixer pockets £150k as he rigs the England Test at Lord's.* A frantic effort meant that around midnight the last edition of the *Sunday Times* sport section headed to the printers with news of the allegations on its front page. By the time I left our east London headquarters to drive back to Kent and Saturday night became Sunday morning, they seemed to

7

be the only topic of discussion on the late-night news bulletins and phone-ins.

If I'm honest, I was not quite as gripped as those on the radio. There was always a pinch of salt that had to be sprinkled over *News of the World* exclusives. Its front-page scoops were often titillating but seldom gave pause for thought. I had also been slightly sceptical about fixing stories in cricket because of the number of people who would have to be in on the conspiracy for it to come off.

On the other hand, this was one newspaper edition that would not be condemned to a second life as tomorrow's fish and chip paper. It was all there in black and white – the captain, Salman Butt, and his two best bowlers named and shamed – and in glorious technicolour – the photos of Mohammad Amir and Mohammad Asif bowling no-balls to order against England at Lord's. And, if suspicion hung over any one country within the cricket community, then it was Pakistan. The way they had played that summer gave the impression they weren't too bothered whether they won or lost.

When play in the Test resumed at Lord's on the Sunday morning, it seemed that that day's copy of the *News of the World* was all anyone in cricket or the media wanted to read or talk about. The action out in the middle was a sideshow. It helped of course that the story had broken during the 'silly season' – that period in the late summer when many public figures, readers and journalists are away on holiday and the appetite for and availability of 'hard' news drops off.

It was still dominating headlines, albeit those on the sports pages, by the end of that week and was given renewed vigour when the limited-overs series between the two countries descended into acrimony the following month. It wasn't until I started talking to some of the England players that I fully appreciated how difficult that period had been for them too.

Over the following months, in 2010 and 2011, my interest in the *News of the World* grew as the drip-feed of phone-hacking and cover-up allegations in *The Guardian* became a torrent. I can still recall the shock in the *Sunday Times* and everywhere at News International when at 4pm on Thursday, 7 July 2011, company chairman James Murdoch announced in an email that the next edition of the paper would be its last. I even had to ask one of my colleagues to read the email again to check that I had understood it properly.

Yet the spot-fixing story was never tainted by the scandal that led to the title's demise. Nor has it been undermined by the criminal conviction which ended the journalistic career of Mazher Mahmood, who had been until then the most famous reporter of his generation.

I owned a flat near the News International building and had rented it out over the years to *News of the World* staffers. I knew from them and from other journalists that its team worked hard (and played hard), were fiercely loyal and were cut-throat in maintaining its position as industry leader. You could fault their ethics but you couldn't fault their tabloid tradecraft. The more I researched the spot-fixing investigation, the more impressed I was by the ambition of its team and Mahmood's tenacity and ability to get the story over the line. For all his hunger to expose criminality, however, I don't think it ever occurred to him or his colleagues that the men they were accusing would eventually end up behind bars.

If I'm honest, I miss the kind of old school journalism which the *News of the World* stood for. It was a world where the hacks doing the digging were often mirror images of the rogues they were exposing: quick-witted, resourceful and – let's not deny it – downright devious at times. Morals, like expenses claims, were made up as you went along. Even if the Leveson Inquiry of 2011–12 had not reined in some of the sharper practices, the dwindling budgets of national newspapers have limited the scope of editors to pursue the kind of operation which Mahmood made his trademark. One reason why the phrase 'the Sunday papers' is not heard so often these days is because the *News of the World* is no longer around to stir things up.

Was my love for cricket soured by what happened at Lord's in August 2010? Only a little. We had already had a similar scandal involving Hansie Cronje ten years earlier (in another game involving England) and there had been plenty of innuendo about international cricket in the intervening period. There had certainly been cynical remarks in the *Sunday Times* office earlier that summer when Pakistan looked as if they were going to blow simple chances to beat Australia at Headingley and England at The Oval.

The lesson I should have learnt from those two Tests and which became apparent as I researched this book is that, of all the cricketing nations, Pakistan is the most infuriating and entrancing. It is a country that has produced all-time greats – Imran Khan, Waqar Younis, Wasim Akram and Inzamam-ul-Haq – and others who would be ranked among the best of their generation – Mohammad Asif and Mohammad Amir would fall into that category. Yet it also seems to be in a perpetual state of turmoil on and off the pitch. Rather wonderfully, it is still capable of producing some brilliant cricket amidst the chaos. It's easy to forget that at the time of the third no-ball bowled at Lord's, Pakistan looked well set to draw a series they had been trailing 2-0.

This book would not have been possible without the co-operation of those who had worked for the *News of the World*. Foremost among them is Mazher Mahmood. From our first meeting at the Copthorne Tara Hotel in Kensington (nice touch, Maz), he could not have been more helpful. Others who offered to share their time and memories were Colin Myler, Tom Crone, Bill Akass, Ian Edmondson, James Mellor, Neil McLeod, Conrad Brown, Matthew Drake, Phil Whiteside, Paul McCarthy and Sam Peters. Rebekah Brooks and Angus McBride of News UK also helped facilitate access to some of the key documents from the paper's archive.

From the England side in the Lord's match, Andrew Strauss, Graeme Swann, Alastair Cook and Paul Collingwood shared their thoughts. Though he arrived in this country shortly after the Test, Shahid Afridi's perspective of his Pakistan team-mates was critical. Former England captain Michael Atherton, now a peerless broadcaster at Sky and cricket correspondent at *The Times*, agreed to meet and was particularly helpful in the telling of Mohammad

Amir's story, as was another of his England predecessors, Mike Brearley.

Both Atherton and Brearley pointed me in the direction of Amir's solicitor, Gareth Peirce. It would be hard to find a better criminal defence lawyer in this country than Peirce, who provided as much assistance as confidentiality allowed.

Mazhar Majeed's brother, Azhar, graciously gave his time. Other key sources of information about Majeed and the politics of the Pakistan dressing room were the journalist Vivek Chaudhary and Southall caterer Dilawar Chaudhry. To sit in Dilawar's TKC restaurant in west London, where touring teams have dined over the decades, and to hear him talk about cricket is to appreciate how strong the feeling of the immigrant community in England is for the Pakistan side and to understand how often they have been let down.

From the International Cricket Council (ICC), Haroon Lorgat, Ravi Sawani and Colin Gibson were invaluable, as was Keith Bradshaw of the Marylebone Cricket Club (MCC). Michael Beloff and Albie Sachs spoke freely about the tribunal they presided over in Qatar. Yasir Patel, who provided legal representation to Salman Butt, spoke to me too. Various other members of the legal and law enforcement fraternities and of cricket officialdom agreed to talk on an off-the-record basis. They know who they are so will I hope understand if I only offer a group thanks to them.

During my time on the *Sunday Times* sport desk, the following have been a great source of support and advice: Douglas Alexander, Stuart Barnes, Alex Butler, Lucy Dupuis, Michael Foley, Stephen Jones, Rebecca Myers, Jonathan Northcroft, Nick Pitt, Peter O'Reilly, Mark Palmer, Paul Rowan, David Walsh, Denis Walsh and Simon Wilde. The friendship of those in News UK's ELP 2017 cohort has been hugely beneficial too. Roger Alton, Jason Cowley and Francis Wheen have been important influences at various points during my career over the years, for which I am truly grateful. Jim Gill of United Agents helped in the early stages of getting this project from an idea to an actual book. Jane Camillin of Pitch Publishing finally got it into print.

Closer to home, I must thank my father for encouraging my love of cricket and my mother and sister for tolerating it. The greatest debt – one I can barely hope to repay – is owed to my wife Denise and our three sons, Patrick, Morgan and Emmet, for all they have given me.

CHAPTER ONE

'THEY DON'T PLAY FOR THE LOVE OF THE GAME, THEY PLAY FOR MONEY, WOMEN AND FOOD'

ON MONDAY, 16 August 2010, Mohsin Khan met Mazhar Majeed at the Hilton Hotel on Park Lane in London. It was late afternoon and was the first time the pair had set eyes on each other. Khan was an Anglo-Indian businessman representing Tata Equity, a private equity firm with links to a consortium in Singapore. The consortium was interested in setting up a Twenty20 cricket league – the shortened form of the game that was proving so popular – in the Emirates. He was 47, well dressed, in a suit but no tie, a good talker and did not drink alcohol.

Majeed was 35, more informally attired in jeans, brown sweat top and a yellow t-shirt, and not lacking in confidence, though he stopped short of arrogance. Like Khan, he was based in England. In fact, he had spent nearly all his life in the country, though his parents were Pakistani immigrants. He was an agent for almost half the Pakistan cricket squad touring England at the time. With so many Asians living and working in the area of the Middle East Khan was targeting, he was an obvious starting point for player recruitment.

Khan had suggested the venue. The Hilton was probably the least grand of the prestigious Park Lane hotels – it was flanked by the Dorchester and the Four Seasons – though it was one of the better known thanks to the brand name. The 28-storey building, looking out on to Hyde Park, had been the first outpost of the

American chain to open in the UK in 1963 and only the second outside the US. It was here, four years later, that The Beatles had first met and fallen under the spell of Maharishi Mahesh Yogi. Eight years after that, the hotel had been targeted by the IRA as part of its mainland bombing campaign. The bomb that went off in the lobby area killed two and injured 63.

The Podium restaurant was located very close to the part of the complex where the bomb had gone off and it was here that the pair met for afternoon tea. Of all the eating and drinking establishments – there was also the Michelin star restaurant, Galvin at Windows, on the top floor, and the more racy Trader Vic's bar and Whisky Mist nightclub – this was probably the most low-key. That suited both parties.

Also present was Khan's assistant Ajit. It was the latter, on behalf of his boss, who had set up the meeting. Two days earlier, Ajit had called what he thought was Majeed's mobile. A woman answered. It was his wife, Sheliza. 'This ain't Mazhar's phone, it's mine. Who are you? How did you get my number?' Ajit answered the first question and dodged the second. Sheliza's suspicions were not wholly allayed but she did agree to put him in touch with her husband so they could talk business. Majeed's interest had been instantly pricked by the talk of earning opportunities for his rostrum of talent.

Forty-eight hours on from that opening call, the mood in their corner of the Podium was rather like a first date – and a blind one at that. With Mohsin Khan nursing a coffee and Majeed explaining that he was fasting for Ramadan, there was no alcohol involved, however. The two entrepreneurs spent the first half hour or so checking out each other's history, long-term intentions and the circles they moved in. Understandably, since he was the one who had been asked out, Majeed was eager to know more about his suitor. 'There's a lot of people out there who know my position, see my position and they're jealous of it,' he said cagily. 'So they try and make trouble for me.'

Khan told him about his backers, their interest in the sport. Majeed liked what he heard but wanted to know how they had got hold of his wife's number, since it wasn't something he usually gave out to business contacts. Khan said he could understand his wariness but he too liked to play his cards close to his chest. Since they barely knew each other yet, he was reluctant to disclose his source. If, however, their conversation concluded successfully, then he would be happy to reveal all at their second appointment.

The agent seemed to accept this as he then went into more detail about his work and the plight of those he represented. Contrary to popular myth, his cricketers were not playing 'for the love of the game' but for 'money, women and food ... How much they are getting paid is a joke.' He said that he managed 'Ten of the players. I do all their affairs like contracts, sponsorship, marketing, everything.' He had done his best to secure them lucrative deals but these amounted to chicken feed compared with what their peers in other countries, most notably across the border in India, were receiving.

Now probably wasn't the most apposite time to be making this point since six days earlier, in Birmingham, a Pakistan side, featuring five of his players, had lost the second Test against England in the most embarrassing fashion. Bowled out for 72 in the first innings, their lowest ever score in Tests against England, Pakistan had been beaten by nine wickets. That put them 2-0 down with two to play in the series.

The financial gulf between the two sides was much starker. While the England players whom they were facing were being paid close to £400,000 a year to represent their country, the Pakistan cricketers averaged around £22,500 each. The England squad's remuneration did not include individual sponsorship deals and other appearance fees. Their opponents could never hope to make up the difference through their own commercial tie-ups because the domestic market in Pakistan was so underdeveloped and unsophisticated.

In India – the yardstick by which so much Pakistani self-esteem was measured – a cadre of star players, meanwhile, were enjoying annual million-dollar incomes thanks to two trends. The first was the focus that Western brands were putting on the burgeoning consumer market in such a vast country. Cricket's popularity meant that the likes of Pepsi, Reebok and Sony wanted to be associated with the game there and its leading practitioners. India captain MS Dhoni would earn $26.5m by 2011 and most of this came from non-playing earnings.

A supplementary form of income had arrived in 2008 with the launch of the Twenty20 (T20) Indian Premier League (IPL). Unlike the elongated Test matches or one-day internationals which stretched across seven hours or more each day, T20 cricket (20 overs per side) meant that all the action could be condensed into a three-hour frenzy packed with explosive hitting, fireworks, dancing girls and pop music blasting out of the PA system. This timeframe appealed to broadcasters and organisers who could stage matches in the evening after work, boosting viewing figures and gate receipts.

By securing huge deals with broadcasters, sponsors and other entrepreneurs, the promoters of the IPL were able to attract the best talent from around the world to come to India to play for six weeks. For nearly everyone in cricket, it was a win-win, unless you were a Pakistani. In February 2009 the government had blocked its players from playing after the foreign ministry judged that their safety could not be guaranteed in India in the wake of the terrorist attacks in Mumbai in November 2008. This state of affairs seemed particularly harsh when Pakistan won the World T20 championship in London four months later. However, copycat leagues were beginning to pop up outside India, again offering the leading international players the chance to pick up quite large sums for just a few weeks of competition. These represented the best opportunities for Pakistan players to recoup the shortfall in remuneration.

This was what Khan and his backers in Singapore appeared to be bringing to the table. 'There will be opportunities for them to earn money,' he said of his putative venture. 'Pakistani players, we can bring them for very cheap as long as there are incentives for them to make money, yeah, in terms of match winnings as well. Then it is easy,' replied Majeed.

The conversation quickly progressed from the getting-to-know-you stage of a first date to open flirting. Khan said he envisaged the prospect of substantial earnings beyond just playing contracts and win bonuses. Majeed took the hint and winked. 'I know what you're talking about because I know what goes on.'

The afternoon had now escalated into a game of 'I'll show you mine, if you show me yours' and Khan took his cue. 'If there's two or three that are on for the other side, the betting side, then good luck, then they'll be really happy,' he said of his paymasters. Majeed flashed some thigh of his own. 'There's more than two or three. Believe me. It's already set up. That's already there.'

The genie was out of the bottle. 'I've got six ready,' Majeed continued, warming to his theme and his companion. 'I've been dealing with these guys for seven years, OK. Who we deal with and how we deal with it is very, very important. That is the main thing. I'm only dealing with certain people.'

'Give us some tips if you've got any,' said Khan. 'If there's anything we need to know in the forthcoming match let me know. Happy to pay, happy to pay.'

Majeed returned to his earlier point. 'If you can find out the information how my number was obtained, from what source, I will sit down 'cos I can see you're a guy I can talk to on a business sense. You get me that information and I'll talk. 'Cos there's a lot of people, as I say. You know what Pakistanis are like. They could record a conversation, go out, it's all over.'

'I know what Pakistanis are like,' nodded the Indian Khan. 'I don't think they're smart enough for this kind of behaviour. But I mean they can certainly spread bad publicity and stir up ... Let's meet Wednesday, Wednesday night. As I say, we are investing a lot of money in this tournament so we don't need any bad publicity. I mean all it takes is a whiff of this and then all that investment has gone down.'

'Get me that information,' said Majeed, 'and you can even meet me tonight.'

'We'll meet Wednesday, inshallah.'

They said their goodbyes and parted. As Majeed left and made his way to the Aston Martin he had parked nearby, he immediately pulled out his phone and listened to his messages. He did not notice the van parked opposite the hotel, just as he had not noticed it an hour or so earlier when he had arrived.

* * *

The email had reached Mohsin Khan's inbox in early August and came with an attachment. That attachment was a collation of 48 texts/emails from a BlackBerry apparently belonging to Majeed. Most of them had a garbled feel and were slang-heavy. Some were quite obviously written by individuals whose first language was not English. Context was also needed because they covered a three-month period. It was obvious, however, what Majeed was up to.

> *20 February 2010 Outbox: Salaam sheikh please make dua [sic] Pakistan win in the cricket match today against England. The game starts at 2pm until 5.30pm London time. And is being played in Dubai. This is very important for me. Thank you Sheikh*

Pakistan were, that day, playing a T20 match in Dubai against England and won by four wickets. Dua is an Urdu term meaning pray or prayer. It was unclear if 'make pray Pakistan win' was a wish or an order. The fact that Majeed considered the outcome of a warm-up game for the forthcoming World T20 tournament 'very important' suggested there was more than just national pride at stake for him.

> *18 March Outbox: It is going so wrong*
> *18 March Inbox: Oh Shit! Why? Omg!*
> *18 March Outbox: I promise u will make double what u have lost today. U will see*
> *19 March Inbox: I've already started get phone calls from*

India. You've put me in a very big mess. You will have to do something now.

19 March Outbox: I thought u were a big player and u cant cover this loss until next time? We are talking millions in the summer with full transparancy.

The above correspondence was sent during and just after an IPL match between Rajasthan Royals and the Kolkata Knight Riders.

25 March Inbox: Come on then mazhar – let's do it. Let's get fucking hold of cricket and squeeze everything we can from it. Azhar

Majeed had a brother called Azhar who was also involved in player management.

10 May Outbox: This will only work if u score in first 2 overs and no wickets. Also even if we bat second inings it is same... Bro also confirm other thing in 7th and 8th over. 1 fall on each... Pleas text me confirm for second thing.

This last message involved communications with mobile numbers outside the UK. One was for a mobile registered in St Lucia, the other in the United Arab Emirates. Pakistan were, that day, playing South Africa in St Lucia in the World T20 tournament.

There were also a message in his inbox which advised caution over financial dealings because two players were 'very much into match fixing alegations' and another which mentioned cricketers and advised: 'we have to have every thing plan and secret plese make sure'

Mohsin Khan's real name was Mazher Mahmood. He was not an Indian businessman, that was just an adopted persona. If he had told him his actual job, investigations editor for the *News of the World*, Majeed would have run a mile.

Insider information was the oxygen of Mahmood's professional existence. The paper even printed a special hotline number in every edition, allowing readers to alert him to any potential wrongdoing. Many of these could be easily dismissed or were handed down to other reporters to follow up. In January 2010, however, a contact, with whom he had dealings previously and whom he later described as a former member of the Pakistan management team, had got in touch about Majeed.

The agent, the source warned, had a shadow life acting as a go-between for Indian gambling syndicates who wanted to fix matches (or certain passages of play) and his players who had it within their powers to do so. This conspiracy ring had already affected the outcome of international fixtures and was planning to do the same during Pakistan's summer tour of England. At this point, the source did not ask for money, nor was any offered. He just wanted Majeed exposed.

Because it came from a reliable contact within the sport whom he knew, Mahmood trusted this one. Yet he found himself constrained. He needed a bit more than unsubstantiated rumour to launch an investigation with all the expense it entailed. He needed a genuine lead or at least a means of gaining easy access to the suspect to check him out. Neither was in evidence in relation to Majeed back in January. Now, with the email, that had all changed. These were the leads Mahmood needed. Just as helpful, he now had contact numbers for Majeed. What he hadn't known was that Majeed had subsequently passed on one of the numbers to his wife, hence the mix-up with Ajit.

A day after the meeting at the Hilton, Mahmood was in Wapping, east London, at the *News of the World* offices, filling his bosses in on the BlackBerry files and his first contact with Majeed. Those bosses were *News of the World* editor Colin Myler and long-serving lawyer Tom Crone. It was rare in the industry for the senior lawyer to enjoy such importance in the editorial decision-making process but, given the nature of the *News of the World's* output, and particularly given the nature of Mahmood's line of work, Crone was a vital cog in the machine. It was also rare for reporters to enjoy open access to the editor. Yet again, Mahmood's importance to the paper necessitated it.

His work in delivering exclusives could essentially be split into two parts: uncovering and exposing criminality, and the celebrity hit job – luring the rich and famous to do (or say they would do) things that they really shouldn't. As a result, he had picked up two monikers, the 'King of the Sting' and the 'Fake Sheikh'. The former spoke for itself, undercover work being an integral part of his work. The latter followed on from that. One of his more popular and effective forms of subterfuge was to pose as a wealthy Arab with huge sums of money to invest in the egos and pet projects of the celebrities whom he targeted. Coming up with the Fake Sheikh's guise had been the easy bit. His natural skin colour allied to an outfit of Arab robes, headscarf and other accoutrements – he had bought the prototype for this costume in 1984 from an Islamic bookshop in Coventry for £9.99 – were all that was needed for first appearances.

This array would have been worthless without visible signs of opulence to back up his credentials. The first step in any sting was usually the creation of a 'front' company in which one of Mahmood's alter egos would be named as the lead investor. Fake websites would be created and swish offices would have to be hired to maintain a façade. This went a long way to convincing celebrity agents that they were dealing with a real player, which itself led to meetings with the stars. These naturally took place in luxury hotels, top restaurants and chic nightclubs around the world. Limousines and chauffeurs would be hired to ferry him and his celebrity victims to and from these locations. There were also a retinue of retainers to make up the Sheikh's entourage – another key element in the charade.

None of this came cheap. An insight into the jet-setting lifestyle the Sheikh led had been provided in his 2008 book, *Confessions of a Fake Sheikh*, which effectively acted as Mahmood's 'Greatest Hits' collection: hiring a villa at the five-star Marbella club in Spain where two of the directors of Newcastle United Football Club had been plied with champagne before making indiscreet comments about their players and fans; hanging around the Executive Plaza hotel in Chicago while TV host Jerry Springer was covertly filmed romping with a porn star and her stepmother; putting Sven-Goran Eriksson up in Dubai's seven-star Burj Al Arab hotel, picking up the tab for a £1,750 meal with him and then hiring a luxury yacht in the marina to loosen the then England football manager's tongue.

The Park Lane Hilton where he had met Majeed had, in March 2001, been the venue for his first meeting with Murray Harkin, business partner of Sophie Rhys-Jones, Countess of Wessex and wife of Prince Edward. That led to an encounter with Rhys-Jones herself who was recorded making a series of indiscreet claims about the royal family and senior politicians, gifting Mahmood another front-page scoop.

By now he was the best-paid reporter in the industry and also one of the most decorated. In 1999, he was named journalist of the year at the British Press Awards, principally for his Newcastle football scoop. Six years later, the *News of the World* picked up the newspaper of the year honour and its then editor Andy Coulson singled out a Mahmood investigation, about a mother willing to sell her baby, as one of the items of journalism that gave him real pride in his job: 'Not to overstate the case, that story, I believe, resulted in a life being saved.'

Paradoxically, he was also one of the least recognisable, even among work colleagues. This visit to the *News of the World* offices was a rarity and he guarded his identity with great care. There were two reasons for this. The first was that several of his undercover operations had ended in the convictions of serious villains. That left him, he claimed, open to reprisals from within the criminal fraternity. He told *Press Gazette* in 2008 that he had already been beaten up once, had guns pointed at him and that a Russian mafia boss had put a £30,000 price on his head. The second risk of exposure was that if any photos of him ever appeared in print then that would be the end of the Fake Sheikh routine. It didn't matter how good the garb was if every agent and celebrity in the West had his face etched on their memory.

As he stood before Myler and Crone, Mahmood explained, as he had done countless times to his bosses before, that he didn't have anything concrete yet but he had a good feeling about Majeed – they would have to trust him on this one. It helped that he was well in credit with the editor. In May alone, he had delivered two exclusives which would have been contenders for scoop of the year. At the start of the month, on the day of the world snooker final, there was an investigation into John Higgins in which the three-time champion was caught on film demanding £300,000 to lose frames in matches to help a betting syndicate. Higgins and his agent had been lured by Mahmood, posing again as a businessman interested in sport, to Kiev where Higgins also revealed how he had tried to bet against himself during one tournament.

Three weeks later, another set-up saw Sarah Ferguson, the Duchess of York, filmed accepting a $40,000 (£25,000) down payment from a wealthy businessman (Mahmood again) in exchange for offering access to her former husband, Prince Andrew. The Duke of York was a British trade envoy at the time and Ferguson believed that she was in line to make £500,000 from acting as the gatekeeper. She needed the money, she said, because she 'hadn't a pot to piss in'.

How Mahmood's source had come by Majeed's BlackBerry messages no one quite knew and clearly that created a grey area legally. On the other hand those messages provided serious grounds for suspicion of illegality. On that basis, Myler and Crone decided this was something worth pursuing. If, as Mahmood had told them, a flash of the cash would get them a seat at the table, then it was worth the outlay. Bev Stokes, PA to managing editor Bill Akass, who handled the financial side of the paper, was told to take out £10,000 from the 'petty cash' till. Mahmood took away his 'seed money' and summoned Conrad Brown to see him.

If there was a second lieutenant in Mahmood's troop then it was Brown. Like many of the other 'freelancers' who dropped in and out of Fake Sheikh investigations, Brown was not a trained hack but tabloid journalism was in his blood. His father Gerry had himself been a *News of the World* journalist and a trailblazer for the kind of muck-raking work Mahmood now undertook. In fact, in his later years, Gerry Brown had been enlisted as part of the team too before his death in 2004.

As well as having a good nose for a story, Brown was also one of the first journalists to appreciate the effectiveness of technology in undercover work, deploying miniature recording devices before their use became widespread in industry stings. His interest in surveillance technology was shared by Conrad who, by his own admission, had no way with words. His son began working with Gerry and 'Maz' in 1993 not long after he left university. When his father died, his importance within the unit grew.

It was Conrad Brown who had been sitting in the van outside the Hilton 24 hours earlier waiting for Majeed to arrive and was still there when he exited. The van was a classic surveillance vehicle, with blacked-out windows that allowed him to film or photograph the outside world but did not allow a view the other way. From this vantage point he had, he would write in a later witness statement, 'captured some very brief footage of Mazher and Majeed leaving the hotel separately using a Sony HDR-X550 hard drive camcorder, which produces high definition video files.' He had also provided Ajit with 'a covert video recording device disguised as a mobile phone, known as a PV900, and showed him how to use it to make a video recording of the meeting. In addition, I helped Mazher hide a Sony MP3 audio recorder in his jacket to make a separate audio recording of the meeting.'

Brown would need his camera again now because the £10,000 which the editor had authorised and Stokes had handed over would have to be accounted for if it ended up in Majeed's possession. The quickest method was for Brown to capture all 200 serial numbers – the money was in £50 notes – as video footage. With that done, all that was left was to get the story straight on how they had got hold of Majeed's number and see if the agent swallowed it.

* * *

Neither Mahmood nor his employers had got to the top of their profession without treading on toes and cutting corners. Born in Birmingham in 1963, Mahmood was, like Majeed, the son of Pakistani immigrants. His father Sultan had arrived in Britain three years before his birth. Sultan Mahmood was a journalist and had soon set up an Urdu-language newspaper, *Mashriq* (The East), in his new home city. *Gharana* (Household), the first glossy lifestyle magazine aimed at Asian women, had followed a few years later.

There were no Urdu language typesetters at the time so the pages were usually handwritten and mostly put together in the family home. Mazher and his brother, Waseem, who both passed the 11 plus, would help their father deliver copies of the publications to Asian-run grocery stores around the city. 'We were thoroughly involved in the social life of the Asian community, and eventually in the wider political world. I remember meeting Harold Wilson. We were very aware of what journalism was about,' said Waseem in 2006.

That his brother might have a different interpretation of what journalism was about would become apparent in 1980. At the age of 17, Mazher enjoyed his first big break in the trade. A conversation overheard in his own home led him to tip off the *News of the World* about a Birmingham-based gang producing pirate videos of the latest cinema releases. 'One of the men I exposed was a family friend, the son of a respected GP,' he recalled. 'My father was furious and threatened to throw me out of the house, as my mother struggled to calm him down.

'I was surprised by my father's reaction; as a journalist himself, one who'd pioneered the first Urdu-language newspaper in Britain, he had always wanted his two sons to follow him into journalism ... But he claimed that my work at the *News of the World* had "blackened the family name", "shamed the community" and that I would be seen as a traitor.'

After freelancing in Fleet Street for five years, Mahmood was taken on as a staff reporter for the *Sunday Times*. 'A three-year stint at *TV-AM*, working as a producer on the David Frost programme, followed,' he wrote in 2008 in the only book he ever published about his career. That was only half the story, though. He had left the *Sunday Times* in 1988 not because he had a job with Frost waiting but because he had been forced to resign. The reasons for this would be regurgitated for many years after by the paper's then managing editor, Roy Greenslade.

The key details, grudgingly acknowledged by Mahmood who had originally preferred to use the term 'disagreement' to describe the cause of his leaving, were summarised by Greenslade thus: 'When Mahmood resigned, he was on the verge of being dismissed for an act regarded within the office as gross impropriety. The facts of the matter were not, and are not, in any doubt. The documentary evidence – which I have – is quite clear. And it is very different from a "disagreement".

'Mahmood made a silly error in a story – the kind that any reporter can make. When challenged about the mistake, instead of accepting the fact (for which he would have received no more than a telling-off), he falsely blamed the news agency and then tried to back up his version of events by entering the room containing the main frame computer in order to alter the original copy. He was found out, and while a meeting was being held in the editor's office to discuss what should be done, he wrote a letter of resignation and left the building. He rightly understood that he would have been dismissed (which was the collective decision of the senior editorial staff).'

After his spell with David Frost, Mahmood returned to the *News of the World* in 1991, this time on the staff. His new employers soon promoted him to investigations editor. In *Confessions of a Fake Sheikh*, his professional memoir of 17 years on the paper, Mahmood was defiant in defence of his methods: 'Subterfuge is a legitimate and basic tool of investigative journalism … Without going undercover my colleagues and I would have no hope of exposing drug dealers, paedophiles and the like.

'Undercover reporting is enshrined in the Press Complaints Commission (PCC) code and is justified where we can show that it is in the public interest and that the material cannot be obtained by any other means. The "public interest" defence includes "detecting or exposing crime or serious impropriety" and "preventing the public from being misled by an action or statement of an individual or organisation". Sometimes the story comes about because of an insider supplying me with the information, and in those circumstances – when they are going to be paid – that too is covered by the PCC code.'

Mahmood would constantly fall back on the PCC code defence when critics of his methods came calling. Roy Greenslade, who would go on to edit the *Daily Mirror* before becoming a respected media commentator, would prove a perpetual thorn in his side. 'Mahmood's methods debase journalism,' he wrote in April 2006. 'They often amount to entrapment and, on occasion, appear to involve the use of agents provocateurs. People have been encouraged to commit crimes they would not otherwise have conceived. As if that wasn't enough, the public interest justification advanced for such activities by the *NoW* is almost always highly debatable.'

Greenslade listed a series of investigations where these charges applied. However, the precipitant cause of his scathing comments was Mahmood's run-in with George Galloway, the former Labour MP now representing the Respect Party in the House of Commons, a few weeks earlier. The venue had been the Dorchester on Park Lane where the politician spent a Saturday night dining with Mahmood, who was posing as an Indian businessman, Pervaiz Khan, with Islamist sympathies. Galloway was known to be a supporter of Muslim causes and later said that Mahmood had tried to coax him into making anti-Semitic remarks and discussing illegal party financing.

The MP refused to be drawn and later reached the conclusion that he had been a target for entrapment – an operation which had Mazher Mahmood's fingerprints all over it. What was more, he had a photo of his nemesis and he intended to release it to as many channels as possible. 'I'm going to publish "wanted" posters next week and I am going to circulate them widely so that no one ever falls for this man again,' Galloway told the media. 'He's an agent provocateur and a disgrace to journalism.'

The *News of the World* denied that Mahmood/Khan had uttered anti-Semitic comments. Lawyers for News International, its parent company, were granted a temporary injunction against publication of his photo. In seeking to extend it further, they argued in court that Mahmood's safety would be jeopardised were his identity to be publicly know. Mr Justice Mitting disagreed: 'I am satisfied that the true purpose of the application [for an injunction] is not the protection of his [Mahmood's] life but the protection of his earning capacity.' Though Galloway was allowed to post his photos they were obviously not seen by a wide enough audience because Mahmood and the Fake Sheikh lived to fight another day.

Around the same time, the paper itself was going through a few difficulties. Founded in 1843, the *News of the World* had for its first 140 years been a Sunday broadsheet, but one which, with its interest in salacious subjects such as crime and sex, embodied much of what would later be regarded as 'tabloid' values. In 1969 it was acquired by Rupert Murdoch, who had also picked up *The Sun* in his first foray into Fleet Street. Murdoch wasted no time in showing where his priorities lay when he bought up the serialisation rights to a memoir by Christine Keeler, the woman at the centre of the Profumo Scandal six years earlier. In 1984 it was transformed into its 'natural' tabloid format and became one of the leading practitioners of 'chequebook journalism' – waving a large cheque in front of anyone who had been involved in a scandal to persuade them to dish the dirt on an exclusive basis.

In 1986 it joined *The Sun* and Murdoch's other two titles in the News International stable, the more sober *Times* and *Sunday Times*, in abandoning the Fleet Street area of London and moving to new headquarters in Wapping where it would shake off the restrictive practices of the print unions. By the late 80s, the *News of the World*, or the *News of the Screws* or *Screws* as it was known for obvious reasons, was selling around 5 million copies each week. By 2006 the internet was starting to make inroads into its circulation and advertising revenue, as it was for all newspapers, but it remained a cash cow within the Murdoch print empire.

It was at this point that controversy intervened. In August of that year, three months after Mahmood's run-in with Galloway, its royal correspondent Clive Goodman was arrested along with a private detective, Glenn Mulcaire. The pair were subsequently charged under the Regulation of Investigatory Powers Act with unlawfully intercepting voicemail messages.

The Metropolitan Police investigation had been prompted by a Goodman-bylined story from November 2005. The report – that Prince William had been lent some broadcasting equipment by ITN's royal correspondent Tom Bradby – was of no great consequence. However, the second-in-line to the throne had discussed with Bradby how such information could have become publicly known and concluded that it was only through someone hacking the voicemail directory on their mobile phones.

The police were alerted and connected Goodman to Mulcaire. Further investigations appeared to show the pair targeting the mobiles of other famous individuals. A month after their arrests, however, company lawyers wrote to the Met saying they had examined how far Mulcaire's links with Goodman or other *News of the World* journalists went but 'extensive searches have revealed the existence of only one piece of paper, enclosed herewith. No documents exist recording any work completed by Mr Mulcaire, monitoring of Mr Mulcaire's return of work, reporting structures or any persons for whom Mr Mulcaire provided information.'

In January 2007 both pleaded guilty to the charges against them. Goodman was sentenced to four months' imprisonment and Mulcaire, six. At the same time editor Andy Coulson tendered his resignation, though he firmly denied that he had known how Goodman had come by his information about the Prince or that other *News of the World* exclusives had come via a similar channel. With those two out of the picture, the *Screws* picked itself up and carried on as normal. Only *The Guardian*, which as a high-minded, liberal, left-wing broadsheet embodied everything the *News of the World* despised, continued to chip away at what it claimed was a cover-up.

Still, when Mahmood mentioned messages downloaded from a BlackBerry an alarm must have gone off in the heads of Myler and Crone. Set against that was the fact that neither at the time of Goodman's arrest nor in any of *The Guardian*'s subsequent reporting had their star reporter been linked to phone-hacking. Even if the texts had been illegally downloaded, it was not at the instigation of anyone at the paper. If 'Maz' said he had a sniff of something big, then past form suggested it was wise to let him follow his nose. So that's what they did.

* * *

It scarcely seemed credible, but just two days after their first meeting, and a mere two hours after the end of the first day of the third Test between England and Pakistan at The Oval in south London, Mahmood was sitting next to Majeed as he called up the visiting team's captain Salman Butt. It was the third significant phone call of the day and marked the moment when the agent was ready to allow 'Mohsin Khan' into his secret world.

The first of those phone calls had come in the morning. Wednesday, 18 August had been agreed as the day for their second date and Majeed was keen to fulfil it. He rang Mahmood and they arranged to meet at 8pm at the Bombay Brasserie on Gloucester Road. This was good because Mahmood knew the lie of the land. It was at the same upmarket Indian restaurant in 2003 that he had followed up another big lead on sporting corruption.

Lured to a meeting with the Fake Sheik to discuss a football match in the Middle East, former FA Cup-winner John Fashanu had, over dinner at the brasserie, claimed that he had made £1.5m working for a Far Eastern betting syndicate. He then went on to list his own fee and those for the players if the Sheikh was interested in fixing a match. Fashanu later said that he had merely been playing along and that he had reported the approach to the police. This was technically true, though he had only gone to the authorities *after* the *News of the World* had contacted him for comment the night before publication.

Majeed would be more circumspect than Fashanu. While much of the night's success would depend on the credibility of the mobile phone 'alibi', it was also important to bolster Mohsin Khan's credentials. To this end, his entourage would be expanded. Fayaz Sayed, another freelancer, was brought in to serve as Khan's business partner; Amanda Evans, a *News of the World* reporter, would play the role of his assistant; Alan Smith, as he had done for Maz countless times before, would act as chauffeur.

The burly Smith chaperoned them into the bar area to meet Majeed before retreating to a silver S-class Mercedes. They sat down for drinks and small talk before adjourning to their table for dinner. This would be the best time to get the tricky business done. It was time for the second big call of the day.

Mohsin Khan began by apologising to his would-be partner that he had not been upfront from the start about how they had come by his wife's phone number. 'We wanted to get in touch with you,' he said, 'but we couldn't get a number through the internet or anyone in cricket.' With a sheepish grin, he told Majeed that they hadn't exactly used normal channels. Khan had a driver whose girlfriend worked in a mobile phone shop. She had accessed one of its phone directories to see if there was anything registered to his name. And there the number was. Strictly speaking, this wasn't legal, but what was a little contravention of data protection laws among like-minded businessmen? Khan was willing to go further to put Majeed at ease. He was now going to call up the driver so he could hear the story first-hand.

The 'driver' was in fact another of Mahmood's stringers, Majeed Singh, who had been primed to expect the call. Majeed Singh fitted the bill perfectly. He was a Sikh who spoke Urdu. The plan was not for him to meet Majeed but, if it ever came to it, he looked and sounded exactly like the kind of discreet and dependable fixer a dodgy Far Eastern syndicate would want on its payroll. Majeed listened and spoke – they both conversed in Urdu – and was satisfied. Time to eat.

The final significant call of the day would occur during the meal. As they ate, the pair discussed arrangements for the planned T20 competition. Majeed said it would be a good idea if he called up Salman Butt. He did this because he wanted to show how close he was to the Pakistan dressing room but also for practical reasons. They would need an idea of the team's itinerary over the nine months to work out when they would be available for the fledgling tournament. As captain, Butt was best placed to provide that. Within earshot of Mahmood, he told his agent that after a series of limited-overs matches against England in September, they would be playing South Africa in Dubai in October and November and touring New Zealand the following month.

The meal and discussions continued. For the second time in 48 hours, there was a flirtatious air. Majeed and Mahmood were like two lovers making eyes at each other, sharing suggestive comments without either actually mentioning the deed they were going to perform. Finally, Mahmood decided it was time to get down to the dirty. He asked Majeed if they could talk more in his car. Majeed agreed and followed him into the Mercedes. Any reservations he might have had were now banished because when Mahmood offered to let him search for recording devices, Majeed said there was no need.

Even if he had taken him up on the offer, it is unlikely that he would have found the Sony MP3 audio recorder which Conrad Brown had expertly hidden within the vehicle. Nor would he have thought to examine the lining of Mahmood's 'bespoke' extra-large Y-fronts which contained a Sony MP3 audio recorder connected to a small microphone in his belt buckle; or indeed what had been inside Mohsin Khan's assistant's handbag – a video camera and another MP3 audio recorder. These had all been installed by Brown just a few hours earlier when the *News of the World* team had met at Mahmood's London home. At this particular moment, Brown was sitting in a 4x4 car, his Sony camcorder having captured the two plotters leaving the restaurant for the Mercedes.

The search offer declined, Majeed got down to business. 'I don't usually speak about these things,' he began in conspiratorial fashion. 'I am very, man of instinct. And I do feel that I can speak to you about this so I am going to speak to you about it. OK. Now, there is very big money it. They've toned down match fixing a lot. They've made it very, very difficult in many, many ways. But obviously, you know, these guys would not deal with anybody ... the only reason they deal with me is professional, they know my background, they've known me for so many years. I've been doing it with them, the Pakistani team now for about two and a half years. And we've made masses and masses amounts of money. I'm not doing no betting, I deal with an Indian party, yeah. They pay me for the information.'

Now he was ready to specify what that information might be. 'Say for example a bracket would open in India, and it would open for 30 runs after ten overs, or 33 runs after ten overs. So what the players would do is for the first three overs, they would score a maximum, they would score 13 or more runs in the first three overs. Right. So then the market goes, expecting it to go high because they are scoring at a higher rate. Then the next seven overs they would score 14 or less. So then the people who know the information would go low and make a hell of a lot of a killing on it.

'Then there's a bowling bracket.' Majeed was now getting excited because he began referring to 'the last Australia match, the second Australia match' and showed a message on his BlackBerry. 'Oh I'm sorry that's another one,' he added before reading out a second text:

Eighth, ninth, 10th bowling, one confirmed with 17 plus one run of no ball in the last over ...

'So say for example Mohammad Asif and Mohammad Amir are bowling, yeah. The market opens at ten overs and, let's say, 32 runs. Asif is going to indicate by bowling a dead ball at the start of the sixth over. That means it's on. In other words he runs up but doesn't bowl the delivery, pretends that he didn't get his stride right and then goes back. That means he's going to do it. Then we know, then we start betting …

'So at the sixth over when he does the dead ball, my people know that the eighth, ninth and tenth over they are going to concede more than 18 runs. They're going to concede more than six runs an over and the last ball of the tenth over is going to be a no-ball. OK. So they know, then everyone's thinking, no they're not because they're conceding only two or three runs an over. So the last three overs they let it all go and they make a killing … So that's brackets. There's brackets and results.'

So what, Mahmood asked, could Mohsin Khan and his people expect from entering into partnership with Majeed? 'Do we get information, like there will be three no-balls in the third over?'

'You will get everything like that. And you get the indication to show if it's on or not. They'll change gloves at a certain point. It all comes through me. I do it all but as I said I only deal with Indian people. We do results now and again. The last one we did was against Sri Lanka in the Asia Cup which was about two months ago.'

Pakistan had played Sri Lanka on 15 June. Sri Lanka had scored 242/9, with Mohammad Amir and Mohammad Asif easily the most expensive of the bowlers. In reply, Pakistan had been bowled out for 226. Their total would have been much lower but for a century by then captain Shahid Afridi, who was not one of Majeed's players. Of those who were Majeed's clients, Butt had been out for 0, the Akmal brothers had scored a combined total of 44 runs with each run out, while Amir had made 5 and Asif was last man out for a second-ball duck.

'And you get a script as well,' he continued. 'In other words, this bowler is going to concede this many runs or more, this batsman's going to do this … If there's a Twenty20, rather than being out for zero it's better that he wastes an over or two and then gets out. But you will never have the whole team …'

'How many have you got?'

'I've got six first-team players. And they are all guaranteed positions.'

'OK, it's against England now, what's happening?' asked Mahmood, scarcely able to believe how well things were proceeding.

'For Friday, you get the information, we deal with everything on the night before or the morning – Thursday night or Friday morning early. We charge anything between £50,000 and £80,000 per bracket. And for results, Twenty20 is about £400,000. A Test match, depending on the situation, can go up to a million pounds.'

'Come on. How do you recover that – a million?' To Majeed this sounded like Mohsin Khan expressing some scepticism, which it was in a sense. Yet this was also investigative journalist Mazher Mahmood probing and prodding for more information. He wasn't to be disappointed

'Let me tell you the last Test we did. It was the second Test against Australia in Sydney. On the last day Australia had two more wickets left. They had a lead of ten runs. The odds for Pakistan to lose that match were I think 40-1. We let them get up to 150 in the morning, and then everyone lost their wickets. That one we made £1.3m. Tests is [sic] where the biggest money is but we are not going to do any results for the next two games because we want Salman Butt to be captain for the long term.'

Majeed's recollection of the Sydney Test was more or less correct. That final day had started with Australia eight down in their second innings and with a lead of 80 – the two batsmen at the crease, Mike Hussey and Peter Siddle, had already enjoyed a partnership of 29. On the final day they added another 94 before Australia were all out for 381, leaving Pakistan to chase 175. They were then bowled out for 139.

Pakistan were said to have 'choked' during their fourth innings chase, though their cause had not been helped by wicketkeeper Kamran Akmal dropping three catches and missing a fairly simple run-out opportunity in Australia's second innings. Akmal would later say that the game had been like a 'scary dream'. The report on the website *Cricinfo* would also put some of the blame on captain

Mohammad Yousuf, 'whose timid tactics in the morning session played into the hands of the Australian batsmen.'

It was clear that something had gone badly wrong on that tour because, though none had fixing charges or even circumstantial evidence brought against them, former captains Younus Khan and Mohammad Yousuf, Shoaib Malik, Rana Naved-ul Hasan and the Akmal brothers were all the subject of disciplinary proceedings for indiscipline or in-fighting soon after it ended.

Mahmood asked about arranging no-balls but Majeed made clear that was small beer. 'No-balls is easy. No-balls, there's not that much money anyway. If you wanted no-balls you could probably get up to 10,000 each. But in terms of results, one-day matches, results are about 450, depending on who we are playing. You can speak to any bookie in India and they will tell you about this information and how much they'll pay. You can make millions, you can make absolutely millions, millions.'

They had come so far in such a short time but Mahmood needed to go further. Braggarts with big mouths were an occupational hazard for him. In Asia, the UK or elsewhere, there were untold young men on the make, eager to say whatever would impress a wealthy contact. Majeed himself liked to give the impression that he knew everyone and everything. He said he had helped set up a £12m book deal for footballer Rio Ferdinand before making an even wilder claim about the Pakistan president, Asif Ali Zardari: 'Everyone knows he killed his wife.'

Yet the detail he had gone into about cricket matches, combined with the BlackBerry messages, looked like corruption. What the story still lacked was evidence to link to his players. Butt could, for example, state he had no idea of his agent's shadow life, while the rest could legitimately claim they had simply underperformed in the matches cited. It was time for Mahmood to put the bait on the hook and cast his line into the water. 'So let's put this to the test, if this is going to work. Would you be able to tell me on Thursday there will be a no-ball in whatever over it is?' Majeed said he would.

'We'll give the boy ten grand, no problem, whatever the rate is,' Mahmood/Khan went on. 'Just give me a no-ball so that our boys have got an indication this is on. Then they'll invest big.'

'Fine. I will let you know on Thursday evening and I will tell you on Friday morning what the no-ball is going to be. I'll give you two if you want. And once you paid then I know that it's real, yeah. The main thing if we do this is to be discreet. The only thing that can ever mess this up is if people talk.'

Majeed had no idea how indiscreet he had been.

CHAPTER TWO

'IT'S TAKEN ABOUT SIX MONTHS TO GET THEM PROPERLY WORKING BUT I'VE GOT THE BOWLERS, THE BATSMEN AND THE ALL-ROUNDERS'

MAZHAR MAJEED was the agent who rose without trace. Born in Croydon in 1975, he was, like Mahmood, the son of Pakistani immigrants, only his parents had settled in London rather than Birmingham. The family home was in Croydon in the south of the capital. His father, who had grown up in Faisalabad, had first worked in a bakery in Notting Hill before opening his own convenience store in Earl's Court.

Mazhar had two brothers and a sister and was the youngest of the four siblings. He attended the local comprehensive, Coulsdon High School. From there he had gone to Middlesex University, where he had studied for a marketing degree. It was an apt specialism because Majeed was all about image and projecting himself. Ambitious for money-making opportunities when he graduated, he found that Western capitalism agreed with his entrepreneurial instinct. He would feel no shame in telling people that his main motivations in life were 'success and money' and his role models were Bill Gates and Lalit Modi, the businessman who had set up the Indian Premier League.

He was unlikely to reach their levels of wealth, but by the age of 30 he was doing well for himself. In 1999 he and a friend, Faisal Hameed, had set up Bluesky Developments, which bought up derelict houses and did them up before selling them on or renting them out. It was a good time to be in the property game because the London market was about to take off. Hameed would later describe his partner as 'a great guy and a straight-up, totally legitimate businessman'.

The profits from the property portfolio had enabled him to expand his empire and Majeed began opening a chain of ice-cream parlours, *Afters*, in Croydon, Tooting and Southall. In 2006 he had bought a house in the upmarket Oaks Road area of Croydon, for £860,000. By now he was married to Sheliza Manji, a European studies graduate of Manchester University. Ann Hewitt, one of their neighbours, recalled that 'they would have lots of people round during the summer. He liked to entertain ... There were hundreds of people at the home.'

With a similar family history and shared hunger for the 'deal', he and Mahmood were almost mirror images. Certainly, Majeed would have looked at Mahmood's alter ego, Mohsin Khan, as an equal, maybe even his better. Money – either to spend or to invest – did not appear to be a problem for Khan. Majeed would have particularly envied his contact network in Singapore because he was himself keen to stretch his tentacles beyond the pockets of London, which they already reached. As well as riches, he craved fame. Given his love of cricket (a passion his father had passed on to him), it was no surprise then that he had tried to insinuate his way into the bosom of the Pakistan national team.

Despite having few contacts in the land of his ancestors, this was not actually that hard. Pakistan were the least organised, one might even have said the least organisable, of all the Test nations. Idolised by their own fans – only India offered any real competition in this department – they were very porous as a travelling unit. The result was that wherever they went in the cricket world they would be surrounded by hangers-on from the local expat community. Some of these were harmless and just wanted to be able to tell friends and family they had been in the company of their heroes. Others wanted to get rich on the back of them.

There was certainly never any shortage of either in England and it was on their tour in the summer of 2006 that Majeed appears to have established a foothold. At this point, Pakistan were passing through one of their more stable periods. Their star batsman, the large and laconic Inzamam-ul-Haq, had been appointed captain in 2003 and begun to turn around an underperforming team. They had come to England on the back of three series victories, one against the same opponents in the previous winter, the others against their Asian rivals India and Sri Lanka.

'Inzy' had been helped by Bob Woolmer coming in as coach in 2004. The hugely experienced, England-born Woolmer had played and coached all over the cricket world and was immune to the politicking that was ever present in the Pakistan cricket hierarchy. He also knew about the dangers of corruption from his time as South Africa coach. In 2000 his captain Hansie Cronje had been disgraced after confessing to taking money from Asian bookmakers. Cronje admitted that $300,000 had been offered to his team to throw a match earlier that year. He added that when 'Bob Woolmer heard about the offer he was very angry about it …'

Woolmer imposed discipline and organisation, but he couldn't have done it without Inzamam taking care of the pastoral side. Religion, namely Islam, became the glue that held a previously fissile ensemble together. For the first time, there was a proper team room in the hotels, where prayer meetings would be held (along with meals and tactics discussions). Inzamam would instruct the younger players to prepare the room beforehand, making sure any mirrors were covered and the prayer mats pointed in the right direction. Then they would all congregate. Even the notoriously unreliable playboy bowler Shoaib Akhtar would show his face.

Dilawar Chaudhry was a Southall-based caterer whose firm had been providing food for Pakistan teams in England for more than 20 years. In that time, he had become familiar with the inner workings of the camp and developed friendships with many of the cricketers. In 2006 Chaudhry saw up close the beneficial effect that these new arrangements had had on tour. Yet he also noted that even Inzy couldn't prevent cricket's equivalents of 'hawkers and peddlers' from getting into the hotel and sometimes into the team room.

Among those to penetrate the inner sanctum were Majeed and his older brother Azhar. The latter was six years older and was registered as an agent in the UK. This was the same Azhar who in March 2010 had messaged Mazhar's BlackBerry with the suggestion that they 'get hold of cricket and squeeze everything we can from it' (to which his younger brother would reply: 'Exactly the attitude I wanted from you yesterday').

The former international Saqlain Mushtaq had introduced Azhar to the Pakistan squad. By 2005, Saqlain was at the end of his Test career but played for Surrey in the English summers. Azhar Majeed had attended a benefit event for his county colleague, Mark Butcher, and left surprised by some of the sums that even county players could command for appearances. From discussions with Saqlain, it was clear that few of the Pakistani players were professionally represented in any of their contractual negotiations in the UK or at home. Azhar realised he could leverage his Pakistani heritage, friendship with Saqlain and sales background to gain their confidence. Once registered as an agent, he was soon up and running, negotiating playing deals with English counties on their behalf.

The squad for that 2006 tour included Kamran Akmal, Mohammad Amir, Imran Farhat and Salman Butt, all of whom the Majeeds would go on to represent, or claim to represent. At 21, Butt was the youngest, while the 24-year-old Akmal was the oldest. They were ahead of their contemporaries in terms of sporting ability but lacked the worldliness that an established cricketer enjoyed. As such, they were easily impressed by public displays of wealth, and Mazhar, who was now tagging along with his brother, was never reluctant to parade his. Talk the talk, buy a round of drinks, take a few out for dinner and on to a casino after – this was often all it took to lure them in. If Azhar became like a benevolent uncle to them, then Mazhar was a slightly older, charismatic cousin. One by one they fell into the pair's orbit.

Other than the brothers' natural sales patter and business acumen, a number of other factors played into their hands in winning them over. The first was the hierarchical nature of Pakistan cricket. The officials of the Pakistan Cricket Board (PCB) were invariably political appointees in a country that was hardly a beacon of liberal democracy in the first place. Some were venal, many were not fit to have oversight of a sport that was entering a period of turbulence. Nepotism was not uncommon. 'Our worst enemy is the PCB,' Inzamam had said to one of his confidants towards the end of the 2006 tour.

With the superstars – Inzamam, Shoaib Akhtar, Younis Khan, Shahid Afridi, Mohammad Yousuf – gobbling up what limited lucrative commercial deals there were on offer, there were few crumbs left for the next generation of stars. This would have grated with Butt, in particular, who was from a relatively affluent background and would have expected better. It all meant that Majeed was that rare commodity in sport – an agent who was actually richer than his pool of talent. With his pad in Croydon, fast cars and 'playboy of the Western world' lifestyle, he was a source of envy and admiration for Butt and the others. What he had, they wanted.

Events on and off the pitch would also conspire to help Majeed strengthen his hold. In 2007 Bob Woolmer collapsed and died during the World Cup in the West Indies. The team had just suffered a shock defeat to Ireland and rumours blazed that the coach had been murdered in a gambling-related hit job. A month later, the captain resigned. With those two gone, the dressing room dissolved into the normal state of cliques and internal squabbling. Before Butt's appointment in 2010, four men would captain the Test team in the three years that followed Inzamam's resignation. None won a series and only Mohammad Yousuf won a Test.

Another key moment would take place in 2009. On 3 March, as it was making its way to the ground in Lahore for the third day of the second Test against the hosts, the Sri Lanka team bus was fired on by what was estimated to be up to 12 terrorists. Five Pakistani police officers were killed and six members of the Sri Lanka team wounded. The attack came three months after Pakistan-based militants had attacked various targets in Mumbai, with the final death toll close to 170. This was the same attack that would lead to their exclusion from the pension fund that the Indian Premier League was fast becoming.

The Lahore shootings forced the International Cricket Council to suspend any international matches in Pakistan. After the atrocity, the team's opportunity to play Tests and limited-overs matches was severely curtailed and that again limited earning opportunities. It also led to them travelling more often to the United Arab Emirates, which began to act as an alternative home. Once outside their own country, their adherence to the Muslim faith was tested by the temptations of the West. Dilawar Chaudhry had once helped one player extricate himself from an argument with a prostitute and her pimp in Soho. There was never any shortage of similar temptations in their new 'home' of Dubai, just as there was no shortage there of shady, wealthy individuals who had the same designs on cricket as Majeed.

Bumbling administrators, a lack of real leadership leading to dressing-room divides, terror attacks at home, constant gripes about inadequate pay – these provided the fertile terrain for the brothers to put down deep roots within the camp.

* * *

By 2008, everything appeared to be going well for them. In September of that year, the *PakPassion* cricket website announced that it was introducing a new column, *The Agent's Views*, to be written by Azhar. It described him as 'a UK based agent who has represented a variety of Pakistani players over the last few years. Some of the players that Azhar currently represents are Salman Butt, Kamran Akmal, Mohammad Yousuf, Mohamed Asif, Abdul Razzaq, Abdur Rauf, Shahid Afridi, Saqlain Mushtaq, Misbah ul-Haq and others.'

Mazhar was not mentioned here but he was far from a sleeping partner. Though he had also taken a majority stake in a local non-league football club, Croydon Athletic, in July 2008, that was really only a vanity project. Cricket was now where it was at for Mazhar Majeed and it was no coincidence that this happened as the fortunes of his other businesses began to nosedive. The precipitous fall in the property market in 2008–09 had left Majeed exposed. The stake in Croydon Athletic was the obvious example of this, but he had also unwisely invested in property in Portugal and Turkey.

By August 2010 it would emerge that he had been a director of 28 different companies, with nearly all of them dissolved. One of them, Valesco Ltd, had been placed in receivership, while another, Able Trading Ltd, was liquidated. Bluesky had been wound up a year earlier with debts of £74,163 outstanding. He also had an overdraft of more than £700,000.

According to one source in whom he confided, it was soon after the economic crash that he first came into proper contact with match fixers in Dubai. This may have been in April 2009 when Pakistan played one-day internationals there against Australia or five months later when New Zealand were the opposition in the Emirates. The fixers were always hanging around team hotels, always Indian and invariably recognisable by their stained teeth – due to the habit of chewing betel nut. One of them had befriended him at the team hotel. As there would be with 'Mohsin Khan', there was the opening chat about cricket and then gambling before the pair quickly moved on to coded references to the financial rewards of a mutually beneficial relationship.

Further chats followed and once the terms of business had been clearly intimated, Majeed was led from the hotel to a Rolls-Royce parked close by. The boot opened to reveal a briefcase crammed with $100,000. There you go, now we are partners, his new friend told him. A business card was handed to him and another meeting was arranged on Park Lane when he returned to London.

Yet Mazhar would also claim that it was Butt who had been the driving force. By June 2009 the batsman had gone from a rising star to bitter and disillusioned pro. During the World T20 in England, which his team would go on to win, he was dropped after three matches. At this point, he and his agent dined together in London. Majeed's account of the night stated that Butt wasted no time lamenting his plight. He was lucky if a sponsor offered him more than £10,000 while others in the squad, less talented than him, were boasting about how many houses they owned. Looking around the dressing room he began to wonder if they had accrued the majority of their fortunes through fixing. If so, he wanted a piece of the action.

It is difficult to tell which of Butt and Majeed was the instigator. It is obvious though that once they had agreed to go down this path they each set about it with great purpose. Pakistan had been dogged for more than ten years by suggestions that players were taking bungs either to fix matches or to provide information to bookmakers and gamblers. If any of this went on during the Woolmer/Inzamam years then it was almost certainly individuals 'freelancing'. What elevated the Butt and Majeed operation was that they co-opted others into a concerted plan. It was this that enabled them to fix brackets and results and make the big money. Mazhar's confidence had been well placed when he told Mahmood, 'These boys are going to be around years and I've got the best boys.' Butt's appointment as captain in July 2010 could only open up more opportunities to cash in.

Majeed wasn't stupid either. He knew that the project hinged on absolute discretion, attention to detail and scorching their trail. That was why he himself had three BlackBerries. This was where the original confusion over the phone numbers had arisen. When Mahmood's source had emailed him at the start of the month, the messages indicated two numbers for the agent – one beginning 07930 and the other 07957. They had called the first, which turned out to be the one now used by his wife. Initial dealings with Majeed were then conducted using the second number. Once he came to trust the undercover reporter, however, he also provided a number for a third, 'safe' phone.

Majeed impressed on his fellow conspirators too the need for covering their tracks. 'We change our phones, and the thing is you've got to get rid of the sim and the phone separately,' he told Mahmood during one of their conversations. 'Obviously there's always a risk in anything we do but all I can do is make them [the players] aware that that is how it could fuck up. How everything can mess up, and they're getting paid well. I'm actually paying them more than other people have offered them because I know to try and cancel that out.'

Majeed had spent much of the previous year following Pakistan on their travels. To the outside world, he was doing what any assiduous agent would – taking care of the off-field needs and interests of his clients. The main purpose of his jet-setting though was to act as the conduit between the Indian syndicates and the players and to micro-manage with Butt the implementation of their plans.

In late 2009, Pakistan were in New Zealand, where they drew a Test series 1-1 and lost a one-day series 2-1. From there it was on to Australia and he was in Sydney for the New Year Test, which Pakistan managed to lose from a seemingly impregnable position. In May 2010 he was in the Caribbean for the World T20 competition. The players would regularly join him for dinner at the villa in St Lucia where he was based.

From St Lucia, it was on to Sri Lanka for the Asia Cup. On 19 June, in Dambulla, Pakistan were set to play India, the first time the two countries had met in almost a year. Indian journalist Bivabasu Kumar found himself sharing a car to the ground with Majeed, who introduced himself as an agent to several Pakistanis. Kumar recalled that 'we instantly hit it off, discussing cricket and the travails of managing cranky players like Asif. While Mazhar agreed that it was difficult to control Asif, he also praised Butt for his charisma on and off the field. He dwelt on the need to keep players informed about the financial dynamics surrounding cricket and how challenging it was to groom them professionally.

'At the stadium, Majeed said he had plans to take Kamran Akmal and some others sightseeing around Dambulla the next day. Clad in a white T-shirt and capris, he stressed the importance of the India–Pakistan match and how vital it was for some of the younger players in the squad. He was especially anxious about Asif as the pacer was making a comeback after a long time and a flop in an India game would be a setback. Whether Mazhar's anxiety was heightened because he had money riding on the game is a matter for speculation, but his discomfort was evident.'

It was possible Majeed did have money on the game, though the only result in the tournament he claimed to Mahmood to have fixed was Pakistan's defeat to Sri Lanka four days earlier. But Kumar's account is instructive because it hints at the differing views the agent had of his players. Clearly, Butt was his most important asset. Not only was he effective in all formats of the game, but he had also been appointed vice-captain at the start of June, making him 'next in line to the throne'. There was something else though that set him apart from the others – he was from a wealthy, upper-middle-class family in Lahore.

The others whom he represented were largely from dirt-poor, rural backwaters and difficult to control (even Asif would have agreed that he was 'cranky'). Their English was poor and, from his conversations with Mahmood, it was obvious he did not rate their intelligence. If there is a power balance in an agent–player relationship, then it invariably tilts toward the player. His relationship with Butt aside, however, Majeed appeared to be the master and the cricketers the servants. This was clear not just from the way he talked to Mahmood about the fixing – that he was giving the orders and they were carrying them out – but also in the contemptuous tone he was prone to adopt when referring to them. There had even been an occasion on one tour when he was reported to have turfed one of them out of his hotel room so he and his brother could share it.

Dilawar Chaudhry had also spotted how close Butt and Majeed were. During the earlier half of the 2010 summer, when Pakistan had been playing Australia in England, he had been at the team hotel when Majeed arrived to pick up Butt in his Aston Martin. When Majeed asked him if he wanted to take the wheel, the 25-year-old showed all the excitement of a teenager being handed the keys to his first car by his dad. Shahid Afridi's contempt for both was evident when he turned to Chaudhry and said, 'Even if you turned up in a yellow, two-door Suzuki I'd still rather hitch a ride from you than him.'

Afridi asked Chaudhry to have a word with the 18-year-old Mohammad Amir, whom he could see falling under the spell of Butt and Majeed. Chaudhry did as promised but while Amir made the right noises and gestures during their conversation, it was clear nothing was going in. 'The boy's gone,' he told Afridi afterwards.

Afridi's concern was long-standing. A month earlier, while the team were in Sri Lanka at the Asia Cup, he had arranged a meeting with team manager Yawar Saeed and bowling coach Waqar Younis to warn them about Majeed. Afridi acknowledged that Azhar had previously been his agent but that was several years back and he had broken with him after a disagreement over a deal Azhar was pushing. Mazhar, he wanted them to know, was worse news than his older brother. The enmity was mutual because Mazhar would tell Mahmood, 'A lot of the boys, they want to fuck up Afridi because he's trying to fuck up things for them, and he's the captain of the Twenty20 and one-day.'

The Pakistan Cricket Board can hardly claim they were unaware of his influence. Officials had had their first meeting with the agent a few months earlier when Majeed had made his first-ever visit to the country from which his parents had emigrated. Normal contractual business had been discussed then, but his presence in and around the camp during the World T20 had also been officially noted by the team security officer, Major Khwaja Najam Javed.

On 27 July 2010 the Urdu paper *Jang* reported that the Pakistan management had advised players not to have anything to do with either brother while in England, such was the level of suspicion hanging over them. *Jang*'s reporter, Abdul Majid Bhatti, later said he had received calls from men who claimed to speak on behalf of the brothers threatening legal action.

The warning from the management fell mostly on deaf ears. Azhar Majeed had been spotted early on during the tour at their hotel. Despite their previous acquaintance, Afridi had blanked him but his team-mates welcomed him. At some point during The Oval Test against England, Azhar would be found in the room of Wahab Riaz at the Royal Garden Hotel. It was past midnight and Butt and Kamran Akmal were also present.

The same Major Khwaja Najam Javed, who had noticed his brother three months earlier in the Caribbean, asked him to leave since this contravened the tour rules that agents were only allowed to meet players in the lobby. Azhar explained that he had only come to drop off pads from Akmal's kit sponsor but did as he was ordered.

Just a couple of days earlier, after the Bombay Brasserie meeting, Mazhar had himself been to the hotel to meet Salman Butt. Mazher Mahmood had offered him a lift from the restaurant in his own Mercedes, which Mazhar Majeed gladly accepted. He even asked Mahmood if he wanted to come in to the meet the captain. Mahmood declined. He had no video equipment on him to film the meeting and there was also the risk that one of the squad or management could recognise him. The story had already advanced at a pace quicker than he could have imagined – there was no need to push it further. Besides, he would only have to wait 24 hours to be introduced.

* * *

The conversation in the car near the Bombay Brasserie had ended with them agreeing a rendezvous the following evening at a Lebanese restaurant on the Edgware Road. Majeed said it was called Sheesaw though its proper name was Al-Shishawi. He said his players would be with him so they could get to know Mohsin Khan. At some point in the evening, he added, 'Me and you can just go for a five-minute walk and we can talk.'

Majeed spent the morning and afternoon of Thursday, 18 August watching the second day's play at The Oval. During that time, Mahmood was doing some background checks on what he had been told the night before. Before getting ready for his assignation on Edgware Road, he emailed Myler and Crone what he later described as 'various articles that had appeared in other newspapers about suspicions that players linked with Majeed were linked to match fixing.'

At 6.49pm he received a text from Majeed. 'Nadeem I won't be able to get to Edgware Road until after 9pm as the game has just finished.' He would go on to call him Nadeem again later that night until Mahmood corrected him. His name was Mohsin.

Amanda Evans would not be required as part of Mohsin Khan's entourage, but Alan Smith and Fayaz Sayed would be reprising their roles. Naturally, they and Alan Smith's Mercedes had all been rigged up in advance by Conrad Brown. There would be two additional figures from the *News of the World* in the vicinity. With Majeed promising to bring along the players, it was time to get some professional shots of them in his company. Photographers Kerry Davies and Alastair Pullen were dispatched to find somewhere discreet nearby and fix their cameras on the restaurant.

The second day at The Oval had ended well for the away side. They had taken a first-innings lead of 86 then removed England captain Andrew Strauss for 4 shortly before close of play. Just over two hours after that, their own skipper Salman Butt was at Al-Shishawi being introduced to a man called Mohsin Khan. Butt was polite and friendly – not surprising since Khan's connections could significantly boost his income. Before they could get properly acquainted, Majeed intervened. He was sorry to interrupt but it was time to have that quiet chat. They left Al-Shishawi and were soon back again in Mohsin Khan's Mercedes. Alan Smith drove them a short distance round the corner, then got out.

Majeed picked up where they had left off the night before. 'Alright, just to show you it's real, I'm going to show you two no-balls tomorrow. OK. Then you just pay as I said minimum for that. Just £10,000 for each. I'm telling you big money can be made. I can even show you proof. You sit with me and I'll phone each player who I've got and I'll even talk to them about it.'

As he uttered these words, he was staring at one of the cameras secreted within the head rest. Only an expert eye would have picked it out but Mahmood didn't want to take any chances. He took this as his cue to produce the £10,000 given to him at the office on Tuesday. He handed it over with the promise of the same to come the next time they met. Majeed nonchalantly accepted it. His gaze was now diverted from the head rest to the task of cramming the cash into the inside pockets of a cream jacket he had borrowed from one of the players at the restaurant. He then said he would call about 8.30am on Friday to confirm when the no-balls would be bowled.

To carry on getting access to information, Majeed explained, Khan and his consortium would need to give him £150,000 to pass on to the players, 'then they give me the authority to work with you. They will only let me do it with a new source because I am open with them completely.'

They quickly moved on to the finer details. A cheque or bank transfer didn't look wise so how did Majeed want the money? 'It has to be all cash, the first payment is like a deposit. These players don't know who you are so I'm going to say to them I've got a new party. I think he's good, yeah, we'll deal with him. After that, payment has to be made within 24 hours either in England or Dubai. These are the two places, in cash. Stay here for the next month because we've actually been working towards this next month for a long time. And I'll give you the exact script, exactly what's going to happen, how it's going to happen.'

For Mahmood, what happened in September was likely to be immaterial. He wanted to nail Majeed and the Pakistanis sooner rather than later, so he steered the conversation back to the current match: 'Right, so tomorrow you are going to tell me which two balls are going to be no-balls?'

'Yeah, I'll just tell you which two. If obviously it will go to plan tomorrow then you meet me tomorrow night. I'll give you a bracket for the following day ... What I'm saying is a deposit of £150,000 in cash needs to be paid ... I pay that to the players ... Then they give me the authority to work with you. Once the authority is there to work with you, I'll give you everything we do after that. Obviously Lord's match starts next Wednesday [it was actually Thursday] and there will be brackets, at least four, five, but there's no result because we're trying to win the Lord's game. Because we want Salman Butt as captain.'

'Sure, it makes sense. It's useful to have him there,' Mahmood said to show he understood the significance of that last part. From the Bombay Brasserie, he had Majeed naming Amir and Asif engaging in fixing, albeit in a hypothetical situation. Now the captain had been brought into discussions. It was time to pin down where he stood in all this: 'Is he on side as well, is he in the fixing? If Salman's at it then it's OK.'

'Of course, of course,' cooed Majeed.

Butt had been appointed Test captain the previous month after the incumbent Afridi had announced his retirement from red-ball cricket. Afridi's decision had been prompted by his team's 150-run defeat to Australia in the match that the two countries had just played on neutral ground at Lord's. His replacement had then won his first Test in charge, beating Australia at Leeds a week later.

It was just the start that Majeed had wanted. Pakistan had now had five Test captains since January 2009 and the win would almost certainly buy Butt more time in the role than some of the previous skippers had enjoyed. It all meant, said Butt's agent, that 'I have got the bowlers, the batsmen and the all-rounders. I've got two, two, two. That's all you need. It's taken about six months to a year to get them all properly on side and all properly working.'

'Well it looks like you are well in with Salman Butt, they listen to you. That's good, it's in their interests as well, it's in everybody's interests.'

'Boss, they need to make money.'

With the plan to meet again the following night agreed, Alan Smith was then summoned back to the car and they were driven back to the restaurant. The evening took on a more relaxed tone as Majeed introduced more of the team to Mohsin Khan. Azhar Majeed was now present with Wahab Riaz, a bowler who had taken five wickets the day before, and Umar Amin, left out of the team for The Oval game. Mahmood chatted with them before Butt asked him and his agent to join him at the table where Fayaz Sayed had stayed to talk with the Pakistan captain while the other two were in the car.

There was no discussion about fixing, but it was clear, Mahmood would later write, that 'Majeed and Butt were very close. They talked about how long they had known each other, and about time they had spent together in Lahore. Butt even knew what Majeed's favourite restaurants were in Lahore. We also talked a little about the tournament I was planning.'

Before they broke up for the night, Azhar Majeed, eager to make sure his brother's associates left happy, offered to take some photographs of the group. Mahmood handed his camera over and Azhar began snapping. One of the images from the night shows 'Mohsin Khan' flanked by Riaz and Amin to his right, and Butt and Mazhar to his left.

The reporter then departed, while the players and their agent milled around on the pavement dining area with the other customers taking advantage of the warm summer's night air to smoke shisha pipes. It was a scene being replicated in nearly all the Arabic restaurants that lined Edgware Road. None of the others, however, at that moment had *News of the World* cameras trained on them.

* * *

Majeed did call, as promised, on Friday morning, but he wasn't passing on details about the no-balls. Not his fault but there had been a change of plan. Blame Waqar Younis. The great Pakistani paceman was now his country's bowling coach. With play due to start in just over an hour at 11am, Younis had 'just sat down with the fast bowlers for half an hour about how many extras they gave last game. They said because after the talk this morning they don't want to do any new balls today. No-balls sorry ... It's just because of this talk this morning he doesn't usually do it, otherwise we done five no-balls yesterday. Yeah, the day before, sorry. But bloody because he had this talk this morning it's just going to look a bit suspicious.'

He insisted, however, that this did not mean that all bets were off. He would be able to arrange 'better proof' on Saturday. It was important at this point for Mahmood to turn up the heat himself. He was, after all, supposed to be playing the part of a representative of some serious businessmen and one who had handed over £10,000 for what now looked like nothing. No-balls were promised and no-balls were what was expected, he insisted. Majeed told him not to worry and that he would be in touch that night.

He was true to his word on that, texting at 11.29pm: 'Can u speak now?' Within a couple of minutes they were talking on Majeed's 'safe' line. With great regret, he had to report that the no-balls were a no-go. England had finished Friday on 221/9. Amir had four balls of an over left and then it would almost certainly be the turn of Saeed Ajmal who, along with Amir, was working his way through the opposition lower order. The problem with Ajmal was 'we haven't got him. He's not with us … There's no point organising no-balls when there's one wicket left to go.'

The situation was still salvageable, he maintained. Pakistan would start their second innings soon after the start of play. Butt was due to come in at the fall of the first wicket and when he did he would bat out a maiden (no runs scored) in the first full over he faced to show that 'he's followed the instructions'.

It was at this point that Mahmood showed how quick-witted he could be. Despite being played out at a predicted time, one maiden could easily be passed off by Butt as defensive batting. A second, again delivered on demand, would be harder to explain. So he asked the agent to ask his client to ensure the third over he faced was also scoreless.

Majeed was rattled by his new friend's anxiety. To assuage him, not only would he pass on the request to Butt immediately, but he would even put the call to him on speakerphone. The introductions at the start of the call were inaudible to Mahmood, but then Majeed could be heard saying, 'Shit alright. You know, just quickly. Can you do quickly or not? Or shall I speak to you in the morning?' Butt's reply was not clear, but Majeed was coming to the point. 'You know the maiden. Yeah what we're doing for the first over.'

'Yeah,' said Butt.

'You know the third over you play yeah. One more maiden.'

'Bro, just leave it. OK? We don't know what the situation will be at that time.'

Saturday, 21 August was only a few minutes old when the journalist sent the following email to his editor:

The Pakistan captain Salman Butt is in on the fixing!!

Majeed just rang me and said that they can't do no-balls tomorrow as it's the last wicket. Amir is on side but he only has one ball remaining [Majeed was wrong, it was four] and the first ball of the day can't be an extra. Then Saeed Ajmal is bowling from the other end who is not in on the scam. The England boys are likely to be bowled out.

Instead he has said that the first over that Salman Butt faces as batsman, he will make it a maiden over. I said that isn't strong enough for me and my lads.

Majeed said just tell me what you want the boys to do and I will make them do it. I asked whether besides the first over could the third over Butt faces be a maiden. Note that Butt is famous for hitting out straight away.

Then with me on the line he called Salman Butt on speaker phone. I could hear him in the background and he is heard on my tape saying the first over is ok but he can't guarantee the third.

I am meeting Majeed at his £1.8 million pad in Croydon tomorrow morning at 8am. He will call Salman Butt in my presence on speaker and give me his number and I will hear him confirming that he is in on the fixing. I will be there at Majeed's place at 8am videoed up.

Incidentally the no balls today were fixed but for Majeed's other party. He had admitted this and says that he couldn't get two more for me because it would look silly.

If we get Butt on tape and if he does play a maiden in the first over, I don't need to spell out the implications. This is massive and will mean the end of the current Pakistani side and possibly the whole tour.

* * *

Twenty minutes by train and only ten miles from central London, Croydon is, depending on your view, either a visionary or depressing example of post-war urban development. When city-centre planning departments refused to allow skyscrapers to be built in the 60s, Croydon stepped in. David Bowie, who had lived there as a child, would say in 1999, 'It represented everything I didn't want in my life, everything I wanted to get away from. I think it's the most derogatory thing I can say about something: "God, it's so fucking Croydon."'

Majeed must have felt differently. He had gone to school there and when he had made his fortune it was here that he chose to buy his dream family home. With two young children, it was now a home for four. Mahmood had obviously allowed for some considerable property market inflation with his claim to his editor that the Majeed family home, which had been purchased for £860,000 four years earlier, was now worth £1.8m.

Located on the edge of Croydon, where south London really became Surrey and concrete gave way to countryside, there was no doubting its attractions. Like all the other properties on or around Oaks Road, it was detached, modern and spacious, backing on to Coombe Wood, with the 114-acre Lloyd Park just a short walk away. Majeed's plot amounted to a couple of acres.

The drive from Mahmood's house wasn't far, but he and Conrad Brown had needed to be up early. They were meant to be there for 8am but would have to pull over for a while on the way. A few miles from Croydon, they stopped at a hotel car park. Here Brown hid two video recorders within Mahmood's get-up. One was located behind a button. The other was concealed in what was known as a *salwar kameez*. This was a traditional Arabic jacket which, like the y-fronts Mahmood had worn at Bombay Brasserie, had been used many times before by the pair and was fitted out with the usual video and audio equipment.

They pulled in to Oaks Road and were let in through the electronic gates guarding Majeed's house. Alongside Brown's 4x4, on the drive were a Range Rover, black Jaguar and Aston Martin DB9, all presumably belonging to the homeowner. Brown stayed in his car, posing as another of Mohsin Khan's drivers.

Majeed was dressed in a navy polo shirt and grey jogging trousers. He led his guest to a ground-floor lounge where a large frame with the word 'Allah' in Arabic was hanging on the wall. He offered a seat to Mahmood, then put his own feet up on a grey and brown Chesterfield settee and began to talk shop.

As agreed, the first full over Butt faced would be a maiden. He would signal that it was going ahead by tapping his bat on the pitch after the second ball he faced. They then moved on to the bigger picture. Mahmood complimented the agent on his portfolio of young talent. 'I tell you, we've got Umar Akmal, Kamran Akmal, Mohammad Asif, Mohammad Amir, Salman Butt, Wahab Riaz and Imran Farhat – seven,' purred Majeed. 'Only a few of them know the full picture. You see what I mean?'

'Yeah, yeah. But Salman is totally trustworthy?'

'A million per cent. There's not any reason to worry about him. He will be captain full time. There's gonna be an announcement in the next two days that he's going to be captain for a year.' If only everyone in the team were like him ... 'Saeed Ajmal you can't ever chat to about the fix. You know some people you can and some people you can't. He's very religious and he'd be shocked if he knew what we do.'

It wasn't long before a call came through on his phone. Majeed held the handset so Mahmood could see the screen. It was Butt. It was a sign of how much he trusted 'Mohsin Khan' and how much he wanted to impress him that he decided to put this call too on speaker phone. 'Boss, just stick to what we said last night, okay. Just the first full over you play, you just make sure you play a maiden. Don't forget that, after the second ball, the signal. Boss, good luck. I'll speak to you soon.' Butt assented to all this and with that he was gone, ready to prepare his team for what should be a victory charge.

Other journalists might have been happy with this, but Mahmood was always conscious of making a case watertight. He therefore feigned concern that the captain hadn't really been listening ('he's half asleep, isn't he?') and asked Majeed to send him a text reminder. Majeed did as requested and sent a follow-up message to reinforce the point that the signal should come after the second ball he faced in his innings, not after the second ball of the over in question.

Butt wasn't the only Pakistan player he tried to contact that morning. A call to Kamran Akmal's mobile went unanswered so Majeed tried the switchboard of the Royal Garden Hotel where the team were staying. There was no answer either when he was put through to the room – it would later emerge that Akmal had been on the toilet at the time. There were also records of incoming calls from Mohammad Amir on Majeed's BlackBerry log.

Majeed was becoming more expansive. He showed footage on his TV of past matches he had helped to fix. He called an Indian bookmaker and asked him for a price to fix The Oval Test. A million dollars was the quote. Then he talked about the Swiss bank accounts through which he channelled money for the players. He had even set up an account for Butt with Clydesdale Bank in England. There wasn't much left to say after that so, like the good *News of the World* man he was, Mahmood made his excuses and left.

Within half an hour, he and Brown were back in the newspaper's offices and ready for play to start at The Oval at 11am. The longer the investigation went on, the greater the chance there was of something going wrong. If the paper had cast-iron evidence of Butt promising a maiden and that maiden then being delivered to script, then there was a strong case for running the story in the next day's edition. While Butt was not the most famous cricketer in the world, he was, after all, the captain of the team England were playing. That surely guaranteed an eye-catching headline. Myler, Crone and their star reporter knocked the arguments back and forth while they waited for Butt to bat.

They did not have to wait long. Resuming on 221/9, England were bowled out on the fourth ball of the morning – a wicket that gave Amir his then-best Test bowling figures of 5-52. Set a total of 148 to win in difficult batting conditions, Pakistan lost opener Yasir Hameed in the fifth ball of their innings, bringing Butt to the crease. The first delivery he faced hit his pad and he survived a close lbw call. Imran Farhat took the first four balls of the next over before a single brought Butt back on strike. He then took a run off the final ball to ensure he kept the strike for the next over.

This was to be the first full over that Butt would face, yet there had been no signal either after the second or any of the balls he had faced. The fears of the *News of the World* triumvirate watching this unfold on their TV screens were realised when Butt flicked the second ball from James Anderson through the leg side and picked up two runs. Tomorrow's potential splash had just been spiked.

A few minutes later, at 11.35am, Mahmood on the phone was asking Majeed what the hell was going on. 'He didn't give a signal,' the agent explained apologetically. 'That's why he didn't do it. He obviously felt the ball was doing too much off the pitch and he couldn't do a maiden so that's why he didn't do the signal. He felt it might be risky trying to defend it with the new hard ball. That it might pop up. There's always signals and the reason for the signal is whether it's on or not.'

Mohsin Khan let it be known that he was not happy. When, he and his people wanted to know, were they going to see 'either a no-ball or a definite something from Salman?' Majeed asked for time to think and promised to call later in the day.

They spoke at 8pm. Pakistan had won the match, though nearly made a mess of it. Butt had been top scorer with 48 but his removal precipitated a batting collapse as four wickets fell for 29 runs. In the end, they limped over the line, winning by four wickets. Still, it was the result that Butt's captaincy needed and kept the series alive.

Majeed, however, was offended that Mohsin Khan did not apparently have faith in him ('I've even let you come to my house and made a phone call with the captain'). He said the players themselves were concerned that Khan and his backers might not come through with 'big money'. There was every chance that it was actually Majeed who was more worried about £150,000 slipping through his grasp. Mahmood said he was still willing to part with the money but he needed to see the plan in action first. The Lord's Test was due to start on Thursday and he wanted one deliberate no-ball on that first day.

'All I'm saying is, I've just had a word with them [the players],' said Majeed, 'and they just said to me, "you know why he's not delivering?" I said because he wants to wait for a no-ball. He [Butt] goes: "You spoke to him on the phone with me this morning and what else did he want? People are bloody offering money left, right and centre without even speaking to anyone, without even, you know, meeting anybody, and just by talking to you and knowing who you are with the team and then they're giving that money … and this guy's not giving anything." That's what they're thinking …'

'Yeah but did you tell them what you said to me, that I'll give you two no-balls?' replied Mahmood on the defensive. 'And today he'll do this and he didn't do it. What did he say? I mean a maiden is nothing, is it?'

'It's not nothing boss. When it's a hard ball like that it's very, very hard to do a maiden. When the ball's coming off your bat and because everyone's round the wicket if that ball goes through in the gap you have to run. That ball can come off the edge and go quite hard away as well. If it was even five, four even overs old it's much easier to handle.'

The point he was making – that paradoxically it was harder not to score at the start of an innings when the bowlers were making the ball swing and move off the seam – was a fair one. The newer the ball, the harder and faster it came out on to the bat and the more likely it was to take the edge. The attacking fields traditionally set in this passage of play increased the likelihood of a catching chance. They also meant that there were easy runs to be harvested if an edge did not go in the direction of the catcher.

Shortly after the conversation ended, Mahmood fired off another email to Myler and Crone who had just put to bed the first edition of the *News of the World* (the splash was now a story about the family of *X Factor* runner-up Olly Murs – 'Olly has wrecked our lives'). He summarised what had been said between the pair and that they would be meeting again on Wednesday. Mahmood then added one intriguing coda: 'My own feeling is that Majeed arranged for the wickets to fall today for the Indian syndicate who rang him three times while I was at his place.'

There would be further communication with Majeed before the weekend was out. At 11.34pm on Saturday, the agent was in conciliatory mood, sending the following text: 'Hi if you free tonight and in the mood please join me and the boys at a party to celebrate the win.' Mahmood/Mohsin Khan declined. Twelve hours later, Majeed was telling him about what had been discussed at the party. If the £150,000 was not handed over within the next few days then the partnership was dead before it had even begun. That being the case, Majeed said he would simply return the original £10,000 and both parties could walk away. Again, it was not clear whether this was really the players or just their agent talking. Still, it got Mahmood's attention and he agreed to hand over the six-figure sum. He wanted to be absolutely clear, however, about what he would get in return: 'So you are guaranteeing me now, that if I give you £150k, you are going to give me two no-balls, well, it depends if they are batting, they might be bloody batting first.'

'Then you can take the second day bowling,' Majeed offered. 'That is to get you confident. Then to get you confident to put the big money on the next bracket. OK?'

'OK, let me talk to them,' said Mahmood referring to his fictional partners. 'Thank you brother.'

CHAPTER THREE

'TOMORROW, THE *NEWS OF THE WORLD* IS GOING TO BREAK THE BIGGEST STORY IN ITS HISTORY'

'SORRY, SON, you're not getting the money.'

Neil McLeod hadn't even opened his mouth before Colin Myler had knocked him back. Editorial conference was due to take place in just under an hour at 10am and McLeod wanted to get his request to the boss out of the way early. His whole week hung on the editor authorising the payment of £150,000.

It was Tuesday, 24 August, the first day of the working week at the *News of the World*, as it was for every Sunday newspaper. It would also be the first week in which McLeod would be in charge of the news team. Usually one or both of Ian Edmondson and James Mellor, head of news and news editor respectively, would have overseen the desk but, this being August, they were on holiday. Edmondson was in Menorca with family, Mellor attending a friend's wedding in Italy.

That was good and bad. Good because it gave McLeod, the associate news editor, a chance to impress Myler, to show that he could fill their shoes. Bad because if he didn't deliver then he risked being marked down. Too many crosses against your name and you were out. That had been the *News of the World*'s employment policy for as long as anyone could remember.

When it came to landing scoops no paper had a budget or record to compare with the *Screws*. If the journalists who worked on it couldn't deliver the stories to defend or extend its position as market leader, then they were shown the door. In 2002 several reporters had received letters warning them that management had conducted an audit of how many stories employees had generated. Those in receipt of the letters were not being singled out for praise. 'It's become a climate of fear here. Everyone's watching their backs,' was how one hack described the atmosphere in the office to *The Guardian*.

They were right to watch their backs because within a few years Matt Driscoll, a sports reporter, was sacked while on long-term sick leave for stress-related depression. In November 2009 an employment tribunal found that Driscoll had been the victim of a culture of bullying, which had started at the top with editor Andy Coulson. News International, parent company of the *Screws*, had been ordered to pay Driscoll almost £800,000, including legal costs, for unfair dismissal and disability discrimination. Coulson was now in Downing Street as new Prime Minister David Cameron's communications chief.

Myler, Coulson's successor, was no less demanding. The 58-year-old was a tabloid veteran who had already edited the *Daily Mirror* and its Sunday title. He had resigned from the latter in 2001 after the collapse of an assault trial involving two Leeds footballers. Myler had published an interview with the family of the victim while the jury were still considering their verdict. The judge deemed the *Sunday Mirror*'s intervention prejudicial and it was fined £75,000 for contempt of court. Myler was lucky not to face personal prosecution. After five years at the *New York Post*, he had returned to London in 2007 to succeed Coulson.

He was, to use Fleet Street's highest compliment, a 'newspaperman', who wouldn't be bounced into doing anything he wasn't sure of. McLeod knew he would need to have a rock solid case to secure such a large sum of money. As he strode purposefully through the newsroom past Myler's PA Belinda Sharrier and into his office, he had been pretty sure that he did. Now he stood in front of him, the wind taken out of his sails, struggling for a reply.

It was on 20 August, shortly before his departure for Italy, that Mellor, who effectively 'ran' Mahmood, had briefed him for the first time on this latest project. In other circumstances, they might have tried to hold the story until Mellor or Edmondson was back from holiday but time was running out. When Salman Butt was unable to pull off the fix at The Oval Test, it meant that there was only one chance left in the series – the fourth and final Test due to start on 26 August. Responsibility to see it through would have to fall to McLeod.

It was clear from Mellor's briefing that Mahmood was already well advanced and Maz had then called him on Monday to confirm that he was reaching end game with Majeed. 'Look, we've already given him £10k and that's got us in the door,' he explained, 'but if we want to play at the table then we're going to have to give him the rest of the money.' How much were they talking? '£150,000.'

Before McLeod could give voice to his astonishment, Maz was off: 'If this thing isn't going to hit the buffers, then we have to show him we are serious players. You're going to have to go in to Colin, tell him what we've got, that the clock is ticking, and make him sign off the cash.' He had worked with him often enough to recognise in his voice that tone of certainty and intensity that signalled Mahmood had the target in his sights and was moving in for the kill.

It turned out that Mahmood had made a private plea to Myler anyway because the editor followed up his opening remark that Tuesday by telling McLeod, 'I know what Maz is saying but £150,000 is a lot of money. You're going to have to find another way to conduct this investigation.' There wasn't a lot to be said to that and he beat a tactical retreat to his desk to prepare for morning conference.

At this point, nine members of the *News of the World* staff knew about Majeed: Mahmood, McLeod, Mellor, Edmondson, Myler, Bill Akass, Amanda Evans, the in-house lawyer Tom Crone and Matt Drake, a reporter who had been roped in as a consultant because he knew more about cricket and betting than the rest of them put together. If it went ahead and ran in the paper when the presses began to roll in just over 100 hours, then this was an investigation which would demand help from other reporters, including those outside his own department. And yet McLeod knew it would be madness to mention it in conference to his colleagues.

Why the secrecy? Since there were several major obstacles, not least the money, to clear first, there was no great need to publicise it internally. Then there was the in-house politics. With departments pitted against each other, there was a fiercely competitive internal culture at the *Screws*. The fug of smoke and whiff of alcohol might have been banished from the editorial floor, but the bile, bitchiness and backstabbing remained ever present. They were the only reason some people went into the office.

The 35-year-old McLeod had spent most of his career as a reporter, out on the road, and was not as attuned as a bruiser like Edmondson to this working environment. So when he joined the editing team in 2007, Edmondson gave him a warning of what to expect. He told McLeod of the time he had received a phone call from one of his reporters in the field demanding to know why a writer from the features section had arrived on the scene to chase the same lead. Edmondson was furious because he had only mentioned the story an hour earlier in conference and not a word had been said to him during or after by his counterpart in features.

Then there were the Fleet Street moles. In May 2002 Eddie Fitzmaurice and James Eisen were told to leave the *News of the World*'s offices after being interviewed by senior executives following claims that they had sold stories to rivals. These allegations were not uncommon among the rat-eat-rat world of tabloid journalism. Myler himself had sacked a crime reporter on the *Mirror* for selling exclusives. Edmondson naturally had a story of his own too. One Saturday, he had been called by an agent demanding to know more on the next day's story on page seven about a celebrity he represented. It was just possible that the agent had heard on the showbiz grapevine that there was something in the works about his client. What he could not have known was where in the paper it was scheduled to appear – unless he had an inside man or woman.

So McLeod prepared his news list for conference without including Maz's investigation. At the 10am meeting, he did his best to talk it up with his colleagues but his mind was elsewhere. How could he find a way ahead that wouldn't cost £150,000? After fruitlessly racking his brains, he devoted the rest of Tuesday to organising and delegating other duties among his team.

Mid-afternoon, he was summoned to see Myler again. In the office he found Maz, Crone and managing editor Bill Akass. For the first time, Mahmood presented his case in full, in person, to all concerned, outlining how far Majeed's influence stretched within the Pakistan dressing room, the sophistication of his operation, as revealed by the messages on the BlackBerry and his conversations with 'Mohsin Khan' and the significance of what he was now promising. As far as Myler could see, the risk was threefold: Majeed could be working a scam; the cash payment could be seen as incitement to break the law; there was no guarantee of getting the money back even if/when it all came off. On the first point, he trusted Maz if he was happy that Majeed was a genuine player. He asked the others for their opinion on the other two.

The most forceful voice here belonged to Crone. The lawyer had studied the evidence and was happy to provide the legal all-clear. This was not a case of entrapment, Crone confirmed, because all the evidence collated so far indicated Majeed was no criminal ingénue. He was up to his neck in it. 'In my 25 years at the *News of the World*, I think this is the best investigative story I've ever seen,' he told the room. 'Something is going to happen in the middle of a Test match and we can report that we already knew it was going to happen.'

It was hard to argue with that. Akass was in agreement on the magnitude of the story, which was why, as the man charged with staying on top of the budgets, he gave his assent to the cash payment. There was a risk that they might not recover some or even any of the money, but if it all came off they were looking at the kind of publicity that £150,000 just couldn't buy.

There was another issue concerning the money that Crone raised. In the event of a criminal trial, it would be evidence. Yet it was evidence that could quite easily be spent, hidden or laundered before the authorities had acted. That made it imperative that the police were brought in *before* the paper went off-stone. Without doing so, they would look legally and professionally irresponsible. Myler agreed. He and Crone would handle police liaison once every brick of the case against Majeed and the cricketers was cemented in place. In the meantime, he would contact management about raising the cash.

McLeod was heading for the lift around teatime when he bumped into the editor. Myler smiled as he acknowledged him. 'We're getting the money, son ... You'll need to be careful about how you draw it but speak to Bill. He'll know.' It transpired that in the intervening hour or so he had walked across to see News International's chief financial officer, Susan Panuccio, on the sixth floor of the Wapping building. An Australian accountant, Panuccio was a little – but only a little – surprised that he should be asking for such a high figure and asked why. Myler gave her the details.

She listened. She gave her approval. That was it. No phone calls were made to Rupert Murdoch or to his son James, then in charge of News International's parent company in Europe. There was a reason why the *News of the World* was the 800lb gorilla in the Fleet Street jungle – because it had the greatest financial muscle and backed its editors to flex it wisely.

*　*　*

In fact, it would be £140,000 that would be drawn. Mahmood had already handed over £10,000 before The Oval Test for what had turned out to be nothing. To maintain the pretence that he was a businessman who wasn't to be messed around, it was decided that he should explain to Majeed that that first payment could not simply be written off. Majeed should think of it now as the initial instalment of the larger fee.

Getting £10,000 in cash had been relatively easy. Securing the rest was going to be more complicated. How do you draw such a sum, ensure it is brought safely to your office in Wapping, then pack it up and organise delivery to its lucky recipient? Like most journalists, Neil McLeod had never had to wrestle with such questions, until now. Back in Wapping on Wednesday morning, he talked it over with Akass, who told him it should be picked up from a branch of Thomas Cook on Oxford Street. McLeod was a little surprised but if the managing editor told him that was where to go then that was where to go.

Akass gave him the appropriate paperwork and asked him whom he proposed to send. McLeod suggested Drake and Phil Whiteside. Drake was already in on the story and Whiteside, as one of the senior reporters, would eventually be enlisted to help out anyway so it made sense to include him. The pair were experienced, reliable and discreet. Akass approved and, within half an hour, after Whiteside had been brought up to speed, a company car, including a driver and two security guards, was waiting outside reception for them. Understandably, conversation was sparse in the 20-minute journey from Wapping.

On the outside, it looked like a regular branch of Thomas Cook, albeit a big one. When you got inside, particularly when you had been led past the retail counters and into the back offices and vaults, it started to feel more like a bank, one of those private ones which have safes for their customers as well as their own reserves. It was impossible not to feel like you were in some sort of heist movie – either as the victim being set up for the hit or the criminal mastermind casing the joint.

The money, broken down into bundles of £2,500 each, comprised of 50 £50 notes, was removed from a safe and placed inside a big black holdall, and they left the small room into which they had been discreetly ushered. The driver was called and summoned to meet them outside the building, with one of the security guards dispatched to wait for his arrival.

Within a couple of minutes, they were on their way back to Wapping. Drake's phone rang. It was McLeod who, unsurprisingly, was finding it hard to relax. *Yes, it all went smoothly, we've got the money, just on our way back*, Whiteside told him. McLeod's response indicated that the news had not alleviated his stress levels: *whatever you do, don't go to the pub, don't go to Stringfellows, don't stop anywhere. Just get back here.* Whiteside wasn't sure if this was a light-hearted remark designed to ease the tension or serious advice – Stringfellows? – but since he liked McLeod he let it go.

Back on level six in the News International building, they were ushered into the bunker, the secure room used by reporters, principally Mahmood, to work on the big exclusives. This private office, with its own internal computer system, which could not be accessed from the outside, was a no-go area to anyone who didn't have clearance. It would be here where most of the legwork would now take place. That started with the second part of the cash operation – the marking of the notes.

There would, it was hoped, be three central planks of evidence to the case the *News of the World* was building: Majeed promising delivery of the fix in exchange for money; the Pakistanis carrying it out as instructed; then the money being found in their possession. The first would be filmed by *News of the World* cameras and the second (hopefully) by those of host TV broadcaster Sky Sports. The third plank, however, required the paper to prove the connection between the money it gave to Majeed and any the police would subsequently find on his person or property or among the cricketers. That meant that all 2,800 of the £50 notes would have to be accounted for. It was now lunchtime and Maz was due at the rendezvous in the evening. It was going to be a long and boring afternoon but this was work as vital as any.

In a previous life, Matt Drake had managed a chippy on the docks in Ipswich. There had been a period when money from the tips collection had gone missing. Drake had decided to test his suspicions about a particular member of staff by secretly marking notes then leaving them around for his man to pick up and pocket. The notes soon showed up in a search of the prime suspect's wallet. So, now, he got the secret marker pen out again and went to work.

Even that wasn't enough it was felt, so another backstop was put in place – recording the serial numbers of each of the notes. This began in earnest with Drake, Whiteside and Frances Carman, the news desk secretary, taking turns to read out the figures and enter them into a spreadsheet. After 15 minutes, they realised that not only was this procedure mind-numbingly boring but it would also take them dangerously close to the teatime deadline set for the money to be transported to Maz.

A quicker solution was therefore adopted – the Conrad Brown method. As with the earlier £10,000 payment, each note was held up to a video camera. The number would be captured and saved on film. Should it be needed as evidence later, the police could go through the recording and shoulder the task of marrying up the serial numbers.

Last but by no means least would come the money shot. This was that magical moment in any sting when the greedy, grasping villain was captured by the secret cameras opening the 'golden' briefcase stuffed with huge wads of cash. McLeod had ordered one of his junior reporters earlier in the day to buy such a case. Wapping wasn't blessed with much in the way of retail outlets and the reporter, unaware of exactly what it was required for, had popped up to the nearby Petticoat Lane market. Sensing some urgency in McLeod's voice, he quickly handed over a fiver for an old, tattered holdall. It took a bollocking and the dispatching of another reporter to find something that looked worthy of carrying £140,000.

It was around seven in the evening when they were good to go. Soon, Whiteside and Drake were back in the company car with the security guards and the briefcase, making their way across town through the rush hour traffic to the Copthorne Tara Hotel. When the car reached its destination in Kensington, Drake got out with the case and waited in the lobby for Mahmood, who returned with Conrad Brown at 9pm. Drake handed over his consignment before he and Whiteside moved on to an Indian restaurant in Balham and let events take their course.

While his colleagues had been busy handling the cash, Mahmood had spent the afternoon making the final arrangements. At 1.31pm he had called Majeed to say he had the money and was keen to meet that night. Majeed said he would be taking some of the players to watch his Croydon team play a pre-season friendly. He could see him at 11pm once he had returned them to their team hotel. Believing they were accommodated at the Royal Garden Hotel, where they had been put up for The Oval match a few days earlier, Mahmood proposed meeting at the nearby Copthorne Tara. In fact, they had moved to the Marriott, Regent's Park, which was close to Lord's. Despite having to travel back again from north to west London, Majeed agreed to the meeting point and time.

The Copthorne Tara is tucked away in west London, behind Kensington High Street, one of the capital's more upmarket thoroughfares. It is also just a two-minute walk from the offices of one of the *News of the World*'s main rivals, the *Mail on Sunday*. It is what you would expect from a four-star hotel: corporate, comfortable but not extravagant. While the swankier Hilton Park Lane had been ideal for pricking Majeed's greed and establishing Mr Khan's credentials, the Copthorne, with its business-like feel, was the perfect place to conclude the deal. It also had the advantage of familiarity, Mahmood having used it before for similar set-ups.

Two rooms were booked, one for himself and Majeed, the other next door where Conrad Brown would monitor proceedings on a screen linked into the video and audio network he would install around Majeed. Proximity meant that if anything went wrong, if Mahmood was rumbled and it turned violent, then Brown could be on the scene instantly to offer help. This had been their standard modus operandi for the best part of a decade.

At 4pm Mahmood had checked in and gone into the 'deal' room where he began taking photos and videos. These he immediately sent on to Brown. The technician took a careful look and concluded that the layout wasn't suitable for his purposes. In short, it was difficult to see where they could place a camera opposite the sofa on which Majeed would naturally be asked to sit.

Changing rooms did not prove difficult, and from 9pm Brown and Mahmood were in place, rigging up suite 1273. By the time the former had finished, there were six video cameras stashed around the room, three of them in tissue boxes, one in a folder (a 'document folio' that had also been placed in the Mercedes in earlier meetings), one in a suitcase facing the sofa where they anticipated Majeed taking a seat and another in a lamp. There were also three audio devices, including two under the sofa. Brown was about to install another listening device into the suitcase when, shortly before 10pm, Mahmood received a text. *Boss can we meet at 10.30 pls.* That was half an hour earlier than scheduled, and there was always the possibility Majeed could arrive sooner. So Brown abandoned that last job, performed one final check-up of his equipment and retired next door.

Half an hour later, Majeed called again. He was outside. Could they do the handover in his car? Not for the first time, Mahmood needed to think on his feet. For obvious reasons, the car was not going to work. But was Majeed genuinely suspicious or was he just too idle to find somewhere to park – never easy in this part of London – and walk to the rendezvous? If Mahmood was too insistent that he come to his room then that might confirm suspicions of a trap. On the other hand, there was the small matter of £140,000 that Majeed was obviously desperate to trouser. Ultimately, that gave Mahmood leverage.

His reply was therefore intended to make Majeed think that Mr Khan might be offended without saying so outright. It also offered a chance to burnish Mr Khan's wealth. 'Look, boss, I've got a very nice suite here. I don't want to walk down the street with £140,000 in cash and give it you in the back of the car. Why don't you come in? I'll meet you in the lobby and we can have a drink in the room and a proper chat about how we are going to work together in future.' Majeed acquiesced. Five minutes later, the pair were taking the lift up to the 12th floor.

Majeed had been busy too during that evening period. In the hours and minutes before the rendezvous, there were nine texts or calls from himself to Butt, with four going the other way. It was a similar story with Amir, who had rung Majeed five times and sent three texts. From Majeed there had been three calls and eight texts.

At 7.57pm and again four minutes later, Majeed called Asif. This flurry of communications was not normal for cricketers on the eve of a Test series decider.

* * *

The idea was that Majeed would be invited to sit down on the longer of the two couches in the lounge area of the suite. There was a coffee table at the centre on which the money would be placed ready for him to check, and on which a tissue box with one of the cameras had been placed. As usual, Mahmood and Brown had choreographed their target's likely movements to verify that he would be in shot at all times.

The meeting would last around half an hour. Majeed was watchful when he entered the room, not exactly suspicious but cautious. He even performed a quick tour of the suite to make sure there was no one else present before obligingly taking up position on the larger sofa. They got down to business. Gone was the brash braggart of their first four meetings. Majeed had now switched to cagey conspirator. His tone was almost *sotto voce*, as if worried that someone in the next room might be listening in. 'I can tell you now exactly what's going to happen ... when we bowl,' he explained. 'I'm going to prove to you, I'm serious ... Boss, I'm going to give you three no-balls, OK right, to prove to you firstly that this is what's happening ... No-balls are the easiest, and they're the most clearest. There's no signal, nothing. These three are definitely happening.'

Mahmood nodded to show his understanding and appreciation, and Majeed began to show his hand: 'So the first ball of the third over of the innings, yeah.'

At this point, Mahmood delivered the first of several replies which were little more than repetitions of what the man sitting opposite him had just said. To Majeed, it probably appeared that his new business associate was simply double-checking the details – he was writing them down as he went along – because with so much money at stake he couldn't afford to make the slightest mistake. For Mahmood, however, this was a routine honed over two decades to ensure that there could be no doubt among editors, journalists, readers, police officers, lawyers and jurors about what was being proposed. 'OK, first ball of the third over of the innings, right. So who's going to be opening?' he said.

Majeed revealed that it would be Amir and Asif. The former usually bowled the first over so that meant that he would also be on for the third. 'So the first ball …?' asked Mahmood/Khan.

'Of the third over,' confirmed Majeed. 'Then the tenth, the last ball, sixth ball of the tenth over.'

'The tenth over. Who's bowling it?'

'Asif will be bowling it.'

Patience, urged Majeed, would be required for the third no-ball: 'The next one will be, you know Amir, he goes over the wicket to right-handers.' England's two openers, Andrew Strauss and Alastair Cook, were both left-handers so it was not clear when that would be. 'Whenever the right-hander comes in, he'll be going round the wicket. OK? The over he goes round the wicket, the last ball of that over will be another no-ball … The first over he bowls around the wicket, the last ball of that over will also be a no-ball … After you see these three, yeah, you'll know that that's no coincidence, yes or no? … I've given you the three … This is exactly what's going to happen, you're going to see these three things happen. Then you're going to see that I'm talking 100 per cent and I'm serious as well as you're serious.'

'So this is nothing to do with our 150 grand, this is you trying to convince us that it's definitely on.'

'Yeah, this is for the ten grand you've given me,' said Majeed. 'Just say I've given you three no-balls. Make whatever you want on it. The 150 is security, what you are giving me to show that you are serious. After that, I'm probably going to give you a bracket.'

'That's included in the cost of the 150?'

'Well, no, what we'll do, we'll finalise a price for each one and we'll just take it off the balance. We'll take it off the 150 till we're square. And then from then on, once we do it, then you pay us, once we've done it.'

There was one thing even the fixer couldn't fix – the toss. The fourth Test was due to start in around 15 hours and, playing the part of a twitchy punter eager to nail down a sure-fire winner, Mahmood wanted to know what he could bet on if Pakistan were instead batting in the morning (in the three previous Tests of the series the side that had won the toss had always batted first). Could Salman Butt deliver in those circumstances? 'No,' said Majeed, 'because it hasn't been organised, I've just left them now, I'm not going to go back. This is more than enough that I've given you.'

'OK, alright, let's see that happen,' replied Mahmood/Khan.

'Yeah, you'll see this happen and then you'll be confident, OK, because there is no way that could be a coincidence …' That phrase, 'there is no way that could be a coincidence', would echo around Southwark Crown Court 14 months later when statisticians testified to its essential truth.

'If Asif isn't bowling the tenth over then I'll have grounds to scream, yeah. We're putting money on it now, on your say so we're going to put money on it,' Mahmood/Khan reminded him.

This prompted Majeed to raise one final caveat. He could deliver the captain and the bowlers but there were two other unwitting partners in this relationship – the umpires. There was always the possibility that either would fail to notice that the bowler – whether it was Asif, Amir or anyone, in fact – had overstepped the mark. 'I can't say it's guaranteed because we're not the umpire, we're not paying the umpire.' On the other hand, he added, 'they [the bowlers] will be well over the mark, they will be well over the mark. Don't worry about it, you will see it.' With that final assurance, it was time for the transaction.

Mahmood opened the briefcase and began to hand over bundles containing £2,500 each. There would be 56 of them to make £140,000, he told him. With the earlier £10,000 included, it would make £150,000. Majeed demurred, 'Well it wasn't what we said because the ten grand was for this.' It could have been awkward but at this point it seems that each party deemed it imprudent to make a scene having come so far. Mahmood/Khan said he would make a £10,000 top-up at a later, unconfirmed date and Majeed settled for that.

Majeed moved the lamp and the tissue box away from the coffee table so he could lay out and count all the notes before placing them back in the case. The camera opposite was still there to capture all this. As he did so, Mahmood pushed for further incriminating evidence of the conspiracy: 'So what, there's no question, Salman is definitely going to put these boys on to bowl these overs, yeah. You've discussed it with him.'

'Boss you'll see. Just relax, I promise you OK ... At the end of the day, you know what's going on, and you know what's going to happen, yeah.'

Majeed said he would phone Amir. 'Get him to confirm, does he understand what we're talking about,' pressed Mahmood/Khan. Majeed said he never discussed such matters on the phone but the exaggerated concern in Mahmood's voice persuaded him to put the call on speakerphone. The conversation went as follows:

Amir: *Hello, hello.*

Majeed: (in Urdu) *Are you sleeping, fucker?*

Amir: *Yeah I was.*

Majeed: (in Urdu) *OK sleep.* (English) *Just, we've spoken about everything before anyway. OK don't mind.* (Urdu) *You sleep, OK?*

Amir: *Alright, OK.*

Majeed turned to Mahmood. 'I got him sleeping. I didn't realise it was tomorrow,' he said, presumably meaning that he hadn't actually appreciated that the Test was due to start the following day. He asked Mahmood to call the next day 'when it's happened'.

By 11.16pm he was back in his car with £140,000 in a briefcase, both provided by the *News of the World*. He immediately called Asif. They spoke for 30 seconds and then he rang Butt. Amir was not going to be allowed his beauty sleep either. There were three unanswered calls to him in ten minutes from 11.38pm. He did not get through to the 18-year-old until 1.24am, though they spoke for only 21 seconds. Five hours later, Amir sent two texts within the space of five minutes. Majeed called him again at 8.14am. Again, their conversation lasted less than 30 seconds.

Mahmood was equally busy – emailing his boss. At 1.24am, the following message landed in Colin Myler's inbox:

> *We have fantastic video of Majeed counting out £140k by making piles of notes on the coffee table in the hotel. He said the money would be a deposit and he would provide information (brackets) the cost of which would be deducted from this sum. He said for the £10k I have already paid he would give me three no balls in the Lords Test.*

After outlining when those would be delivered, he threw in another juicy morsel to leave his boss salivating:

> *[Majeed] also confirmed that Pakistan will lose the ODIs coming up, as Afridi will be captain for those and the boys want Salman Butt as captain so they are happy to lose the matches. He will provide full details of how they plan to lose later. Majeed was nervous in the room and looked around, even moving one of our cameras hidden in a lamp. However he left happy and even told me that I looked nervous and that I shouldn't worry as he will deliver.*

* * *

Forty-eight hours after his initial conversation with Colin Myler about Majeed, Neil McLeod was making his way back down to his editor's office. This time, there was none of the fretting about how to play the boss. McLeod had also now seen Mahmood's memo as well as some of the highlights from Conrad Brown's video production. It looked like journalistic gold, but it was as worthless as glitter if the Pakistan players didn't do their bit.

Play was due to begin at Lord's in just under two hours. Myler asked him what the plan was. With his knowledge of the sport and the gambling world, Matt Drake would be sent to Lord's. Watching proceedings from the media centre was out of the question. If a news reporter from the paper suddenly appeared then questions would start to be asked by the cricket correspondents. Though they wouldn't get any answers they might raise a flag with their own editors. Instead, Drake would have a ticket for the stands and pose as a punter. His brief was to sit, observe, score, listen to the radio commentary in his earpiece and note anything of interest.

Photographer Kerry Davies would also be positioned in the ground, parallel to the wicket. His purpose was twofold. Firstly, he was there to snap the Pakistan trio and ensure that the paper had its own exclusive pictures of the crime being committed. There was no guarantee, for instance, that the host broadcaster, Sky, would have its own cameras fixed on either of the popping creases to capture the exact moment at which a bowler overstepped for a no-ball.

Davies was also there as a legal backstop. Majeed had been quite right to warn about an umpire failing to spot an illegitimate delivery. Nine years earlier, Pakistan had beaten England at Old Trafford after four batsmen were given out on the final day to what were clear no-balls. On this occasion TV replays had belatedly exposed the umpires' failings. Davies's presence meant that even if the no-balls were not identified by match official or broadcaster, the *Screws* could still build an argument if it had photographic proof of Amir and Asif going over the white line at the agreed moments.

There would also come a point soon, McLeod went on, when he would have to involve other staffers. There would need to be background checks on Majeed and the players and other research. There would be investigative leads to be followed up. Then there was the task of transcribing and editing the recordings of Maz's meetings and phone conversations. Myler could see his point but told him to hold off while they waited for the game to take its course. He did say that he would brief sport editor Paul McCarthy, whose team would inevitably be asked to contribute.

There was one final thing, Myler said. 'In conference this morning, I'm going to give you a bollocking. Sorry, son, it's nothing personal. It's just you can't put any of this on your list. And if we're going to keep up the pretence that you've got nothing else up your sleeve then I need to give you a hard time.' He would be true to his word.

Next to be summoned was McCarthy. 'What we are about to discuss stays only within this room,' opened Myler with a hint of menace. 'Do not mention it to anyone – staff, family or friends?'

'Understood, boss,' replied McCarthy. This should be good, he thought.

As luck would have it, McCarthy was due to head for Lord's once Thursday's conference had concluded. He hadn't planned to tell the boss since he had envisaged a day of boozing and bantering with his chief sportswriter Andy Dunn and Adrian Bevington, head of communications for the Football Association. Once Myler had briefed him on Maz's investigation, he could see he had no choice but to come clean. In fact, he could turn the situation in his favour. He explained he was going to St John's Wood to meet Bevington, whom the editor knew and liked, to dig for dirt on England's disastrous World Cup campaign two months earlier. While there, he could act as an extra pair of eyes and ears on the ground.

Myler concurred. Besides, even something as trivial as the sport editor cancelling a day at the cricket at short notice was the kind of signal they didn't want transmitted to the outside world. The instruction, as it had been to McLeod, was clear: carry on as normal.

Bollocking to McLeod duly delivered, morning conference broke up naturally before 11am. There was no way Myler would have let it go on any longer because that was the scheduled start time at the Test. Unfortunately, when he got back to his office and turned on the TV, he saw dark clouds over the Lord's pavilion and the covers sitting across a damp outfield. There would almost certainly be no play before lunch at 1pm.

He kept the TV on in case that changed and carried on with other editorial duties in the meantime. One of those was reading the full transcript of last night's meeting at the Copthorne Tara, which was sent to him soon after midday. Outside the editor's office, Mellor, Akass, Crone and Mahmood kept themselves busy in the same way.

It was an agonising wait for all, but shortly after 1pm the covers came off and the captains, Andrew Strauss and Butt, made their way out to the middle for the toss. The first bit of good news came when Butt called heads and the coin landed in his favour. The Pakistan captain announced that his team would bowl first. Given the conditions and the frailties of his batting line-up (only once in ten Test innings across the English summer had they surpassed 300), this was understandable. At the same time, you had to wonder if Butt's decision was motivated by a desire to get 'the business' out of the way early in the piece. Both teams were unchanged from The Oval Test.

At 1.40pm, Strauss and Alastair Cook strode out to open the England innings. Myler, Crone and Mahmood were now gathered round the television in the editor's office, the door shut, the blinds pulled down. McLeod and Whiteside were on the newsroom floor, pretending to be casual viewers of the game – neither was known to be a cricket fan so it would have looked odd if they had watched intently. Drake and Davies were at their posts while McCarthy was settling into his seat and his first beer, also inside the ground.

Amir was handed the new ball, which meant he was on course for no-ball #1 in the third over. No one dared to relax, especially when he opened up by sending his first delivery well down the leg side for five wides. There was an unease among the *News of the World* family. This was not normal. Was the lad up to something? The rest of the over passed off without incident. Nerves were settled further by the sight of Asif coming on from the other end for the second over. That should ensure he also bowled the tenth, as the plan dictated. Apart from one ball on to Cook's legs, which allowed the England batsman to get off the mark, the second over was a good one.

Part one of the three-card trick was approaching. 'The first ball then,' said Colin Myler to no one in particular. Kerry Davies focussed his lens on the popping crease around which Amir was due to plant his front foot. In the Upper Compton stand, Matt Drake did the same with his binoculars and pressed the radio earpiece firmly in place. *Sit tight now, drink your beer, give nothing away,* thought Paul McCarthy.

There was no discernible difference to Amir's run-up and it appeared to end with another good ball – decent line and length, moving away from Cook a little. But what was this? Billy Bowden, the umpire at the non-striker's end, was raising his arm just above shoulder height to indicate a no-ball.

In the Sky Sports commentary box, Ian Botham noted, 'No-ball is the call. Front foot no-ball. Because of the one-dayers, you don't see that too often now. The bowlers who play both forms of the game, because they have got into the discipline of keeping behind the front line. Because in the one-day game it's a free hit. It's just an extra delivery and a run in this form of the game.' Alongside him was Pakistan's Ramiz Raja. 'He's inexperienced, we know that, Mohammad Amir. Though, extremely clever in the mind. Maybe ...'

At this point, Sky flashed up a freeze frame showing clear daylight between the heel of Amir's front foot and the popping crease. Later estimates would put the gap at nine inches, a huge distance in the context of fine margins. 'Oh, it's a big no-ball,' said Raja. 'Maybe he's finding it a little difficult because of the wet patches in his run-up to get it absolutely right. There's a little bit of wetness around. Maybe that is the reason why he could be struggling a little to maintain good consistent line and not to overstep.' In the editor's office the replay left them flabbergasted.

There wasn't much time to discuss it anyway because the very next ball took Cook's edge and flew to Umar Akmal, brother of wicket-keeper Kamran, at third slip. It was not a difficult chance but Akmal put it down and Amir could not hide his anger. To add insult to injury, the second legitimate ball of the over also took the edge, but the ball found the gap between the third and fourth slip. A boundary resulted.

The next six overs passed off largely without incident, the Pakistani pair bowling a controlled line, which the England openers treated with caution. 'It's not doing a lot, Henry,' Geoffrey Boycott told Henry Blofeld in the *Test Match Special* commentary box, 'nothing that's really that bad ...'

The score was 25/0 when Asif ran in to bowl his fifth over, the tenth overall. No runs were scored off the first five deliveries. On the sixth Andrew Strauss scurried down the wicket for a single after pushing a straightish ball into the covers. When Strauss got to the bowler's end, he was greeted by the sight of Bowden's fellow New Zealander Tony Hill also signalling for a no-ball. At this point, David Lloyd and Mike Atherton were the men calling it for Sky. 'Just oversteps [two inches was the estimate in this instance] on the front line and looks as if he wants a bit of sawdust, it might be quite greasy,' commented Lloyd. 'When you see his foot position at the bowling crease, I think he's in a perfect position. Just see where the sawdust goes down on the back foot first. But just look at that front foot where it lands, which means that his arm, if his left leg lands there ... he's way over ... his arm must be over the stumps. He'll be bowling wicket to wicket.'

'Seen a couple of biggish no-balls actually,' remarked Atherton. 'One from Amir. He was over that front line by a good half a foot or so.'

At the other end, Amir having served his initial purpose, Butt replaced him with Wahab Riaz. With his second ball, Riaz also transgressed, though by two inches. 'Well Wahab is a different type of bowler from Amir and Asif,' explained Atherton. 'He's got a lower arm, he's not going to hit the seam as much because of that. And he certainly, in the first game at The Oval, he didn't look like a bowler who would swing the ball back at the right-hander i.e. away from either left-hander. Another big no-ball.'

Asif would continue from the Nursery End and it was he who made the first breakthrough, piercing Strauss's defences with a beauty. The wicket had more significance than anyone outside those in the know could realise since it meant that the final no-ball could happen sooner rather than later. What was it Majeed had said the night before at the hotel? 'The third one will be, you know Amir, he goes over the wicket to right-handers. Whenever the right-hander comes in, he'll be going round the wicket. OK? The over he goes round the wicket, the last ball of that over will be another no-ball … The first over he bowls around the wicket, the last ball of that over will also be a no-ball.'

Strauss's departure had brought a right-hander, Jonathan Trott, to the wicket. Trott managed to see off the remaining five balls of Asif's over, taking a single off the last to keep the strike. It should now have been Wahab Riaz to continue. His first over had not been the best but it had hardly been the worst either, going for four runs. It was not uncommon for even the best bowlers to need a few looseners to find their rhythm. Riaz wouldn't get the chance to find that rhythm because Butt had decided to re-introduce Amir.

Was this going to be it, wondered Drake in the crowd where a father and his two sons alongside were giving him strange looks, wondering why the man next to them appeared to be watching every ball as if his life depended on it. He wouldn't get to find out then because three balls into Amir's over, the umpires were consulting their light meters, a trickle of rain was falling and the players were heading for the pavilion. Twelve and a half overs had been bowled, England had scored 39 runs, three of them in the form of no-balls, including one delivered innocently enough by Wahab Riaz, and lost one wicket.

Drake called the office, surprised that no one had been in touch after the second no-ball, as they had after the first. There was a reason for this and it spoke volumes about the jittery, feverish mood that had now enveloped management. When Asif began that fateful tenth over, Myler had had one eye on the clock as he was already late for an important meeting with the editor of the paper's *Fabulous* supplement. He had waited for and watched the Pakistani deliver what was promised on the sixth and final ball of the over. But, hold on, why then was Asif running in again to bowl one more before the umpire called over? That was not supposed to happen … And where did it leave them now? With that question weighing on his mind, he headed to his meeting, muttering 'he hasn't done it' to McLeod as he walked past his desk.

Myler's mistake – understandable in the pressured, febrile atmosphere that comes when you bet £150,000 on your paper's reputation with a south London wide boy – was to overlook the fact that Asif's no-ball was in reality always going to be the *penultimate* delivery since he would have to send down another one to make it six *legitimate* balls.

Myler's passing comment had now got McLeod querying what he had just witnessed. He daren't shout to anyone on the desk to double-check and, before he could verify it himself, Drake was on the line. 'I thought you might have called … We've got it, Macca.' *Got what?* 'The second no-ball, just before they went off. Asif in the last ball of the tenth over.' *Are you sure?* 'Of course, I'm sure. I might not know much but I know cricket.' *But Colin said he then saw him bowl another one so it couldn't have been the final ball.* This momentarily stumped Drake but then he twigged where the misunderstanding might have come from and explained to McLeod.

McLeod was relieved but realised that he was now in a tight spot. He would have to explain to the boss how he had managed to confuse himself without making it sound as if Myler, who thought he knew his sport, had committed the kind of mistake usually made by the uninitiated. Tact would be the order of the day. He walked over to Belinda Sharrier, the editor's PA, to ask where he was and what he was doing. Her reply indicated that it wasn't likely to be a quick meeting. Taking a couple of deep breaths first, he informed Belinda, 'You're going to have to get him out of that straight away and ask him to come back here. It's important. I'm afraid I can't tell you what it's about.' What McLeod didn't know was that the last time, the only time, anyone had ever done this to Myler was when news came through that his father-in-law had died.

Within two minutes, with a face like thunder, Myler was back in his office asking McLeod what was so bloody important. A minute later, Thunder Face was transformed into Smiler Myler.

Three hours later, at 5.45pm, play was abandoned for the day. Butt, Amir and Asif now had important calls to make. With play officially over, they could retrieve their mobile phones handed over to the security officer at the start of the day. This protocol had been introduced a few years earlier as part of the International Cricket Council's clampdown on in-game fixing and other forms of insider information.

Butt and Amir didn't waste any time. The latter called Majeed ten minutes after close of play, though they spoke only for 35 seconds. Four minutes later, his captain was trying to get through, failed, but did make contact at 6.22pm. Back in his hotel room, Amir texted Majeed at 7.40pm and they had three short chats in a half-hour period from 9.05pm. Less than ten minutes after the last of those chats, Asif rang him and they spoke for 37 seconds.

The subject of these frequent but brief discussions appears to have been the third no-ball because at 10.15pm Majeed was on to Mahmood. After some understandable bragging ('You bit more comfortable now? Told you, once you showed your hand, I showed my hand'), he assured Mr Khan that the last part of the plan would be executed.

'OK, what we going to get tomorrow then? Tomorrow we've got the third no-ball?' asked Mahmood/Khan.

'Yeah, I'll give you the other no-ball, yeah right. And you need to give me ten more, OK.'

Since Majeed had delivered so well so far, it didn't seem fair to Mahmood to quibble over ten grand (which he would never pay anyway) and he agreed that seemed fair. 'So third no-ball exactly the same?'

'I'll tell you right now what it is. Right, it's going to be Amir's third over and third ball.'

Mahmood again repeated what he had been told and just in case there was any confusion Majeed added, 'It'll be his third over [of his opening spell], not the third over of the game.'

Still they were not yet done. At 10.45pm a text appeared on Mahmood's phone. 'Yaar after you finish your current over then 3 overs. Text back.' The number was that of Majeed's BlackBerry. Yaar was Urdu for mate, Mahmood knew that, but the rest left him perplexed. Then it came to him. So busy was Majeed sending texts back and forth that he had mistakenly forwarded on to him a message intended for one of the players. 'Wrong person,' Mahmood replied. Realising his mistake, the fixer immediately sent the same message to Amir who, as instructed, texted back.

At 11.34pm Majeed made his last phone call to Mahmood to make sure that Mr Khan knew exactly where he stood. 'Bruv, just to tell you so there's no confusion yeah, right, he's finishing the over he's currently bowling yeah … 'cos rain stopped play so he's still got three balls left of his current over, yeah … so once that's over then the third ball of the following three. Do you get what I'm saying? … So we don't count the one that he's doing now.'

* * *

Half an hour before the start of play on Friday, Mahmood received a text from Majeed: 'Pls call me on my other number when u get a chance'. He did so instantly to find his business partner telling him there was 'no point doing the third one now'. This comment was not calamitous since the evidence of the first two was compelling, but two-thirds of the deal wouldn't be half as a good as the full hat-trick. Mr Khan would have to bring some pressure to bear. He tapped into Majeed's eagerness to continue doing business with his invisible partners in the Far East. 'I've already told my boys. They're ready for it, ready to place,' he stressed.

'Are they making money on it? I thought you couldn't make money on the no-balls.'

'On this one they will. Not much but …'

'So you can place on no-balls then? What sort of monies?'

'We'll talk when we meet but there's definitely something on it, yeah. Definitely on it. If you can do it, it'd be good. It's already laid on that end. I can't keep cancelling them.'

'Alright, we'll do it then.'

The third part of the hat-trick would, it appeared, go ahead, but if Majeed had gone further with his line of questioning about betting on no-balls then it would have been like pushing one brick out from a wall and seeing the whole edifice collapse. 'I thought you couldn't make money on the no-balls,' he had said, and he was right. No bookmaker, legal or illegal, was likely to take that bet because no-balls were not only an odd thing to set a market for but because they were so obviously open to *individual* corruption. So seduced was he by Mr Khan's image and money (and the prospect of more to come) that it never occurred to Majeed to stop and think about this.

The weather at Lord's, meanwhile, was not a huge improvement on the day before – grey clouds, moisture in the air though no precipitation, perfect conditions for Amir's brand of swing bowling – but play would start on time. At 11am the teenager had the ball in his hand and was measuring his run-up to finish off the over cut short by rain the day before.

Fifteen minutes in and for the second time in nearly 24 hours the *News of the World* editorial hierarchy were thinking: *What's Amir up to?* The 18-year-old had four wickets from his first ten balls. His third delivery had swung late and caught Alastair Cook's edge ('Perfect line outside off and lovely shape away from Cook who pushed forward with the edge pouched safely by Kamran Akmal,' reported *Cricinfo* on its ball-by-ball feed). Jonathan Trott then played out a maiden from Asif, who looked equally impressive. On the first ball of Amir's next over, Kevin Pietersen was dismissed, caught behind for a golden duck. There was to be no hat-trick, but when Paul Collingwood was given out leg before a couple of minutes later, Amir already had three wickets in five balls.

It was a devastating spell against which the game's finest batsmen would have struggled – you couldn't accuse the England batsmen of being in on any fix. Sport editor Paul McCarthy, who knew a bit more than the other journalists about international cricket, wondered how a man who was apparently on the take and poised to deliver for his paymasters could produce such heroics. McCarthy's wonderment only grew when, in his next over and with his tenth ball of the day, Amir removed Eoin Morgan to leave England 47/5. What the 18-year-old lacked in morals, he certainly made up for in talent and *cojones*.

It was at the point that Pakistan were celebrating Morgan's wicket that Majeed texted simply: 'Not on'. Mahmood was on the phone to him immediately. Now no one seemed to know what was going to happen as the disjoined nature of the fixer's explanation showed: 'So the captain might go up and say listen if you get a no-ball … you're bloody … what if you do a no-ball you get a wicket? So much is happening out there at the moment.' The point he was making was that the no-ball was 'not guaranteed'.

A lucky four for Jonathan Trott off Asif took England past the 50 mark, and another single meant that the same batsman was on strike when Amir took the ball for his next over. According to Majeed's *original* prophecy ('he's finishing the over he's currently bowling yeah … 'cos rain stopped play so he's still got three balls left of his current over, yeah … so once that's over then the third ball of the following three'), they should be moving into the final act.

Ball one: The left-armer, coming from over the wicket, moves it across the batsman who allows it through to the keeper.

Ball two: Better line, better length from Amir and Trott is drawn into a shot only to pull his bat inside the line at the last minute.

Moment of truth …

Ball three: A short preamble as Salman Butt leaves his place in the field to speak to Amir. 'A quick conference between captain and the bowler. Hasn't resulted in the field being changed. Not yet,' says commentator Michael Holding. Amir bustles in and it's a short one. Trott is caught in a tangle as he wrestles with the fend and the hook shots. The ball drops down to where short leg (mysteriously moved to midwicket at the start of the over) would have been and Trott and Matt Prior scramble through for a single.

The real action though is at the bottom of the TV screen where umpire Bowden's raised arm is a signal of joy for those watching in one corner of east London. On time and on the money, the boy's only gone and done it. No one in Wapping notices that Amir responds to the call with a quizzical, rueful look at the popping crease.

Sky Sports are now replaying the delivery. Amir's front foot must be at least ten inches beyond the legal line – another whopper. 'How far over was that? Wow,' says an incredulous Holding. 'It's like net bowling,' says Ian Botham, eager as ever to lambast a bowler for this particular failing. At this point, a thought occurs to Paul McCarthy: will anyone outside of the paper's magic circle twig that such a huge overstep can only be deliberate? He wasn't going to darken the mood by asking the question out loud in the editor's office where everyone was now fighting with their inner selves not to mimic the high-fiving with which the Pakistanis had been celebrating wickets.

Back at his desk, McCarthy still couldn't quite believe what he had seen. It had been like a Derren Brown stunt. First came the extravagant opening gestures – the fall of the wickets – and then the act itself with its signature sleight of hand. He had been involved in many *News of the World* undercover operations before but none that had stuck so closely to the playbook, none of this magnitude. Now the hard work would begin.

* * *

As promised, Colin Myler and Tom Crone took care of the police connection. To non-journalists and indeed many hacks, the closeness between the Metropolitan Police Service (MPS) and *News of the World* seemed beyond the call of duty. The paper had always been strong on crime stories and many of those naturally emanated from the capital. In some cases, often involving Mahmood, the *Screws* would be exposing crime and that necessitated, as it would now, contacting the police in advance of publication. The most high-profile example of this came during a 2002 investigation into a kidnap ring allegedly targeting David Beckham's family. In that instance, three officers from the Met's kidnap and special investigations team had been called in weeks before the story went to press.

That made it natural that the two institutions should cultivate one another, and it was hardly a shock among their peers that *News of the World* reporters were later found to have paid MPS officers for confidential information. What did surprise them was how personal the relationships between the leadership teams at the paper and police had become. The key figure here had been Sir John Stevens, Met commissioner from 2000 until 2005. In his autobiography, Stevens admitted that he had 'worked hard to foster good relations with newspapers and had made himself "available" to editors including Rebekah Wade [now Brooks] at *The Sun* and Andy Coulson of the *News of the World*.'

Just how available was evident in *Confessions of a Fake Sheikh*. Mahmood recalled that in 2004 he had been invited by Stevens 'for a private drink together with [editor] Andy Coulson. We sat in his plush offices at the Yard and Sir John praised my work, singling out the Newcastle United bosses story as one of his all-time favourites. He also told me that he felt my work on the Beckham kidnap case had been excellent ... Coming from the most decorated officer in the land, I considered it a huge honour.' In 2005, soon after he had stepped down as commissioner, Stevens began a weekly column for the paper. That column was ghost-written by the then deputy editor Neil Wallis, who resigned in 2009 to begin a contract assisting the force with its communications and PR. It would later emerge that while wearing his Met PR hat, he had also been paid £25,000 by his former employers for providing exclusives about investigations.

There were other ties. Crime reporter Lucy Panton was married to a Scotland Yard detective. Questions would be asked about the wisdom of allowing assistant commissioner John Yates, a guest at Panton's wedding, to review the Met's investigation into phone-hacking at the paper after *The Guardian* had brought new evidence to light in 2009. In 2011 it emerged that the present Met chief Paul Stephenson himself had enjoyed meals with News International executives and editors on 18 separate occasions during the investigation. He would resign that year after a torrent of adverse publicity about his relationships with the News International hierarchy and *News of the World* in particular.

None of that was on anyone's agenda, horizon or conscience on the evening of Friday, 27 August 2010 when Colin Myler pulled out his mobile and dug out Stephenson's number from his contacts folder. The commissioner took his call straight away. 'Paul, it's Colin. Hi, how are you? Listen, we've got a very big corruption story and it's something your people really need to look at before we go to print.' Their discussions went on a little further, with Myler indicating the urgency and the gravity without giving away any particulars. It ended with Stephenson saying he would call him back.

It was about 9pm when Stephenson informed him that one of his assistant commissioners, Cressida Dick, would be along with a team at 8am the following day to see what they had. Before he hung up, he asked: 'This wouldn't be a sporting story, would it?' Myler chuckled and told him Tom Crone would reveal all to his officers in the morning.

Eleven hours later, assistant commissioner Dick and detective superintendents Nigel Mawer and Matthew Horne were at the front gate of the News International headquarters. There to meet them, with about 12 hours' sleep in the past three days under his belt, was Neil McLeod. The police car was not marked but they would have immediately stood out as representatives of the law to any seasoned hack. This being Saturday morning, there were plenty of those from the *Sunday Times* arriving for work. With secrecy still the order of the day, it was deemed prudent to squirrel them on to the premises via the side entrance and up the back lift.

McLeod had been told to take them to the fifth floor where Tom Crone had his office next to the editorial space that housed the *Fabulous* magazine and from where Myler had been extracted the previous day. *Fabulous* was the lifestyle supplement pitched mainly at female readers, with fashion a staple of its content. As the detectives followed McLeod to where Crone had set up his evidence room, they passed hanger after hanger of skirts, dresses and other types of ladies' designer gear. 'This place is just like CID,' joked DSI Horne, trying to break the ice.

They did not go into the lawyer's but into a nearby meeting room. Here the police officers met the lawyer Crone, Mahmood and Brown. In front of them, on the table, were print-outs of the transcripts in which Majeed had unwittingly incriminated himself and his players. To further bring the case to life, Brown had edited a short film combining his own video recordings with Sky's footage of the match. Crone summed up the essentials of the investigation, Mahmood provided more detail and then Brown showed the film on his laptop.

Once it had finished, questions inevitably followed. On more than one occasion, Crone was impressed by Cressida Dick's familiarity not just with the sport but with the Pakistan team. He had no idea that Dick, who would follow Stephenson's successor, Bernard Hogan-Howe, into the top job, was a cricket fan. More to the point, she was a Pakistan fan, having been at school in Oxford in the mid-70s when their greatest player, Imran Khan, was making a name for himself at the university. Even more to the point, she had actually been at Lord's on the Thursday, as a paying spectator with her friend Sue.

After half an hour of listening to the *News of the World*'s case, Dick asked if she and her detectives could take the transcripts and other files into a quiet room and talk among themselves for a while. 'Of course. Here, use my office,' Crone said, ushering them in. Twenty minutes later, they re-emerged. Dick resumed her place at the table. 'We have decided you are not wasting our time. We will now take away all this evidence, go back to Scotland Yard and scope our operation. We will be at Lord's this afternoon when the cricketers leave the field and we will also visit Mr Majeed's house.'

They gathered up all the files that Crone and Brown had prepared for them, took down Majeed's address and BlackBerry details, then asked Mahmood for one final act of assistance. It was critical to their operation that Majeed was at home in Croydon when they called round, so would 'Mohsin Khan' mind calling him to arrange a meeting there? If there was a full day's play at Lord's then Pakistan would probably get off the field at around 6.30pm when they would be met by representatives of the Met. Mahmood was asked to arrange the meet at the same time. He was then to call again at 6.25pm to say he was five minutes away. He warned Dick that her officers might have trouble getting through Majeed's securely gated entrance. 'Oh, I don't think our people will have any trouble,' she said with a wry grin.

As Crone was walking the police to their car, he apologised to DSI Mawer for messing up their day off. 'That's OK,' he said. 'You know if Cressida wasn't here today she would be at Lord's wearing her Pakistan shirt.'

* * *

By now, the weather had turned for the better at Lord's and so had England. Once the third no-ball had been completed, no one at the *News of the World* had really given too much thought to the game itself. This was a shame since it had marked the start of the home side's resurgence. Shortly before 11.30am on Friday, when Amir had overstepped for the second time, England had been 52/5. At 1.45pm they were 102/7, Amir removing Matt Prior and Graeme Swann in three balls. By close of play, the hosts were 346/7.

The heroes were Jonathan Trott, a feisty competitor who had shared a few choice words in the middle with his opponents throughout the series, and Stuart Broad. Trott would start day three on 149, while Broad, known more as a bowler than a batsman, was also not out and with a century to his name. It was the 24-year-old's first Test ton and on reaching 100 he had looked to the sky and said, 'That was for you, Miche' – a tribute to his stepmother who had died of motor neurone disease seven weeks earlier.

While Trott and Broad spent Saturday morning resuming their assault on Pakistan's attack, Paul McCarthy was in with Myler. 'Tom Crone has signed almost everything off on the Pakistanis so we are good to go,' explained the editor. 'The plan is to do nine pages at the front of the book but we'll want something in sport too ...'

'Of course. I've got Sam Peters, our cricket man, at Lord's. He will need to be told at some point. Then there's Richie ...'

Richie was former Australia captain Richie Benaud. One of the game's great leg-spinners and leaders, he was now its foremost commentator. If anyone had a right to be called the 'Voice of Cricket', it was Richie. Here was an Aussie even the English had come to respect and embrace. Benaud had been writing for the *Screws* for more than 50 years. From the outside it looked a strange fit. The *Screws* wasn't regarded as a 'cricket paper' and brand Benaud – as Richie would never have called it – didn't sit comfortably alongside tales of suburban orgies, politicians cheating on long-suffering wives and assorted showbiz scandals. And yet Richie had a taste for the anti-establishment, as evidenced by his decision to back Kerry Packer's breakaway World Series regime in the late 70s. He also had a liking for red-tops, having started his working life as a crime reporter for the Sydney evening newspaper, *The Sun*.

At least once every summer, Myler and McCarthy would take Benaud and his long-time collaborator David Norrie for dinner at Langan's in Mayfair. McCarthy had never seen the *News of the World* editor star-struck … until then. The editor was naturally delighted that the Australian would be enlisted.

'Yes, we will need a Richie column – either for news or sport. Have you spoken to him?' he asked.

McCarthy shook his head. 'No, I was waiting for your say-so. Sam Peters ghosts him now and the pair usually sit down late afternoon to write the column.'

'Presumably, they're both on their way to Lord's as we speak.' McCarthy nodded. 'Well,' Myler continued, 'I'm not sure they will find in the press box the privacy they need. What's your plan?'

McCarthy hadn't formulated one yet but he was used to thinking on his feet in front of the boss. 'I don't see that we've got any choice other than to bring them here. They need to see the evidence first hand if either of them is to write a fully informed piece. I was going to wait until lunchtime to see how it pans out in the match itself. England are on top at the moment and I can always get someone else to do the live report. It's not as if that's going to be the main read …'

'OK, let me know when Richie's coming and we'll bring him in here.'

Soon after midday, McCarthy picked up the phone in his office and pressed the button that put him straight through to his cricket correspondent. 'Sam, where are you at the moment? Yes, I know you're in the press box but are you somewhere quiet? OK, find yourself somewhere private first ... Are you OK? Right, listen to me and don't ask any questions. There is a car coming to Lord's, it will probably get there during the lunch interval. It's going to bring you and Richie over to Wapping ... I said don't ask any questions and don't worry about what happens in the afternoon and evening sessions, we can take care of that on the desk.

'Secondly, and more important, you need to get Richie out of there without anyone noticing. Nice and casual. As soon as this call is over, take him into a quiet corner and tell him about this conversation and explain that the editor – that's Colin Myler not me – needs him in Wapping to look at a big story that news have been working on. You'll need to look at it too. It's going to be a long night. The driver of the car has your number.'

As luck would have it, Benaud was sitting next to Peters so the task of moving him into a discreet recess of the media centre wasn't difficult. Once there he shared the details of his conversation with McCarthy. Benaud was a little surprised but took it calmly enough, as he did most things. One job he would have to do first, he informed Peters, was to call his wife Daphne who was also at the ground. At this point, the cricket legend pulled out his mobile phone and turned it over where a list of names and numbers was taped on. Richie, it transpired, had not mastered the contacts folder on the phone itself so had devised this 'analogue' system.

Once Daphne had been informed that her husband would be gone for some time, the pair furtively made their way to the North Gate where the car was waiting for them. Inside the vehicle and away from the ears of fellow journalists, Peters was keen to discuss what might lie in wait for them in east London. Once the match had started, he had been surprised to receive several calls from the news desk asking him about the Pakistan team. Calls from the news desk were not common. Questions about the politics of the tourists' dressing room were even rarer. Now his mind was hurtling to the conclusion that the reason for their inquiries was corruption. He was eager to get Benaud's view.

'Richie, I think we've got ...' he began. Before he could blurt out any more, the wily 79-year-old had raised his finger to his lips and nodded in the direction of the driver. It was a gesture that said trust no one. Peters stopped and inwardly bowed to the doyen's sagacity. Discretion was definitely the better part of valour and he dropped the subject.

Matt Drake was downstairs by the same side entrance that the police had used, waiting for the cricket correspondent and columnist to arrive. As there had been with Dick's arrival five hours earlier, there was an urgency to usher them into the building as quickly and clandestinely as possible before journalists from the *Sunday Times* spotted them and sensed that something was afoot. Incredibly, it was Benaud's first ever visit to his employer's offices.

Drake led them up to where McCarthy was waiting. He then shooed them straight into the editor's office. Myler got up to greet Richie, delighted by his presence. He shook hands with Peters too as if he was one of his regular confidants, but McCarthy wasn't sure the pair had ever met. Until now, there had been no need for them to be introduced. 'Tomorrow, gentlemen,' he said with a rhetorical flourish, 'the *News of the World* is going to break the biggest story in its history.' Like Dick, they were then invited to inspect the evidence. McCarthy watched Richie watching the film. He didn't give much away. 'This is what we are splashing on,' said Myler after sufficient time had elapsed. 'What do you think?'

Just under ten years earlier, Benaud had been interviewed on Australian TV about the disgrace of Hansie Cronje, the South Africa captain who had accepted bribes and instructed two of his players to help lose a match. His observation back then was devastating: 'I've spent just about every minute of my waking life figuring out how to win cricket matches and now I find out there's some bastard out there working out how to lose them.'

Come on, thought McCarthy, we need something just like that now.

'Well,' said Richie, 'I reckon it could be the biggest scandal ever to hit cricket.' McCarthy wanted to hug him, but then the Australian added, 'If true ...'

Time stood still for a moment, then all eyes turned on Myler. If anyone else had queried the editorial integrity of his paper (in his own office!) he would have ripped out the most sensitive and vital parts of their anatomy. Myler looked at Benaud like a boy who'd shown off his A-grade homework to his dad only to be asked if he had cheated on it. Very calmly he said, 'Richie, I can assure you it's all true.'

'Well then, everybody, Sam and I had best start cracking on.' McCarthy didn't dare look Myler in the face as he ushered the pair out. Drake bumped into the Australian in the toilets almost immediately after. 'So it's true then,' said Benaud drily. 'I'm afraid it is.' He looked saddened rather than shocked, and Drake remembered that he had probably been working for domestic TV on the Australia v Pakistan Test in Sydney earlier in the year, which now looked as if it too had been shaped by non-cricketing forces.

While what seemed like every section head, reporter, sub-editor, designer and picture researcher available was working on the cricket story – the secret was now out in the office – there was one employee of the *News of the World* left at Lord's. Phil Whiteside had been sent to see what unfolded when the police fronted up to the Pakistan team. He had not been able to get a press pass or a ticket for the game so was forced to keep a vigil on St John's Wood Road close to the Grace Gates, which served as the main entrance and exit point for players and spectators.

Unbeknown to him, the police arrived at around four. Although the match was part of a series organised by the England and Wales Cricket Board, who also had their offices at Lord's, the running of the ground fell under the auspices of the Marylebone Cricket Club (MCC). Australian Keith Bradshaw was its secretary and was on duty on matchdays. He was doing one of his normal afternoon tours to make sure everything was in order when he received a call from his PA. *Could he come straight back to his office where the police were waiting to talk to him about a matter of some urgency?*

Bradshaw beat a hasty retreat to the pavilion where he found Cressida Dick and a couple of other officers. The assistant commissioner told him that they were now entering into a lockdown situation. The game would continue as normal but any internal and external communications and actions could only be made with her consent. He was not to inform anyone of this. Dick then asked where the players' mobile phones were kept. He told her and they discussed retrieving them from the safe.

On the pitch, events had moved on significantly. England had been bowled out shortly after lunch for 447. Pakistan's response was poor to the point of embarrassing. At about the time the police were arriving, they were 46/3. Salman Butt's dismissal for 27 then set off a collapse that saw the last seven wickets fall for 28 runs. Only twice had they scored less than 74 in a Test innings against England, and one of those had come earlier in the summer in the match in Birmingham. With England skipper Andrew Strauss forcing his opponents to follow on, it meant that Dick and her team were in the same building as the three main suspects, a 30-second walk from where they were sitting in the visitors' dressing room, waiting for their turn to bat again.

The plan, once play concluded for the day, she told Bradshaw, was to pretend that there was a security situation. That would require the Pakistan team to remain in their dressing room until it had been resolved. This should not take too long, Dick advised, but they absolutely could not be allowed to leave until other members of her team had located a person of interest elsewhere in London. Bradshaw would later work out that this was a reference to Majeed. Nor could they be allowed their mobiles at that point.

Second time around, Pakistan were just as dismal. At 6.20pm, they were 41/3 – Butt was already out for 21 – when Mohammad Yousuf pulled a short ball from Steve Finn straight to Trott at deep square leg. As if the heavens were offering judgement, a huge downpour then arrived, forcing them off. The umpires had no hesitation in confirming there would be no more cricket that day.

With all the away side now back in their dressing room, Keith Bradshaw sought out team manager Yawar Saeed to explain that there was a complication with security. It was nothing to fret about and they expected to have it under wraps very shortly, but it would require the squad to wait in their dressing room in the meantime. Saeed and the players took it in their stride, which wasn't unsurprising since such issues seemed to follow the team wherever they went.

After a quarter of an hour, Bradshaw got the nod from Cressida Dick that the person of interest was now in the company of her officers. The Pakistanis were at liberty to move. Half an hour later, their coach left the ground for the short drive to the Marriott Hotel. Phil Whiteside followed.

The tourists barely had time to order room service before the police were moving through the hotel to begin their search of the players' rooms. Phil Whiteside was in the lobby, and although it was clear that officers of the law were on the premises it was hard to find out much more.

Also in the lobby was Azhar Majeed, unaware of his brother's arrest. Azhar had taken his sons to watch the day's play and was due to have dinner with them, Mazhar, some of the players and a mutual friend from Birmingham. They had gone to the hotel at the same time as the team and his boys had been introduced to Kamran Akmal. Spotting a representative of the ICC's anti-corruption and security unit also on the premises, Azhar marched up to him demanding to know why he was apparently on the PCB's blacklist. Not long after, as the word spread about the nature of police inquiries, team security officer Major Khwaja Najam Javed had shouted at him: 'Are you happy now?'

* * *

In Wapping the last touches were being put to the first edition. *Front page:* A giant headline, **CAUGHT!**, above the money shot of Majeed counting out the cash with an inset of Kerry Davies's photo of Amir's second no-ball. *Pages 2-3:* **Cricket in the dock: Greedy fixer strikes his bargain to cheat fans.** *Pages 4-5:* **Cricket in the dock: Three no-balls that will shake world of sport.** *Pages 6-7:* **Cricket in the dock: Mastermind pockets his money after**

pay-off. *Pages 8-9:* **Cricket in the dock: Match-rigger boasts of syndicate's shady fortune**. There was more in sport where the headline 'Ban 'em for life' spoke for itself. By 7.30pm, it was ready to go to the printers.

The night was only beginning for Paul McCarthy. Though he had only been on the periphery of Mahmood's investigation, he was about to get star billing in the *News of the World*'s PR operation. These were the days before social media was the dominant voice, when the most obvious way for a newspaper to amplify a 'world exclusive' was through TV. Much as they might hate to admit it, the hacks knew that TV trumped print or the internet for impact every time. BBC, ITV, Sky – Hayley Barlow, the paper's pugnacious PR chief, had them all lined up and McCarthy was going to be her leading man.

Print-outs of the relevant pages along with Brown's video would be released to the 24-hour news networks to put out on their 9pm bulletins. At the same time, that video would be uploaded on to the paper's own website. The story would then get wider consumption on the late evening ITV and BBC newscasts. After that, McCarthy would be wheeled out to any channel chasing more context and insight. The thinking was simple: he already had experience and exposure, having appeared many times on television; he would also be billed as sport editor, which should enhance the story's credibility. The interviews would be conducted outside, in front of the main gate. The cover of darkness would underscore the idea that this was a breaking story which could go anywhere overnight. The backdrop of the gate would ensure that no viewer could fail to see the huge News International sign with its logos for the *Screws*, *Sun*, *Times* and *Sunday Times*.

McCarthy was killing time before the cameras came calling by reading back over his own sports pages. If he had one disappointment from the day it was when he read Benaud's column again. Despite the editor's reassurance, it was as if Richie still couldn't quite believe what he had seen. There was the expected condemnation and call for action ('The ICC has a lot of work to do to restore confidence after this latest, lousy bit of skulduggery.' No shit, Rich!) but the killer line – the sentence that would be picked up by news agencies, broadcasters and other media and echo round the world – was nowhere to be found.

He was wondering whether to call up Benaud and ask him to go in harder for the second edition when his phone rang. He looked at the caller ID, Colin Gibson. 'Gibbo' was hack turned flak. After nearly two decades on Fleet Street, where he had risen to be sports editor of the *Daily Mail*, he had crossed the fence to work as communications chief for the Football Association. He then took up a similar position at the ECB. From there he had migrated to Dubai, home of the International Cricket Council, though his ICC duties ironically meant he was now in London.

'I've had a message from a bloke on your news team saying they are going to need someone to comment on a very big story. What's it all about?'

'Sorry, Gibbo, you'll have to speak to them yourself, this is front-page stuff.'

'OK then. But when they say big, just how big are we talking? Bigger than Sven and Faria Alam?'

Sven was former England football manager Sven-Goran Eriksson whose affair with Alam, who also worked at the Football Association, had been another *Screws* special. The reporters assigned to the case could not believe their luck when they discovered that Alam, a PA, had also been having an affair with the FA chief executive Mark Palios. Gibson had more reason than anyone to remember that story. He could have shut down all lines of inquiry by stating that private lives were meant to stay private. Instead, he had tried to trade his boss, Palios, out of trouble by offering the *Screws* what he called 'chapter and verse' on Alam and Sven. 'The pay-off obviously is that we leave MP [Palios] out of it,' he told one of its executives. 'I've got the details, I've got the places, I've got the phone calls, I've got everything. He's keen, we're all keen, to see the deal go through.' Asked if Alam would talk to the paper, Gibson replied, 'If she won't, I will, on her behalf.'

Little did Gibson know that Alam was already out selling her story to other interested parties. Once the *Screws* got wind of this, the putative Palios deal went out the window. Even better, they had the conversation of the FA's chief spin doctor plotting to save the suit and shaft the England manager on tape. When the transcript appeared in the paper, Palios and Gibson were dead men walking.

'Gibbo,' said McCarthy chuckling at the memory of that tawdry little episode, 'it's bigger than Faria and Sven, and this time it probably won't cost you your job. Probably.'

Within half an hour, Gibson had got wind of the exocet missile coming his and the ICC's way and was in a cab heading to the Royal Garden Hotel in Kensington. While his team had moved to the north side of the capital after The Oval Test, Pakistan board chairman Ijaz Butt had remained there while the Lord's match was on. Like Gibson, Giles Clarke, chairman of the England Cricket Board (ECB), was now aware of the breaking news and had realised he too would need to consult immediately with his opposite number on damage limitation and contingency plans. They were joined at the Royal Garden by Cressida Dick, who had deemed it prudent to speak with the main authority for Pakistan cricket.

Clarke and Butt had already spent the previous evening at a dinner party in Hampstead, hosted by former England captain Mike Brearley. In fact, it was quite the gathering of the cricketing great and good, with fellow former England captains Mike Gatting and Mike Atherton in attendance. Also present was Pakistan World Cup-winner Ramiz Raja who, like Atherton, had been commentating for Sky when one of the three no-balls was bowled. Most of the guests had departed around midnight, but Butt and Clarke had stayed on and spent most of the next hour reciting Urdu poetry – the latter having studied the language at Oxford.

There was obviously a rather different mood in Butt's suite at the Royal Garden. Even if the scandal hadn't involved a live match against England, Clarke would probably have been there anyway because he was on friendly terms with Butt and he knew that in a foreign capital he would need help around him. He was right to be worried about his Pakistan counterpart because Butt was essentially in denial about what looked like compelling evidence. Cressida Dick kept telling him to study the *News of the World* footage on Sky News but her urgings fell on deaf ears. 'Just make sure he watches Sky,' were her parting words to Gibson.

At about the same time as the ICC, ECB and Pakistan officials were holding their crisis summit and Paul McCarthy was walking out to face the cameras, Dilawar Chaudhry was sitting in his restaurant, TKC, in Southall, keeping an eye on business. To the right of the table where he was seated was a TV screen which, with there being no cricket in England or anywhere else to see at this time of night, was playing Sky News. The funny thing was that Sky News now appeared to be showing a story about cricket and he drew nearer to see what it was.

His first call was to Shahid Afridi, who had come to dine with team-mate Abdul Razzaq at the restaurant earlier that summer. 'Shahid, have you seen the news?' he asked. Afridi had just arrived at Karachi airport with Razzaq to catch a flight to London for the forthcoming one-day series with England. The fixing accusations were the only news on the TV screens at the terminal. 'Yes,' he replied. 'This was inevitable.'

CHAPTER FOUR

'HOW COULD THE REST OF YOU NOT KNOW WHAT WAS GOING ON?'

'THIS IS going to be fucking weird but let's just get the job done. They're not going to hang around – they will want to get out of here quicker than we do.' This was not the normal rhetoric that England captain Andrew Strauss reserved for the team's huddle at the start of each day's play. Then again, Sunday, 29 August 2010 wasn't a normal cricket day.

For Strauss, the day had effectively started around 10pm the night before. At the end of Saturday's play, his media duties fulfilled, he had driven to his home just outside Marlow in Buckinghamshire. Most of his team would spend the night in the team hotel, the Landmark, but the England hierarchy tried to allow players, especially the captain, to stay at home during Tests when convenient.

Lord's was Strauss's home ground. Since moving out of London five years earlier, he had made the drive from St John's Wood to his house in Berkshire countless times. On a Saturday night, he could do it in little more than half an hour. With England on the brink of victory, he was looking forward to seeing his sons Sam (four) and Luca (two) before they went to bed. Once paternal duties had been completed, he sat down for dinner with his wife Ruth and then slumped on the sofa to watch some TV before going to bed.

He didn't have anything particular in mind to watch when he turned it on so settled in for the evening news. Five minutes later, once he had had a chance to take in the detail and enormity of what was leading the bulletin, he was on the phone to Andy Flower. The England coach had only just been apprised of developments and was awaiting instruction from ECB chair Giles Clarke, currently in conference with Ijaz Butt, assistant commissioner Dick and Colin Gibson in Kensington. Flower told him to sit tight and wait for further orders. When those orders eventually came through, they were to assume that the Test would continue, to be at the ground early the next day, and to prepare for any eventuality. So much for a good night's sleep at home.

Strauss was at Lord's that Sunday morning before some of his team had even made it down for breakfast at the Landmark, just 15 minutes from the 'scene of the crime'. Graeme Swann and James Anderson were among the stragglers. Neither was aware of what had been leading the news channels for almost 12 hours and only got wind of it from their team-mates as they were leaving the breakfast room. Even then the pair hadn't really understood the gravity of the situation. So when they picked up the *News of the World* they began chuckling about the 'Fake Sheikh' as they recalled his sting on England manager Sven-Goran Eriksson four years earlier. The feeling was that *News of the World* exclusives should be treated with a mixture of caution and cynicism.

The two left the hotel at around 9am. The rest were already gathering in the players' dining room at Lord's with MCC secretary Keith Bradshaw, who had responsibility for the ground and had arrived at 7am for an emergency meeting with Colin Gibson of the ICC and representatives of the ECB to discuss arrangements for the day. There was no sign so far of the Pakistanis, whose hotel, they discovered, had been searched by police the night before. Bradshaw and those present were watching Sky News, whose cameras were fixed on the Pakistan team bus – outside the hotel but not moving. Everyone was thinking the same: are they coming?

Strauss informed them that they had to assume that they would be coming even though he was beginning to have his doubts. One by one his men filed in to their own dressing room. Swann and Anderson eventually wandered in too, baffled to find that no one had yet changed into matchday whites or any of the kit usually worn for warm-up drills. All of a sudden alarm bells began to ring among the two most nonchalant members of the squad: the sheikh might have been fake but this was the real deal.

Pakistan did come but they cut it fine and did not enter the pavilion via the normal team entrance. As the minutes ticked down to the 11am start, a few briefly appeared on their own balcony before retreating back inside. None came down to pitch level to practise apart from the two not-out batsmen, Umar Akmal and Azhar Ali, and their warm-up could be described as light at best. By now England were out on the playing surface going through their usual routines. Word had come down from the powers-that-be that the match would proceed at the conventional start time.

'The most surreal atmosphere I have ever played in,' was how Swann described it, with Strauss's pep talk adding to the unreal air. The off-spinner had already been nursing a dislike for Salman Butt, who was perceived as arrogant to the point of downright unpleasant by many of the England team. The day before, the Pakistan captain had been bowled by a delivery from Swann which pitched on leg stump and clipped off. Butt had initially stood his ground, refusing to believe that the ball had turned so much. 'You're embarrassing yourself, I'd get off the pitch if I were you,' Swann told him.

If Butt had been embarrassed on Saturday then it's hard to believe how he felt as he watched his men walk out to bat and, not much later, trudge disconsolately back on that Sunday morning. Pakistan started the day and their second innings on 41/4, still 321 runs behind England's first innings total. Even before the newspaper revelations, no one expected them to last the day. That they held out for little more than an hour and a half, however, added to the impression that this was a team which – either through apathy or darker motives – was indifferent to the final outcome.

Strauss wasn't wrong about them not wanting to hang around. Their lower-order batsmen were, as Swann saw it, 'just teeing off', adding 106 runs at five an over with wickets falling regularly. Barely 20 minutes of play had elapsed before they were 64/6. Mohammad

Amir, escorted through the pavilion and down the steps by an official with a walkie-talkie, was now on his way to the middle.

Amir had performed creditably with the bat as well as the ball in the previous Tests, one of the few to offer resistance to England's seamers after they had cleaned up the top order. There would be none of that now. During his brief time at the crease (three minutes for 0 runs), he tried to catch his opponents' eyes, offering a sheepish smile as if looking for a friend. At that point, Swann knew he was guilty. To his eye, the Pakistani had the look of a puppy sitting next to a pile of poo.

Through all the boundaries struck, not one Pakistan player showed his face on the team balcony. Through the fall of all six wickets, the applause from the crowd never rose above modest. There was little celebration from the fielding side either as they closed in on victory. One England player compared their general reaction to each dismissal to Denis Law after he had scored the goal that sent Manchester United down. The last wicket fell to Swann at 12.36pm. With that, England had claimed victory by an innings and 225 runs, and the series 3-1.

The cricket 'bible' *Wisden* would report in its match summary: 'In a sombre atmosphere Pakistan were wrapped up before lunch on the fourth day for their heaviest Test defeat. They made little attempt at a fight, arriving late at the ground and doing no warming up or practising before the resumption: paying spectators had every right to feel robbed.'

Now the prize-giving formalities were also about to leave everyone short-changed. These would normally have taken place on the outfield. One by one, rival captains, man of the match, players of the series for the respective sides would be called forward. Hands would be shaken; trophies, cheques and bottles of bubbly presented; and interviews given. That was how it worked across the cricket world. Not today. Instead, players, officials, MCC members and the odd cameraman were squeezed into the pavilion in the Long Room, the grand hall through which players make their way from the dressing room to the pitch.

The Long Room's historic aura and grandeur had once prompted Australian Justin Langer to say that walking through it was like 'being bearhugged by an invisible spirit'. On this day, Lord's officials were more worried about being ambushed by hostile spirits. So concerned were they that the revelations in the *News of the World* would trigger a chorus of heckles aimed at any Pakistani that the series wrap-up had been relocated to this discreet recess. 'We could not guarantee the safety of the Pakistan players if we did it outside. We were worried they were targets,' said the MCC's Bradshaw. Bradshaw's concerns were understandable though may have been a little excessive because when the Mohammads Amir and Asif had walked out to bat earlier that morning, the only overt outbursts had been what *The Guardian* described as 'a few token pantomime boos' and a joker crying out 'No-ball!'

For England's players and management, this should have been an upbeat occasion. Two of the side would see their names go up on the prestigious honours board for the first time – Stuart Broad for his maiden Test century, Swann for his five wickets in the second innings. It would also be the last time home fans would see the Test team before they flew out to Australia for the winter's Ashes – an opportunity to give them the stirring send-off that a near-perfect demolition of Pakistan deserved. Instead the mood was more funeral than fiesta.

Overseeing proceedings was ECB chair Giles Clarke. No one in international cricket officialdom did pompous quite like Clarke (Rugby School, Oxford University, The City). Given the self-importance of the blazers who ran the game, that was saying something. But for all the ECB chairman's natural conceit, if ever there was a day when he was entitled to a display of righteous indignation this was it. Clarke was later criticised for making the ceremony in the Long Room all about him, with his pointed refusal to look the opposition in the eye or shake their hands. Yet he had good cause for his antipathy. A few months earlier, he had been appointed by the ICC to chair its Pakistan task force. Set up after a series of terrorist atrocities in the country had forced a suspension of home matches, its function was to find a place for the nation within the international community. Clarke's appointment reflected his standing and influence within the sport and also the fact that, having studied Arabic and Urdu, he literally spoke the Pakistanis' language.

To this end, he had gone out on a limb by offering England as a venue for the two 'home' Tests they had played against Australia in the first half of the 2010 summer. Logistically, it had been a nightmare because the knock-on effect was that the final two matches of England's subsequent series against Pakistan would have to be back-to-back fixtures at The Oval and Lord's. It was the first such time that this had happened in the capital and brought with it all sorts of complications. As well as souring England's series win, the allegations in the *Screws* had now added a dark layer of complexity to Clarke's wider remit. It didn't help that his Saturday night had been a restless and late one, with the fraught meeting at the Royal Garden, and he was furious with Cressida Dick.

The assistant commissioner, he thought, should have informed him immediately of her intention to come to Lord's the day before. The ECB clearly had more skin in the game than the MCC, and Clarke was a much bigger hitter than Bradshaw, enjoying close ties to Downing Street – he was a Conservative Party donor. The more he heard about her carry-on in the pavilion the previous afternoon and rumours that she had considered arresting the Pakistanis while the match was still on, the more he was convinced that a major international crisis had only just been avoided. He was also annoyed with Bradshaw for not alerting him to what had been going on. The Australian's argument that he was constrained by the terms of Dick's lockdown did nothing to pacify his rage.

The dawning of a new day had not brought much clarity to the thinking of the Pakistan Cricket Board. Team manager Yawar Saeed and assistant coach Shafqat Rana had been the only representatives of their country to remain on the team balcony during the morning session. At one point, Saeed was caught on camera reading the *News of the World*. The front page with its giant headline CAUGHT! was clearly visible to viewers and Saeed seemed to be engrossed in the second of the four spreads at the front.

Unusually, editions of the *News of the World* were everywhere that day. Even members in the MCC enclosure, who might have had second thoughts about using it to line their cat litter, were walking round with copies. What was more extraordinary was to see the Pakistan manager brandishing one so blatantly. This was as close as the team's leadership had come to an official acknowledgment of the claims. In the Lord's media centre it prompted jaw-dropping amazement. As crisis management went, it was even more lamentable than their team's performance so far. This was a PR gift to the *Screws* and gave the Monday papers their front page there and then.

Despite this gaffe, despite the visitors' appalling batting display, despite the fact that the vibe in the Long Room that lunchtime was similar to the kind you feel at weddings when both sets of in-laws make no secret of their mutual distrust, Clarke was determined to keep the show on the road. Never let it be said that *he* had not stood up when it mattered.

The problem was that no one else was interested in coming to the fore. At first, the only Pakistani representative hanging around the Long Room for the presentation was Dilawar Chaudhry, caterer, confidant and comforter to the team. Nor did the series sponsors or broadcasters now appear willing to share responsibility for the awards ceremony, which meant it fell to Clarke to take over MC duties. Mohammad Amir was told that as the winner of Pakistan's man of the series award he was expected to show his face. The prospect filled the teenager with dread. When the security officer told him it was time to leave the dressing room and go down to the Long Room, he refused. It took a fair amount of reassurance from the guard – 'No, no, come with me, nothing will happen' – to prise him out.

If there was one person who wanted Amir there even less than the cricketer himself, it was Clarke. He handed over the winner's cheque as if giving him a turd. Amir accepted it in the same spirit. No handshake was proffered. Looking on were the few MCC members who had hung around for the ceremony like rubberneckers at a car crash.

Strauss was ushered away for the traditional post-match press conference. He wanted to speak of his anger that Pakistan had led his team to question the sacrifices they were making for each other and for the game itself. He wanted to tell the media how they had lost all respect for their opponents, even if most of them were apparently blameless, for turning cricket's highest form of competition into a shambles. Instead, he did his best to sound dignified and to avoid any outward sign of the bitterness gnawing away within. Yet as he answered the journalists' questions, it began to dawn on him that the ordeal was not yet over. There were seven limited-overs matches to come and the scrutiny of both sides was only likely to be intensified. Even so, he could have no idea that the next four weeks would amount to one of the toughest periods of his captaincy.

* * *

Hanging over the frost in the room that day was nearly three decades of animosity between the two countries. These went deeper than the historical tensions usually associated with a former colony taking on its one-time imperial masters. Twenty-eight years earlier, at the same ground, Pakistan had won their second ever Test against England, their first since 1954. They would lose the 1982 series 2-1 but it could easily have gone in their favour. It was the first time that the country, led superbly by Imran Khan, had pushed England hard, so it was perhaps not surprising that this new injection of competition should have prompted some bad blood.

There were two sub-plots at work here, both of which would be played out for the next decade. The first, unsurprisingly, centred around the divisive figure of Ian Botham, who was Mr England. During the Lord's Test, he had complained to the umpires about the state of the ball, after part-time seamer Mudassar Nazar had unexpectedly got it to swing. He also had words with Imran who, according to cricket writer Simon Wilde, 'replied that England's bowlers might get the ball to swing more if they looked after it a bit better'. It's fair to say that Botham was not used to this kind of condescension.

Another Pakistani with whom he exchanged cross words in the match was batsman Javed Miandad. In fairness to Botham, Miandad could start an argument in an empty house. Botham's team-mate Derek Pringle would recall, 'He wanted to fight him because Javed was winding him up. At one point, Beefy went to sweep, the ball bounced off his pad and Javed, while appealing for lbw, picked it up and threw at the stumps. It hit Beefy and there was a bit of squaring up. A few overs later, he was out and Javed gave him a send-off. Beefy came back threatening to do him serious harm.'

Eighteen months later, Botham was sent home early from England's tour of Pakistan with a back injury. Asked what he thought of the country, 'Beefy' said, 'Pakistan is the kind of place to send your mother-in-law for a month, all expenses paid.' He did not mean it as a treat for the lady in question. The all-rounder was subsequently fined £1,000 and would later pay for the comment in another way. Dismissed cheaply (and, he would maintain, wrongly) for England in their defeat to Pakistan in the 1992 World Cup Final, he was sent on his way by Amir Sohail with the words, 'Who is coming in next? Your mother-in-law?'

In 1987 Pakistan won their first-ever series in England. Yet again, there was an ugly moment involving the home side's star all-rounder. In the Test at Headingley, Saleem Yousuf claimed he had Botham caught behind even though the ball had clearly touched the ground after the keeper's first failed attempt at a catch. The umpires understandably declined the appeal. Botham wrote in his autobiography that he had called Yousuf 'a cheating little bastard, warning him that if he ever tried that stunt again I would knock his block off.' Pakistan made a complaint about the Englishman's language.

Though he only featured in the first two Tests, Botham's shadow hung over the summer of 1992. In the second of the one-day internationals that preceded the Tests, he dismissed Miandad, described by the *Daily Mirror*, for which Botham wrote a column, as 'Cricket's Colonel Gaddafi'. Miandad claimed that he was told to 'fuck off' by Botham as he departed. In the days before the first Test at Edgbaston, the *Mirror* was also claiming that 'the huge Asian community in Birmingham [had] offered £500' to any Pakistan bowler who could dismiss Botham and £100 for each six hit off his bowling.

It would only get worse, as the tabloids feasted on hints and accusations from the England camp of ball-tampering against the tourists who had flummoxed them with their use of reverse swing. The first official innuendo came at the end of England's 2-1 series defeat when coach Mickey Stewart refused to rule out illegal practice by Pakistan's bowlers. It then fell to Botham's friend, Allan Lamb, to lay the cheating claim out in the open. In the fourth one-day international, played after the Tests, Lamb complained to the umpires about the state of the ball. It was then changed after consultation with both England and Pakistan management. Pakistan consented to the change but rejected the charge that one of their players was responsible for altering its condition.

No one else inside the ground was aware of this until a tabloid reporter was tipped off. *'Got 'em by the Ball'* was the resulting headline in *The Sun*, whose correspondent claimed that the umpires 'were convinced the Pakistanis illegally tampered with the ball'. The ICC's refusal to release the official report into this incident created a vacuum that was filled by more invective against the away team. The *Mirror* demanded that the 'International Cock-up Council' throw Pakistan out of the international community. It then paid Lamb for an interview in which he maintained that their two premier bowlers, Waqar Younis and Wasim Akram, 'gouge the damaged ball with their nails then smear the surface to fool the umpire'. The rest of Fleet Street might usually have poured cold water on claims made by a rival, but cricket journalists were largely supportive. Headline-writers had never had it so good, with those on *The Sun* stating that it was time to *'PAK OFF THE CHEATS FOR FIVE YEARS'*.

These personal and nationalistic tensions resurfaced in 1996 when Botham sued Imran Khan for libel, claiming his old rival had effectively called *him* a ball tamperer and racist. After an acrimonious and incident-packed trial that made the front pages more than the back, the former Pakistan captain was found to have successfully defended himself.

That 1982 series had also triggered the first of many quarrels about umpiring and appealing. This was in the era before neutral umpires and it was far from the first or the worst time that the quality of officials had created controversy between any two Test nations. The problem was that it would not go away between these two particular countries.

At the start of the summer of 1982, the Test and County Cricket Board (TCCB), the forerunner of the ECB, had acquiesced to India's demand that umpire David Constant should not stand in the first Test against them. He was back, however, for the second and third Tests against Pakistan of that summer and the bile began to flow. Constant objected to their frequent, vociferous appealing (England were not innocent of this either), while the Pakistanis were suspicious, with some justification, that his decisions favoured the home side. After defeat in the decisive game at Leeds, Imran said, 'I don't want to give an excuse for us losing the series but Constant made what, for us, were some costly mistakes in this match.'

There was more of the same next time around. As India had done, Pakistan objected to the selection of Constant in 1987 but the TCCB refused to withdraw him, to the obvious displeasure of tour manager Hasib Ahsan, who stated that his men 'have no confidence in Constant'. Though it was shocking to hear in such bold terms, it was hardly surprising that Ahsan described him as 'a disgraceful person' after he turned down a Pakistan appeal in the fifth Test.

Three months later, it was the turn of a Pakistani umpire to be thrust into the spotlight. England, led by Mike Gatting, were now the tourists and had lost the first of three Test matches. On the second day of the second match in Faisalabad, Shakoor Rana stopped Eddie Hemmings from bowling because, as *Wisden* recorded, 'he claimed that Gatting had been unfairly moving the fielder behind the batsman's [Salim Malik] back. Gatting informed the umpire that he was, in his opinion, overstepping the bounds.'

Who was in the right was lost in the slanging match that ensued as the photo of the pair eyeball to eyeball, pointing at one another, went round the world. Coach Mickey Stewart would later allege that Rana had called the captain a 'fucking cheating bastard'. The umpire said that Gatting had spoken with equal disrespect. Stewart also wrote that 14 of England's dismissals in the series had been 'victims of umpires' errors', and that their opponents had been summoned to a meeting with the President, General Zia, who 'ordered [them] to win the match'. No play occurred on day three as the diplomats – at sporting and political levels – strived to find a compromise that would allow both parties to save face. One of those involved was the secretary of the Board of Control for Cricket in Pakistan (the earlier incarnation of the Pakistan Cricket Board), a certain Ijaz Butt.

In 1992 Roy Palmer became the latest official thrown into the eye of the storm. The third Test at Old Trafford was Palmer's international debut. On the fourth afternoon Aqib Javed aimed a series of short-pitched deliveries at tailender Devon Malcolm, one of which led to him being no-balled by Palmer under Law 42.8 ('If the umpire considers that a bowler deliberately bowled a high full-pitched ball, deemed to be dangerous and unfair'). Aqib Javed's captain Miandad and a few team-mates made vocal protestations to the umpire.

It was what followed, however, that turned a point of disputation into a controversy. At the end of the over, Palmer handed back the bowler's jumper in a manner that Pakistan manager Intikhab Alam maintained had 'insulted' Aqib. Even the *Mirror* admitted that 'Palmer, clearly annoyed, thrust the sweater at the bowler in a dismissive fashion.' This prompted Aqib and a furious Miandad to further remonstrate with Palmer and a brief, ugly standoff ensued. The *Sunday Telegraph* branded their team 'the pariahs of cricket'.

In the next match, at Headingley, a pig's head was thrown into the enclosure in which Pakistan supporters were congregated.

That was the same Test in which Ken 'brother of Roy' Palmer gave Graham Gooch not out as England nervously chased down a small total in the fourth innings. TV replays clearly showed that Gooch had been run out. Rashid Latif was fined after throwing his cap to the ground in anger when David Gower was let off a strong appeal for caught behind.

The feeling on the home side and among much of the tabloid press was that their opponents' appealing was at best frivolous. At worst – and this was a series in which the warring parties were inclined to think the worst of each other – they believed them guilty of cheating and trying to intimidate the umpires. However, the great Indian batsman Sunil Gavaskar, an unlikely friend of his neighbouring country, said that, given the decisions that went against them, 'the Pakistanis' behaviour was very restrained at Leeds'.

Relations returned to something closer to normal when Pakistan came back to England in 1996 and the truce just about held for a decade. The formal introduction of first one neutral umpire in 1994 and then two from 2002 undoubtedly helped (one of the key proponents of neutral officials had been Imran Khan who had grown tired of the probity of Pakistani officials being queried).

Even that couldn't prevent another ball-tampering scandal though. On the fourth day of the Oval Test in 2006, with England batting and the Pakistanis in a strong position to win, umpire Darrell Hair – an Australian who lived in England and had 'previous' with Asian teams – deducted the latter five runs for altering the state of the ball. It was a hugely controversial decision and a first in Test cricket. The call came shortly before tea. The away side went into the pavilion for the interval but, in protest at the ball-tampering penalty, refused to come out after a rain delay. Andrew Strauss was also captain that day and as the impasse set in he received a phone call from his county chairman, former England spinner Phil Edmonds. 'Straussy,' he was told, 'you need to get them [Pakistan] back out there.'

Strauss protested that he had scant influence over his opponents: his opposite number Inzamam-ul-Haq spoke little English and had largely kept himself to himself that summer. Edmonds tried to explain that what was unfolding was bigger than just cricket. It was an early insight for Strauss into the complex political history that enveloped encounters between the two countries.

Inzamam eventually led his men back on to the pitch almost an hour later, but the umpires refused to join them, judging that their initial non-appearance amounted to forfeiture of the game. Of the England players appearing at Lord's in 2010, five – Strauss, Alastair Cook, Kevin Pietersen, Paul Collingwood and Ian Bell – had featured in the controversial game four years earlier (Mohammad Asif also played). It's unlikely they were impressed by Pakistan as a cricketing nation.

So what you had in that corner of Lord's on that Sunday were two tribes who viewed each other with long-standing suspicion. In the culture of English cricket lingered the impression that there was something permanently dodgy about the way their opponents played the game. On the other side were the Pakistanis, fed up with never receiving the credit they deserved and being judged guilty until proven innocent. That the English press, and the tabloids in particular, were responsible for maligning their reputation made it easy for them to dismiss the *News of the World* as a malevolent, chauvinist rag.

* * *

Could matters get any worse in the late summer of 2010? They certainly could. Shortly after his side's heavy loss at Lord's, Salman Butt gave a press conference with team manager Yawar Saeed. 'These are just allegations. Anybody can stand up and say things about you – it doesn't make them true,' Butt said. 'There is nothing I have seen, or been shown, that involves me.' Asked whether he would be standing down as captain, he was defiant: 'Pakistan have won a Test match from Australia after 15 years and from England after nine years – so does that mean I should resign from this current situation?'

Ijaz Butt backed him by saying that he would only suspend the three cricketers under suspicion if they were found guilty. Butt knew that the outcome of any inquiry would not be known until well after the tour was over. Clarke and the England players were understandably unhappy about this.

Among them was Paul Collingwood, due to lead them in the T20 series starting the following Sunday. He had been out in the middle in November 2005 in Faisalabad when Shahid Afridi – also down to play in the T20s – had been banned for 'deliberate damage to the pitch'. While the umpires had been distracted by an explosion-like noise from the stands, Afridi had performed a surreptitious pirouette with his spikes to create scuff marks to assist his team's bowlers. He had not taken into account the TV cameras picking up his antics.

'Colly' had also played in that game ten months later at The Oval when Pakistan voided proceedings. When the umpires officially adjudged them to have forfeited the match, he was delighted. England had, as a result, won the series 3-0 and, he thought not unreasonably, it was time to go out and celebrate. His captain Andrew Strauss, mindful of what Phil Edmonds told him, advised against that. 'Come on, Straussy, it's not our fault if Pakistan want to sit sulking in the dressing room,' Collingwood replied. 'We've won fair and square. Why shouldn't we go out and celebrate?' He knew as soon as he said these words that his skipper would not be moved.

When the first of Amir's no-balls had been replayed on the England dressing room TV on Thursday, it was Collingwood who had taken one look and cried out, 'That's fucking match-fixing, that!' There was widespread amusement then, but no one was laughing now. Whatever reserves of trust, whatever depths of humour he had left had been drained altogether by the apparent conspiracy between Butt, Amir and Asif. Instead of the pride and excitement he should have felt about captaining his country, Collingwood now felt nothing but anger. He called the ICC's Colin Gibson, whom he had known when the latter was head of communications for ECB. 'Are the three Pakistanis still free to play in the T20 series?' he asked.

'At the moment,' Gibson cautiously replied, 'yes.'

'Well if that's the case then I'm not sure I or the rest of the team want to go ahead.'

As an ICC employee, Gibson was meant to be above personal loyalties. Yet he could understand Collingwood's reluctance. He knew too that he wasn't the kind of character to make empty threats. He passed on his concern to his bosses.

On 2 September, with anti-corruption and security unit (ACSU) investigators now in the capital, and with the rest of the team playing a warm-up match in Taunton, the three under suspicion along with Ijaz Butt were meeting their high commissioner at the Royal Garden. Giles Clarke was also in and out of negotiations. The day ended with the trio being left out of the squad for the two T20 and five one-day internationals that month and then officially suspended by the ICC and charged under the council's anti-corruption code. It was also confirmed that the three would be interviewed under police caution the next day – Mazhar Majeed had been formally arrested on the Sunday then released on bail. He was also detained as part of an HM Revenue and Customs investigation into money laundering at Croydon Athletic FC.

In keeping with the tone of the week, these developments were punctuated by several hysterical outbursts. The Pakistan Sports Minister, Ijaz Jakhrani, for example, gave an interview to Indian news channel CNN-IBN, hinting that there were darker forces at work: 'Let's wait until the report comes. After that we will be in a position to see if it is spot-fixing, if it is match-fixing or if it is a conspiracy against these players or against the country.'

The talk of a conspiracy and a smear campaign was even more voluble on the internet and in Pakistan there could only be one instigator – India. Rumours abounded that Mahmood was an Indian agent deployed to sully the good name of their neighbours and rivals. This dimension had struck *News of the World* managing editor Bill Akass when he had been wheeled out on the Sunday morning to speak to the world's media. With his Pakistani interviewers, he was immediately put on the back foot. The tone of their questioning implied that he had to work not just to defend the story's veracity but to justify the very nature of his paper's journalism. The Indian media, meanwhile, could not disguise their appetite for dirt on their neighbours.

Back in London, the Pakistan high commissioner had been mounting an offensive of his own. 'They are extremely disturbed about what has happened in the past week, particularly in regards to their alleged involvement in the crime,' said Wajid Shamsul Hasan of the accused. 'They mentioned they are entirely innocent and shall defend their innocence as such. They further maintain that on account of the mental torture that has affected them they are not in the right frame of mind to play the remaining matches.'

So was the high commissioner saying that his compatriots had been framed? 'Yes!' He queried the apparently incriminating footage on the *News of the World* website. 'We are not seeing on the video what the date or time is. Do you have answers to these questions? It could have been dated before the match or after the match, or at a different time.' At the same time, his minions were handing out to the media and anyone else assembled copies of an unflattering article about Maz Mahmood written by the press commentator Roy Greenslade, who had been managing editor of the *Sunday Times* in the 1980s when Mahmood had been fired for misconduct. Wajid went on to express his disdain for the ICC. '[They] had no business to take this action … the ICC just try to play to the public gallery.'

If Wajid sounded as if he had a personal grudge against Mahmood then that's because he did. Or rather it was against Sultan Mahmood. Like Mahmood father and son, Wajid had been a journalist before he had become an adviser to Benazir Bhutto. That role had then offered him a ticket into the loftier circles of the diplomatic corps and he had been appointed to his post in London in 2008. Wajid believed that Sultan Mahmood had falsely spread rumours that, like many Pakistanis seduced by life in government, he had embraced Western and non-Muslim habits such as drinking.

It should also be said that the high commissioner was trying to fill the void created by the absence of leadership from the PCB. That had been evident from Saturday night when the police had raided the team hotel. Yawar Saeed had been unable to get hold of Butt and had then turned to Wajid for help. He had arrived on the scene promptly since he lived in nearby Swiss Cottage. Once there, he had worked with the PCB barrister who had travelled over for the tour to ensure that the police observed all the legal formalities and the players were aware of their rights. Five days on from that, after wave after wave of claims about his country's integrity, his aim was not just to throw some mud back at the accusers but to remind the English media of the principle of innocence until proven guilty.

An ECB statement, read out by Clarke in front of the hotel, was issued at the same time: 'The England and Wales Cricket Board welcomes the announcement of the Pakistan Cricket Board's squad for the NatWest T20 and NatWest ODI series. We look forward to an extremely competitive series, full of excellent cricket and, we can assure cricket fans across the country, in the most competitive spirit long associated with contests between England and Pakistan.

'As chairman of the ICC's Pakistan task team, I look forward to working with Haroon Lorgat, the ICC chief executive, Ijaz Butt, the chairman of the Pakistan Cricket Board and everybody involved in Pakistan cricket in taking forward cricket in Pakistan so that a proper plan exists for the whole of Pakistan cricket, given all the many and varied issues which have addressed it. We naturally have many challenges at ICC to face. Cricket fans across the world can be assured that we will be doing so.'

On 4 September, the day before the first T20, Butt's replacement captain, Shahid Afridi, tried to salvage some scrap of dignity for his team and the game. 'On behalf of these boys I want to say sorry to all cricket lovers and all the cricketing nations.'

If those running the sport thought they had bought themselves some quiet time, they were wrong. A few hours before the start of the first T20, the morning of 5 September brought part two of the *News of the World* investigation. The Pakistanis had been bumped off the front page by news of footballer Wayne Rooney's liaison with two escort girls. Instead they were relegated to pages 8–11 of news, the back page and two spreads in the sport section.

The main revelations were as follows: the ICC was going to bring 23 charges against the trio and were also investigating a fourth Pakistan player; between £10,000 and £15,000 of the sum the paper had handed over to Mazhar Majeed had been found by police in Butt's hotel room, and smaller sums discovered in the rooms of the other two; text messages found on Majeed's phone appeared to indicate earlier attempts at spot-fixing.

There was also an interview with batsman Yasir Hameed, who had played at Lord's. Hameed was damning of his team-mates: 'They were doing it [fixing] in almost every match. God knows what they were up to. Scotland Yard was after them for ages ... I've been offered huge amounts of money, up to £150,000. I wouldn't get involved. That's why I was out of the team for two years! If I was playing for any other country, what would I be now? I'd be the team captain.'

Hameed immediately claimed that he had been duped – Mahmood had secured the interview at a hotel in Nottingham by posing as a potential bat sponsor – and misquoted. He passed on the mobile number, which had been used to contact him, to the Pakistan media, which then made it public. It was a revenge of sorts since it was one Mahmood commonly used and he was now forced to abandon it. Hameed would later file a complaint with the Press Complaints Commission about the article.

England would go on to win the T20 match that Sunday, but Collingwood refused to shake the hands of his opponents as was traditional at the end of a game. Mohammad Yousuf, one of the more experienced Pakistanis, told him he was out of line. Collingwood was too cynical to care. 'I'm sorry,' he replied, 'but how could the rest of you not know what was going on in your own dressing room – with the no-balls? I just don't believe it.' Yousuf, known as Yousuf Youhana until he embraced Islam, became defensive and offered a straight denial.

England won again in Cardiff two days later. On 10 September, Butt, Amir and Asif flew home. 'They have not been charged by the police with any offence,' explained Ijaz Butt. 'They have fully co-operated with the police in their inquiries and maintain that they are innocent of any alleged wrongdoing. They have agreed with the police to return to England if the police request them to do so to further assist in their enquiries.' Ijaz Butt himself had already been home for a couple of days. The Lahore-based newspaper, the *Nation*, reported that when he arrived back in Pakistan 'he was greeted by cries of "Shame" and one demonstrator threw a shoe at him'.

The players themselves were keen to avoid such hostility. The same paper revealed that they had arrived 'in the wee hours of Saturday [11 September] seemingly avoiding angry scenes at the Lahore airport, where protesters had gathered with rotten eggs and placards. Team captain Salman Butt, bowlers Mohammad Asif and Mohammad Amir were led from their plane to a waiting bus and driven away through a cargo entrance within minutes of landing. "It seemed as if they had done something really great," a protester who waited for hours to greet their arrival, said. Some waved shoes while others had brought rotten eggs. Their numbers soon swelled as taxi drivers and many at the airport joined and the crowd started shouting "Long live thieves and gamblers".'

Back in England, without their first-choice captain and two strike bowlers, the tourists were crushed in the first two one-day internationals. On the morning of 12 September, the day of the second ODI at Leeds, Scyld Berry in the *Sunday Telegraph* laid bare the concern over Pakistan felt by the game's administrators: 'Pakistan will suffer the first fallout from the spot-fixing controversy this week when ICC chief executives meet in Cape Town. They are expected to be told, politely but firmly, that they will not be returning to England next season.

'England was going to be Pakistan's second home as long as the security situation in their country was desperate, according to the original plan of the England and Wales Cricket Board. The Pakistan v Australia Test series held this summer was intended to be the first of several neutral series staged here. But in Cape Town it is believed that the ECB's chief executive David Collier is not going to offer Pakistan the same facilities for 2011, as a consequence of the recent decline in the tourists' popularity.

'Earlier this year the ECB had hoped that Pakistan would play India in this country next summer, which would have been a real money-spinner as the two countries meet so seldom and have such large and passionate followings. But such fixtures are neither possible nor desirable after three Pakistan players were suspended by the ICC while they are being investigated by the Metropolitan Police.'

The atmosphere was made even more paranoid and polluted by events in and around the third one-day international at The Oval on Friday, 17 September. Before the game, *The Sun* newspaper – probably the *News of the World*'s most bitter rival, despite being a daily as opposed to a Sunday publication, and despite sharing the same parent company – had alerted the ICC to a tip-off it had received about likely spot-fixing.

The ICC was left with no choice but to trigger another investigation, and a conference call involving Lorgat, Gibson (both back in Dubai) and Clarke was held to discuss calling the match off. Without any specific details about the spot-fixing being provided and mindful too of the revenue that would be lost, Clarke was resistant. In fact, he was positively irritated with Lorgat. Why, if he didn't have any real proof, was he calling him up? Why was he calling now, just an hour before the scheduled start time? To scratch the match now would be to invite derision and disappointment in equal measure. Well, said Lorgat, I just wanted to run it by you, it could just be nothing. Clarke grunted and hung up. The players themselves knew none of this.

Pakistan won the match. Their celebrations were soon overtaken by the first edition of *The Sun* hitting the streets that night with its exclusive. 'Cricket chiefs launched an investigation during England's one-day match against Pakistan yesterday amid fears it was fixed by an illegal betting syndicate. The International Cricket Council acted after a *Sun* probe exposed evidence apparently showing that bookies knew details of Pakistan's innings BEFORE the match even began. Incredibly, it comes after three Pakistani stars had already been sent home in disgrace amid claims of match-fixing.

'The new investigation will centre on suspicious scoring patterns in Pakistan's innings and on two suspect overs during yesterday's match at The Oval. Illegal bookies in India and Dubai apparently knew in advance what would happen so they could launch a betting coup. But *The Sun*'s undercover team was able to pass details to ICC inspectors before the match began. Cricket chiefs then watched as Pakistan's score mirrored the target that bookies had been told in advance by a fixer. It is not thought that the overall result was fixed, only scoring rates in parts of Pakistan's innings. Pakistan eventually won by 23 runs.

'*The Sun* is withholding details of the alleged fix while the investigation continues – but we can reveal that horrified ICC chiefs launched their investigation before the Pakistan innings had even finished. The probe centres on an individual within the team camp who is believed to be the ringleader, taking money from bookies and ensuring their orders are carried out. ICC chief executive Haroon Lorgat last night thanked *The Sun* for its investigation and pledged tough action on any players found guilty.'

Though the ruling body's concern had been understandable, there were several factors which did not quite add up about the newspaper story. For all the talk of a *Sun* 'probe' by its 'undercover team' and a 'dossier' passed on to the ICC, no evidence of a rigorous investigation – unlike that splashed across nine pages of the *News of the World* – was ever presented by the paper. It was also noticeable that the title did not even accord its exclusive front-page splash status – a giveaway sign that it wasn't wholly sure of itself. The former England bowler Mike Selvey noted in *The Guardian* that all it seemed to amount to was 'an alleged conversation between two unidentified parties used as the basis for the accusations of impropriety … It simply does not stack up.'

The *Sunday Telegraph* tried to make it stack up, or at least raised the 'mystery of two slow overs' in its 19 September edition. Scyld Berry wrote that the ICC inquiries are 'believed to focus on a two-over segment in which surprisingly few runs were scored. The passage of play involving the 39th and 40th overs of Pakistan's innings appear to invite closer scrutiny. In the 39th and 40th overs of their innings, Pakistan scored no more than seven runs – having scored 58 off their previous eight overs, on what was widely acknowledged to be a pitch made for batting.'

This was tenuous stuff. Seven runs for that period was below par but hardly egregious. There was also the fact that Pakistan had lost a wicket during the segment, which would have been expected to generate a slight deceleration in the run rate. There were two other blindingly obvious points. The first was that any fixer would almost certainly have to buy off most if not all of the team because he could have no idea who would be batting at a certain stage (other than the opening pair in the first over). Then there was the role of the opposition in all this. Any England bowler could accidentally scupper the plan by bowling a wide or no-ball or by producing a series of unplayable deliveries. Even a batsman trying to restrict the runs scored could see a defensive prod end up as an edge and the ball disappearing for four.

On 13 October the ICC would declare of The Oval game that its 'ACSU has verified all the available information and concluded that there was no compelling evidence to suspect individual players or support staff.'

* * *

Located next to Marylebone train station and a short stroll from Baker Street tube and Madame Tussaud's, the Landmark is probably the nearest five-star hotel to Lord's. Cut through Regent's Park on foot and you can be at the St John's Wood venue in around a quarter of an hour. Because of its proximity to Lord's and because of the money being poured into the elite team, England players had been staying here before and during Lord's matches since the turn of the millennium. If you wanted a discreet, comfortable retreat in London to help you switch off for the night from the intensity of international cricket then this was your place.

Sadly, as they gathered on the evening of Sunday, 20 September, the eve of the fourth ODI, no one in the England camp was in the mood for relaxing, and for good reason. The cloud hanging over The Oval match had swiftly been blown away by a tornado of an intervention from Ijaz Butt. The Pakistan chief was in Dubai, meeting with the ICC. Having dined with Haroon Lorgat on the evening of the 18th – the day *The Sun* had published its exclusive – he then decided it was time to turn the fire on his country's opponents.

'There is loud and clear talk in the bookies' circle that some English players were paid enormous amounts of money to lose the [Oval] match,' he said in interviews with TV and the Associated Press that appeared on the Sunday. 'No wonder there was total collapse of the English side. We have taken it in hand to start our own investigations. We will shortly reveal the names of the people, the parties and the bodies involved in this sinister conspiracy and we also reserve the right to sue them for damages. We won the match and we are under suspicion. England lost, their players should be investigated. You don't lose a match if you are doing fixing. We have co-operated so far with all this investigation but after the third ODI we get this feeling it is not a conspiracy to defraud bookies but to defraud Pakistan cricket.

'Did you ask the other people who made allegations against our players whether they had any proof? What did they say? We have thought about this properly and we have positive proofs here before us just like they say they have also.' Butt was alluding to the fact that England, so dominant in the series before The Oval, had gone from being 201/5, needing only 41 off 12 overs to win, to 218 all out. It didn't look good, but of the 'positive proofs' of match-fixing, Butt produced none. He wasn't done though. He also asserted that 'the media in certain countries is biased and not fair' (probably true in all cricket-playing nations) and that the PCB 'feel august cricket bodies are also involved in this conspiracy, which will damage the great game of cricket'.

At the start of the series, Strauss had warned his players that they would have to play with no emotion. The smallest spark could start the biggest fire, he impressed on them, don't rise to anything.

All that went out of the window now. Once he got wind of Butt's observations, the skipper, ensconced at the team hotel, was on the phone to coach Andy Flower to explain that he had had enough. Conversations with other senior players confirmed that they too were in the mood to boycott the rest of the series.

Soon after that call, Strauss, Flower and Clarke were locked in a private room at the Landmark trying to steer a way through the crisis. Clarke said he understood the players' anger and reluctance to play but insisted that the ECB had a responsibility to fulfil the final two fixtures. If the current group of players did not wish to proceed then they would not be judged adversely, but other cricketers would be found to wear the England colours. Flower acted as an impromptu mediator. Clarke asked to address the whole squad and Strauss consented.

That was fine for all bar one of the England party. Eoin Morgan, a Middlesex county player, lived in London and had therefore been granted permission to stay at his home that night. Now he was being summoned to come to the Landmark as soon as possible. Even on a Sunday evening, though, Morgan found the cross-town traffic heavy going. After an hour crawling through the gridlock, he was not in the best mood when he arrived at the hotel. 'What the fuck's happening now?' was his eye-rolling opening salvo.

Hugh Morris, managing director of the England men's team, and David Collier, chief executive of the ECB, were probably closer to the players but Clarke determined that the situation called for someone of his stature and with his powers of oratory. He began deploying them. 'Gentlemen, tomorrow there will be 28,000 at Lord's. Most of them have come to see you bat or bowl, their heroes. Many will be dads or mums taking their sons or daughters to see England play for the first time. Imagine how you felt when you were a child in that situation. If you're a father, imagine being in those dads' shoes. Do you really want their first experience of going to an England match to be ruined by the first XI not turning up all because of some worthless remarks that no one with a brain thinks have any truth in them?

Salman Butt batting during Pakistan's second innings against England at The Oval Test which they won. Butt was asked by Mazher Majeed to bat out a maiden but did not do so

Mazhar Majeed counts out the £140,000 handed to him by 'Mohsin Khan' at the Copthorne Tara hotel, London, on the night of 25 August 2010

Salman Butt and Mohammad Amir in discussion moments before Amir delivered his second no-ball at Lord's on 27 August 2010

'Wow!' was the response of commentator Michael Holding on seeing a replay of Amir's second no-ball – the third of the three that Mazhar Majeed had promised in England's first innings

Mohammad Amir celebrates dismissing Matt Prior during his remarkable spell of bowling on the second day at Lord's. It was his fifth wicket of the innings and another, Graeme Swann, would follow two balls later

Mohammad Amir returns to the Lord's pavilion to silence after being dismissed for a duck on the day the News of the World's *allegations went round the world. Pakistan would lose the match and series half an hour later*

CRICKET IN THE DOCK: GREEDY FIXER STRIKES HIS BARGAIN TO CHEAT FANS

I'll give you 3 no-balls.. they're all organised. If you play this right you'll make a lot of cash

MATCH-FIXER MAZHAR MAJEED on Wednesday night

OUR MAN · THE CAPTAIN · THE FIXER

A PLAYERS WHO SHAMED GAME

NAMED NAMED
NAMED NAMED

See the shocking video at notw.co.uk

© OUR LAWYERS ARE WATCHING   THE CHEATS DELIVER: PAGES 4 AND 5

CRICKET IN THE DOCK: MASTERMIND POCKETS HIS MONEY AFTER PAY-OFF

COAT IN THE ACT

Mr Big stuffed the £10k in his jacket then went to meet players

City of illegal betting

See the shocking video at notw.co.uk

© OUR LAWYERS ARE WATCHING   PLAY BOY BOASTS OF SYNDICATE'S FORTUNE: PAGES 8 AND 9

CRICKET IN THE DOCK: MATCH-RIGGER BOASTS OF SYNDICATE'S SHADY FORTUNE

Tests are where the big money is.. we made £830k when Pakistan collapsed in the Aussie match

ANDY DUNN
Cricket sports writer

"Amir kiss of Lord's turf was one of betrayal"

Endemic

Avarice

See the shocking video at notw.co.uk

© OUR LAWYERS ARE WATCHING   OUR VIEW: A GAME IN TATTERS – PAGE 12 · CRICKET'S SHAME – BACK PAGE

CRICKET IN THE DOCK: THREE BALLS THAT WILL SHAKE WORLD OF SPORT

① **NO-BALL, THURSDAY THE FIXER'S PLEDGE 1**
'So the first ball of the third over, yeah. Amir is going to be bowling. No signal'

② **NO-BALL, THURSDAY THE FIXER'S PLEDGE 2**
'OK. Then the last ball, sixth ball, of the 10th over. Asif will be bowling it'

③ **NO-BALL, FRIDAY THE FIXER'S PLEDGE 3**
'Right, it's going to be Amir's third over and third ball'

Our team will throw two ODIs

THE CHEATS DELIVER

OUR LAWYERS ARE WATCHING

COAT IN THE ACT: PAGES 6 AND 7

Tour manager Yawar Saeed, right, reads the News of the World *on the Pakistan team balcony on the final day of the Test series, in the company of his assistant Shafqar Rana*

An unimpressed ECB chairman Giles Clarke hands the Pakistan man of the series award to Mohammad Amir inside the Long Room at Lord's

The three accused left the Holiday Inn in Taunton on 1 September 2010 to make their way back up to London for police questioning and meetings at the Pakistan High Commission

Salman Butt is surrounded by the world's media as he arrives at the Pakistan High Commission in London for a meeting with diplomats and PCB officials on 2 September

Salman Butt is driven away after facing police questioning at Maida Vale on 3 September 2010

Mohammad Asif is ushered towards a car after leaving police questioning at Maida Vale on 3 September 2010

Mohammad Amir is led towards a car after leaving police questioning at Maida Vale on 3 September 2010

England captain
Andrew Strauss
cannot conceal
his frustration with
batsman Fawad Alam
during the first one-
day international at
Chester-le-Street

'You will get little sympathy from our own media who will just say that the best response would have been to play and ram those words down the Pakistanis' throats by beating them. Let me tell you, if you walk away from this one, then imagine how the Aussies will be stirring it up when you get out there this winter. Those of you who have toured Australia before will know exactly what I mean.'

Clarke then left the room, allowing Strauss and his men to discuss further. He returned to Lord's where he hosted a video-conference call involving at one time or another all of his 14-man board. They backed him, and chairman of selectors Geoff Miller was told to draw up a back-up XI in case the first string opted out.

By now, the captain had calmed a little and was reconsidering the options. It was important, he told his troops, that England occupy the moral high ground. *We have to be seen to be the bigger men.* He was therefore inclined to play the next day. However, they chose to act, he thought it only right that they went ahead on a one-in, all-in basis. The mood had shifted and there was broad agreement. No one said they were vehemently opposed to playing. Game on. 'Chairman,' he told Clarke, 'we have come to a decision as a team and we will play as a team.'

There would be a rebuttal though. Working with representatives from the Professional Cricketers' Association, Strauss went away – it was close to midnight now – to draw up a statement that would make it clear to Butt that he couldn't go around making accusations of impropriety without the slightest proof. That statement was released the following morning: 'We would like to express our surprise, dismay and outrage at the comments made by Mr Butt yesterday. We are deeply concerned and disappointed that our integrity as cricketers has been brought into question. We refute these allegations completely and will be working closely with the ECB to explore all legal options open to us.

'Under the circumstances, we have strong misgivings about continuing to play the last two games of the current series and urge the Pakistani team and management to distance themselves from Mr Butt's allegations. We do, however, recognise our responsibilities to the game of cricket, and in particular to the cricket-loving public in this country, and will therefore endeavour to fulfil these fixtures to the best of our ability.'

Off-field antics at Lord's, however, would yet again overshadow the action in the middle. Jonathan Trott set the scene in his autobiography, *Unguarded*: 'The atmosphere was horrible – full of tension, with deep animosity between the sides – and a few of us were struggling to shrug off the resentment we felt about having to play against Pakistan.' At about 10.30am, half an hour before the match was due to commence, a few players from either side were winding up their pre-match preparations on the Nursery Ground practice area behind the Lord's Media Centre. Trott, as was his wont, was meticulously and neatly packing his batting equipment into his bag when Pakistan bowler Wahab Riaz strolled into view. Riaz was one of the players who had been 'managed' by Majeed and had been questioned by police six days earlier.

Graeme Swann was not far away, going through the last of his drills with England fielding coach Richard Halsall. The interaction between the two was broken by the sound of raised voices from the nets. The clamour came from Riaz and Trott, who were by now squaring up to one another. Before Swann, Halsall or batting coach Graham Gooch, who was also on the scene, could tear them apart, Trott had picked up one of his pads and, gripping it with both hands, slapped it across Riaz's face. The slap was executed with the same ferocity he would have used to pull a short-pitched ball to the boundary. Riaz was about to launch his retaliation when the others stepped in and pulled them off each other.

Trott's side of the story was as follows: 'Wahab Riaz walked past me by the nets on the Nursery Ground and tried to eyeball me. "You going to accuse us of match-fixing again?" I asked. "Your mum knows all about match-fixing," he said. It was a ridiculous answer but it was all I needed. I smashed my pads across his face – they made a great sound – and grabbed him by the throat. I guess I was looking for an opportunity to lash out and he had provided it. I'm not sure how things would have played out, but Graham Gooch, the England batting coach, rushed over to separate us. "That's not how we do things, Trotty," he said.'

In 2016 Wahab gave an account of the set-to which hardly contradicted that of his assailant. 'He [Trott] was a bit rude and when it comes to being rude, you can never beat the Pakistanis on it. We are the most rude when it comes to it. We are nice but if somebody is rude we won't spare it. He [Trott] was angry, he was not scoring runs, he was getting out early in the ODIs – he was doing well in the Tests. It was a frustration he tried to take out on me.'

That was not the end of it. Word had reached the England dressing room of his confrontation even before Trott's arrival back in the pavilion. Collingwood and most of the team were close to hysterics. Flower and Strauss did not see the funny side. Nor did Giles Clarke. No sooner had he arrived at Lord's than match referee Jeff Crowe pulled him aside: 'There's been a bit of an incident.' Pakistan, Clarke learnt, were now threatening to withdraw from the fixture. The chairman must have thought he'd heard it all now and a very clear message was passed on to the England dressing room: right now there was a plane ticket for the winter tour to Australia with Jonathan Trott's name on it. If he didn't make immediate amends, it would be ripped up.

Flower and Strauss were more sympathetic and retreated to a recess where Trott revealed his wound-up state – 'I just fucking lost my shit.' Strauss was not surprised. Trott had scored his highest Test score in the Lord's Test, a century which had immediately been devalued by the *News of the World* exposé. He had also been in the middle of some of the sledging exchanged between the two teams over the summer. This is what happens when you push people to the limit, thought Strauss.

On the other hand, it was critical that England did not come across as the villains of the piece. To that end there was only one course of action: Trott would have to go into the opposite dressing room and apologise to Riaz. Collingwood had been following the discussions with his fellow batsman and found his anger welling up again. Here we go again, he thought, Pakistan casting themselves as the victim of a problem they've created.

Strauss's political antennae proved as sharp as ever, however, because Shahid Afridi hinted that his side could have raised a bigger row had Trott not said sorry. 'It could have been a police case because it is a crime to hit someone, but we showed a big heart and did not press for it,' Afridi said once news of the incident was out in the open.

Grudging apology delivered, the game went ahead. Pakistan won to level the series 2-2. Yet again England had squandered a strong position, going from 113/0 to 227 all out to lose by 38 runs. The Pakistan media decided it was their turn to put the hosts on the skewer and roast them over the fire. 'If it appears tomorrow in the newspapers that the England team have fixed this match and their players were involved in this, how would you feel?' asked one reporter of Strauss in the post-match press conference. He showed admirable restraint to deliver the straightest of bats in his response.

Before the series decider two days later, Strauss's talk to his men was simple. 'After being 2-0 up and throwing away the next two, after everything that has happened, there is no way we are losing this one. We are finishing on a high.' And they did, winning by 121 runs. Pakistan subsided from 63/0 to 135 all out – a collapse in which Ijaz Butt this time saw nothing untoward. England were not intent on rubbing their opponents' noses into this final humiliation but in the dressing room at Southampton they belted out the team songs with unbridled fervour.

In his final press conference of the summer, the England captain, who had now been playing international cricket for four months without a genuine rest, was unequivocal about what needed to happen next: 'This summer has clearly demonstrated when there is a sniff of something in the air it devalues the whole game and nobody wants to play cricket in those circumstances. The ICC must leave no stone unturned. We are keen to move on from this series and very keen not to have a repeat of this at any time in the future, which is why it's so important the ICC take a very strong lead from now on and don't take a breather now this series has finished.'

On 27 September, now back home after the end of the tour, manager Yawar Saeed resigned. Two days later, Ijaz Butt issued a statement of his own: 'I wish personally and on behalf of the PCB to withdraw the comments I made. I wish to make it clear I have never seen any evidence of wrongdoing by any England player or the ECB at any time. I deeply and sincerely regret my statements have been interpreted to cast doubt upon the good names of the England players and the ECB and hope that this public withdrawal will draw a line under the matter.'

At the start of October, the England squad chosen for the winter tour in Australia flew to Germany for an outdoor bonding trip. The purpose was to imbue them with the resilience – physical and mental – to come out on top down under. 'If we had known what we were going to go through in the month before, we wouldn't have needed the Germany trip,' Strauss told me. 'We were very close to the edge but it toughened us up. 100 per cent, it brought us closer together. But now I think about it, it must also have been utterly horrendous for the people in the Pakistan team environment.'

Three months after the Germany camp-out, England celebrated their first away Ashes series victory since 1986/87.

CHAPTER FIVE

'DO YOU THINK
CRICKET IS CORRUPT?'

IT WAS 28 August, the Saturday night the story had broken. After his crisis meeting at the Royal Garden Hotel with Cressida Dick, Giles Clarke and Ijaz Butt, Colin Gibson of the ICC was now on the phone to his boss plotting their damage limitation strategy.

Haroon Lorgat had been chief executive of the game's governing body for two years. He had played first-class cricket for Eastern Province and Transvaal before becoming an accountant and working his way up the Ernst & Young ladder until his ICC appointment. The organisation was based in Dubai but Lorgat had flown to South Africa on the Thursday night prior. A Muslim of Indian descent, he was keen to spend the last week of Ramadan and the festival of Eid at home with his family in Cape Town.

He had been tipped off about the impending crisis earlier that day by Ronnie Flanagan. Announced as chair of the ICC's anti-corruption and security unit (ACSU) just three months earlier, Flanagan had previously served as chief constable of the Royal Ulster Constabulary and of its subsequent incarnation, the Police Service of Northern Ireland. That meant that he had good contacts inside the Metropolitan Police Service, one of whom tipped him off: a raid would be taking place on the Pakistan dressing room at Lord's. Flanagan should expect a corruption inquiry.

That had been mid-afternoon but there hadn't been much he or Lorgat could do until the story was out in the open. Now, six hours on, with the story not so much out in the open as running around with wild abandon, Lorgat was asking of his communications chief, 'Do you think I need to come to London?'

'Haroon,' replied Gibson without hesitation, 'you need to come to London ...'

The 50-year-old spent Sunday morning in a teleconference with his president, Sharad Pawar, and vice-president, Alan Isaacs, who were respectively in India and New Zealand. He then caught a taxi to Cape Town airport. Unfortunately, the only flight to London he had been able to get a seat on was that run by Emirates, which took him back via Dubai and meant he would not reach London until Monday lunchtime.

In his absence, Gibson acted as the face of the ICC. He hadn't been out of Ijaz Butt's suite for more than six hours before he was up again and heading to Lord's for an early Sunday breakfast meeting in the Writing Room at the pavilion. The meeting had been convened to discuss how they were going to get through the final day's play without any further unforeseen embarrassments. Bradshaw of the MCC was there, as was Steve Elworthy, acting head of communications for the ECB, and various security officials.

Gibson then moved on to the media centre, working the room, to ensure that none of the press left there at the end of the day without the official line firmly imprinted on their consciousness: *ICC taking the News of the World allegations extremely seriously ... Anti-corruption personnel already working on an investigation ... Will seek the co-operation of law enforcement officers in England and beyond.*

He wasn't done with the media. Shortly before 2pm, he was back facing them, acting as impromptu chair for the Pakistan team press conference, there to jump on any mines before they exploded. Moments before, Gibson had been into the Pakistan dressing room to check that Salman Butt would attend, as was normal for a team captain. He said he would and that Yawar Saeed would accompany him. Gibson looked him straight in the eye and said, 'You know the question you're going to be asked: Did you cheat? There are only two answers you can give. One is the one you want to give and the other is the truthful one. You have to decide which one you are going to give.'

Butt looked him back in the face and said, 'We didn't cheat.' Gibson said that would be fine but he should expect to be asked the question not just that day but for most of the rest of his life. They then left for the Thomas Lord Suite in the building behind the pavilion, with Saeed, suffering with a bad knee, limping behind.

The room was understandably packed. It did not help that Saeed's hearing was also weakened, meaning that Butt often had to tell him what the question was. They did not have to wait long for *the* question. After Saeed had issued a boilerplate denial of the *News of the World* claims, Butt was asked directly by one of the press pack, 'So you're saying they [the allegations] are false?'

'Of course, they are allegations …'

'The allegations involving you personally – you're saying they are false …'

'They involve quite a few people and they are still ongoing, and we'll see what happens …'

'Yes, but the allegations involving you personally, are they false or are they true?'

'I haven't heard any allegation except just taking my name. There's nothing I have seen or shown on TV, nothing that involves me. Definitely we have given our best that we could do on the days and we have tried our best. It's just been that the conditions have been difficult for the batsmen. Remember that this has been a very inexperienced team, especially the batting has been the main thing which hasn't been going as well as expectations. I've been saying in all my press conferences that the guys are young, with the least experience, and in these difficult conditions they might struggle.'

Even allowing for English being his second language, it wasn't the most robust of rebuttals and led *The Guardian* to note that 'all summer, commentators have praised the captain for his fluency, frankness and confidence in explaining his side's poor form. Yesterday he appeared sheepish.'

One man who didn't appear sheepish was Michael Holding, sitting in the Sky Sports booth while this was going on. Holding, one of the finest fast bowlers in the game, had been on commentary when Mohammad Amir delivered the third and final no-ball. 'How big was that?! Wow!' he had said on seeing the replay.

Two days on from that moment, with the Test over, he and former England captains David Gower and Nasser Hussain were discussing what the newspaper revelations meant for the sport. 'People need to come out and speak the truth,' Holding insisted. 'They need to tell the world exactly what is happening and take action with what is happening. You hear about a life ban being given for disruptions within the team, bad team spirit. You don't ban someone for life for bad team spirit. You have to tell the public what is happening – this person had been found doing this and we are not interested in this person representing us.

'That comes not just with the Pakistan Cricket Board, but any board, the ICC, everyone. The ICC don't want to take harsh decisions but everyone needs to put their foot down and say let's clean it up … People are tarnishing the sport. There has been a lot of lip-service about cleaning it up and some action has been taken. But there are a lot of other things that can be done. It's time to bite the bullet and do what has to be done.'

Hussain pointed out, 'If you are going to clean it up, you can't leave the disparity in pay' – referencing the fact that India's leading one-day bowler, Zaheer Khan, was earning millions from the IPL, while Mohammad Amir, he said for exaggerated effect, might be on '£2.50 for a Test match or whatever'.

Holding agreed but it was his comments on Amir which would linger longest in the memory. 'It just doesn't look good. Someone has sent an email in to say that Mohammad Amir hadn't bowled a no-ball in his entire Test career before this series … And then he went over by a distance. It is so sad, an 18-year-old with that sort of talent – and then for him to be getting involved in this. I'm absolutely sure someone has dragged him into this. And it is so sad …' Holding couldn't say any more, so choked up was he by the plight of the teenager and of the game he had served with honour and distinction. It was the footage of him fighting the tears which turned up the heat significantly on the ICC to take serious action. It was also the first suggestion that Amir's youth dictated that he be judged differently from his two team-mates.

This was the state of affairs Haroon Lorgat inherited when he arrived. Like Ijaz Butt, he was booked into the Royal Garden, where he was brought up to speed by Ravi Sawani, chief investigator for the ACSU, who had flown in from Dubai the previous day. The hotel and the Pakistan High Commission were to be the main hubs of activity in the week they were in London as the ICC and the country's diplomatic corps struggled to get a grip on affairs.

'Make no mistake – once the process is complete, if any players are found to be guilty, the ICC will ensure that the appropriate punishment is handed out,' Lorgat said in his first London press conference delivered just a couple of hours after he had flown in on the Monday. 'We will not tolerate corruption in this great game. The integrity of the game is of paramount importance. Prompt and decisive action will be taken against those who seek to harm it. However, the facts must first be established through a thorough investigation and it is important to respect the right of due process when addressing serious allegations of this sort.'

The cricket chief's message was soon overtaken by comments from Australia. Word had got out that the home side's stirring Test win in Sydney at the start of the year might be under scrutiny. That prompted their captain Ricky Ponting to say, 'The way we won was one of the more satisfying moments that I've had on the cricket field. And now when some of these things come to light is when you start to slightly doubt some of the things that have happened.

'The thing that I'm most worried about if any of this is proven to be true is some of the individual performances that took place in that game.

'You look at Mike Hussey's second innings hundred and Peter Siddle's batting and the way he was with Mike Hussey that day and Nathan Hauritz taking five wickets on the final day to win us the game. All of those individual milestones will be tainted as well.'

Ponting's team-mate Shane Watson also pitched in. Cricket Australia had admitted that a year earlier, in London, Watson and wicketkeeper Brad Haddin had been the subject of approaches from individuals linked to illegal Indian bookmakers. The players had reported the approaches who had passed them on to the ICC. Nothing had been heard since, leading Watson to say, 'The ICC Anti-Corruption Unit is not really working. That's totally to do with the ICC, so they need to step in and really get to the bottom of it. They need to do it as soon as possible because we don't want it to affect the game any more than it already has.'

Another Australian weighed in. Malcolm Speed, Lorgat's predecessor, said there appeared to be a 'fairly compelling case' for the entire Pakistan team to be suspended immediately. 'It looks as though it [corruption] is endemic, that several of the team members are involved and have been for some time. So perhaps they need a rest.'

On Monday night, the Pakistan team bus, with the three accused on board, pulled out of their St John's Wood hotel and headed for Taunton for a one-day match against Somerset on Wednesday. The bus was sent on its way by a small crowd who had gathered to shout 'thieves' at the squad and would have thrown eggs at the vehicle too had they not been confiscated by police. At the same time as the coach was making its way down to the West Country, a three-man team from Pakistan's Federal Investigation Agency was getting ready to head to London to assist Scotland Yard with their inquiries.

* * *

Suspending the country as a whole, as Speed had suggested, was never seriously considered, but it was clear that the only way to defuse the situation was to suspend the three players as soon as possible. To do that the ACSU officers had to ratify that there was a *prima facie* case for them to answer and that meant going to the *News of the World*.

On Tuesday, an ICC delegation, led by Lorgat and including Sawani, headed to Wapping. Colin Gibson, with his Fleet Street connections, acted as the convenor and the exchange he had brokered was simple: the paper would co-operate with the organisation's inquiry, but Lorgat would have to give an exclusive interview in return.

At Wapping, Sawani was introduced to house lawyer Tom Crone. He asked if he could see all relevant tapes and transcripts. Crone told him that he could look at everything that had been presented to Cressida Dick and her team. What's more, he could even take them away with him, as the police had done. To Sawani, the lawyer's co-operation was a thing to behold. He and his officers were not used to media organisations, or indeed anyone caught in their web, being so accommodating. He got out of Wapping before anyone at the *Screws* could change their mind.

At the same time, Lorgat was briefing Paul McCarthy and Sam Peters for an article that would appear in the paper five days later. At one point, Lorgat surprised the pair by turning the interview process around and asking them, 'Do you think cricket is corrupt?' Neither gave an answer, which indicated that they considered the Lord's Test a one-off.

Lorgat's interview was intended to put a lid on the story, but it wasn't going to appear in print for several days and in that time a feeding frenzy developed. In Pakistan, actress Veena Malik, whom Mohammad Asif had been seeing until an acrimonious split earlier in the year, gave a television interview in which she talked about his links to an Indian bookmaker called Dikshit: 'Asif used to call up [him] and other bookies as well on the phone of his servant. I have evidence of the messages he exchanged with the bookies.' She maintained that he had told her that there was good money to be earned from spot-fixing.

Hasan Raza, an ACSU representative in South Asia, subsequently met with Malik who said on 2 September that she had 'handed over Asif's voice recordings with the bookie and some other related information to the ICC official. From head to toe, Pakistani players and officials are involved in match-fixing. I had gone with Asif to Bangkok before Pakistan's tour of Australia. Asif told me he was offered $40,000 by an Indian bookie to underperform in Australia but he demanded $200,000. The Pakistan Cricket Board had evidence of this but no action was taken against him.'

Further details were leaking out about Majeed, who had been arrested along with his wife and a man believed to be his brother by customs officials investigating not just the scandal but also money laundering. The *Daily Mail* reported that 'one mobile used by Majeed is said to show "intense" use only when the Pakistan national team was playing. There was apparently a "large" bill for the past month, compared with little use in the last nine months.

'The bill also apparently surged in November last year when the team was on a tour of Australia. The phone was also allegedly used heavily in 2008 when the team was playing against Australia, Zimbabwe, India, Sri Lanka and Bangladesh; in June last year, when Pakistan featured in the Twenty20 World Cup in England; and in September last year, when a tournament featuring Pakistan was held in South Africa.' The *Mail* also quoted former Australia fast bowler Geoff Lawson, who had taken over from Woolmer as Pakistan coach but had lasted only 15 months in the role. 'It would not surprise me if illegal bookmakers have told players that, if they do not perform X and Y, their families will be kidnapped or harmed,' said Lawson.

The ICC was caught in a bind. It wanted to suspend the trio as quickly as possible but it needed to have its case watertight and, with Pakistan involved, there was a political dimension. Lorgat's Indian ancestry was already being used by some in the country to fan theories of a conspiracy cooked up by its nefarious neighbour. For his part, Lorgat understood something of the pressures that the Pakistan officials were under. Ijaz Butt was the brother-in-law of Ahmad Mukhtar, the country's defence minister. President Asif Ali Zardar was reported to be taking a close interest in the case.

Ravi Sawani was not consumed by such diplomatic considerations. He had studied the evidence – by now the ICC also knew that banknotes marked by the *News of the World* had been found by the Met among Butt's possessions – and was growing impatient for the suspensions to be served. He expressed that impatience formally in an email. The gist of his message to his bosses was: *We can't wait an hour longer than is necessary. The longer we leave it, the more it puts us in a bad light.*

Finally, on Thursday, 2 September, notices of suspension of the three were formally issued to Ijaz Butt at the Royal Garden. A statement explained that the three were 'officially notified of the offences they are alleged to have committed and have been provisionally suspended pending a decision on those charges. In accordance with the provisions of the code, this means they are immediately barred from participating in all cricket and related activities until the case has been concluded.' The accused reserved the right to contest the provisional ban and would have the chance to defend themselves at an independent anti-corruption tribunal.

Before Lorgat flew back to Dubai, he and Flanagan put on another united front for the media at Lord's the following day. 'I do not see this as the tip of an iceberg but I think it is something from which we must learn. It's not a contagion,' Flanagan said to general scepticism.

With the suspensions now served, the ICC must have hoped that the start of the T20 series between England and Pakistan on Sunday, 5 September, followed by the one-day matches, would herald something like a return to normality. That wasn't to be. Even before relations between the two countries descended into acrimony there had already been two unhelpful interventions in the media.

The first was the interview given by batsman Yasir Hameed to Mazher Mahmood, which had appeared in the same edition of the *News of the World* as the interview with Lorgat. Hameed had said that his team-mates were 'fixing almost every match'. Shahid Afridi, now back at the helm as limited-overs captain, responded with a brutal assessment of Hameed: 'He is 30–31 but mentally he is 15–16. I don't know who he was sitting with or in what situation he gave this message but we have known him for a long time. We know we can expect anything from him and he does this kind of thing. People know what type of character he is.'

The following day, Hameed emerged from a meeting with Ijaz Butt and the Pakistan high commissioner to say that he had been tricked by Mahmood, who had posed as a sponsor offering a £50,000 deal with Etihad Airlines when they met. Soon after, the same 'sponsor' called with an offer of £25,000 if he gave a statement against Butt, Amir and Asif. When he declined, he received a text: 'Please call me. Incidentally you are in video drinking wine and saying all the quotes. Denying it is just stupid and we will be releasing the video to TV. Better that you just stand up and speak the truth.' The significance of the wine drinking was that Hameed was apparently a Muslim who had not just been touching alcohol but also doing so during Ramadan.

The Pakistan high commissioner had put all this down in a statement containing the number of the mobile phone that had sent the message. Immediately, journalists began calling the number which, to their astonishment, took them through to the Metropolitan Police. The phone belonged to Mahmood.

Word was also out that a fourth Pakistani was of interest to the anti-corruption investigators. His identity soon came out, as *The Guardian* reported on Tuesday, 7 September that the ACSU had 'written to the Pakistan wicketkeeper Kamran Akmal and the suspended captain, Salman Butt, requesting that they hand over records of mobile telephone calls made during this summer's Asia Cup in Sri Lanka. The unit wrote to the players last month, before the *News of the World*'s allegations about spot-fixing, but it has yet to receive a response from the Pakistan camp.'

* * *

Once back at their headquarters in Dubai, the ICC leaders were cut off from the crescendo of name-calling between England and Pakistan during their one-day series in September. Even so, there was another unwelcome sound buzzing around them and it was the clucking of chickens coming home to roost. In short, corruption within the Pakistan camp had been a ticking bomb that it could have defused. Now, the *News of the World* had detonated it in the most explosive fashion.

The spotlight inevitably turned on Sawani and his ACSU team. The ACSU had been set up ten years earlier in response to the Hansie Cronje affair – at that point the worst scandal in post-war cricket history. On 7 April 2000, Indian media reported that police had a recording of a conversation between Cronje, South Africa captain, and Sanjay Chawla, a representative of an Asian betting syndicate, in which the pair discussed fixing. The South Africa Cricket Board rushed out a statement in response describing their captain as 'a man of enormous integrity and honesty. He and his team-mates Nicky Boje, Herschelle Gibbs and Pieter Strydom are emphatic that there is no substance to allegations that they were involved in match fixing during the One-Day International series in India.'

Even to those outside South Africa, Cronje's honesty and integrity seemed beyond doubt. That all changed four days later when he confessed that he had accepted close to $15,000 for passing on information about matches to a London-based bookie. Cronje was immediately suspended and it was announced that the fifth Test between his team and England two months earlier, which had involved both sides forfeiting an innings and then England being asked to chase an agreed total, would be the subject of a future inquiry.

Just a couple of months later, that inquiry – the King Commission – would reveal that Cronje's decision to engineer a result in the fifth Test (England won by two wickets) was not driven by a desire to entertain the final-day crowd at Centurion Park but by inducements from his bookmaker friends. It didn't end there. There had been other payments from various shady Asian figures for information and there was plenty of evidence that Cronje had gone much further in what he agreed to deliver in return.

One of his team-mates, Pat Symcox, testified that he had been approached by Cronje about 'throwing' a match against Pakistan during the 1994/95 winter. He also described a team meeting in Mumbai in 1996, when Cronje told his men that there had been an offer of $250,000 to lose a one-day international. Another, Herschelle Gibbs, a much younger player who was of mixed race, told the commission that he had accepted his captain's offer to score less than 20 runs in a one-day match in India just three months earlier in exchange for $15,000. Bowler Sean Williams said he had been promised money from his captain if he bowled badly in the same series.

As the King Commission was hearing its final round of disclosures, the ICC announced that it had appointed Sir Paul Condon to head up its own anti-corruption investigations. Condon had been commissioner of the Metropolitan Police, the most senior position in British policing. His main area of interest looked like it was going to be Asia because at the same time that the South Africans were undertaking their investigations, the Pakistan and India authorities were beginning to locate the source of the contamination.

Cronje had told the commission that former India captain Mohammad Azharuddin had introduced him to a bookmaker, who offered a financial inducement to throw a 1996 Test between the two countries. Azharuddin described the allegation as 'rubbish', but he was already under the spotlight for claims made in an Indian publication. *Outlook* magazine alleged that Bombay police had details of telephone calls between him and three other players and bookmakers during a match between India and South Africa in 1997. Azharuddin was allegedly recorded as telling one bookie to 'put my money on the other side', i.e. his opponents. In November 2000 he admitted that he had fixed one-day internationals in 1996, 1997 and 1998. The first two had been on behalf of Mukesh Gupta, whom Cronje had identified as one of his contacts.

Across the border, the Pakistanis had been turning over a few stones themselves. The Qayyum report had been commissioned to blow away the cloud of suspicion that had hung over the national team since the mid-1990s. The starting point for Mr Justice Malik

Muhammad Qayyum was the accusation by three Australian players that captain Salim Malik had tried to bribe them to rig matches on a 1994 tour of Pakistan on behalf of an Indian bookmaker, 'John'. There were also rumours that the team's lame display in the 1999 World Cup Final had little to do with their own ineptitude that day or the superiority of their opponents.

On 24 May 2000, Qayyum's report was published, found Malik guilty ('everyone seems to name him as the main culprit in match-fixing') and recommended that he be banned from cricket for life. It came as no surprise to anyone, especially *News of the World* readers who just three days earlier had been treated to an exposé undertaken by one Mazher Mahmood. The reporter had 'infiltrated an international match-fixing ring headed by cricket legend Salim Malik' whose incriminating conversations had been taped at a secret meeting at a Kensington hotel (the Hilton on this occasion). In a statement that would later look hugely ironic, a PCB spokesman hailed 'this sort of journalism [which] assists us in tracking down culprits. We need to change our image.'

Another to receive a life ban was Malik's team-mate Ata-ur-Rehman, who had initially claimed he had accepted 100,000 rupees from his then captain Wasim Akram to bowl badly in a match in 1998. Rehman later said that he had been asked by PCB chair Khalid Mahmood to retract his statement against Akram, who was one of the nation's idols.

Akram was not the only star implicated. So too was Waqar Younis, subsequently bowling coach of Pakistan at the time of the *News of the World* story, and Mushtaq Ahmed, who at the same time happened to be working for England as a spin bowling consultant. Even Inzamam-ul-Haq was a subject of interest. All four were fined for a lack of transparency. Qayyum stated that a shortage of 'positive proof' meant that charges of fixing could not be satisfactorily proved.

Qayyum recommended that henceforth 'the captain should be a person of impeccable character ... Similarly the manager should be a person of impeccable character. A manager should realise there are people on this earth who would lie even on oath ... The pay structure of the PCB to its players be revised. Instead of being only based on seniority, when paying players, their performances, past and recent, should be worked into the pay structure too ... The Pakistan Government should investigate gambling in Pakistan.' He also observed that the PCB 'should not consider sending Pakistan to venues which are reported to be dens of bookies'. This was a clear reference to the UAE states of Sharjah and Dubai, which would become the team's home from home from 2009.

When the *News of the World* allegations were published in the summer of 2010, Qayyum told the media: 'Had my report on match-fixing been fully implemented, this latest episode would not have happened. I suggested the Pakistan Cricket Board keep tight vigil on the players and recommended some of the players should not be given any responsibility in team matters, but some of them are still involved in the team's coaching.'

Qayyum was right to attack the indolence of the PCB, but he was also being a little disingenuous. There were many who believed that he had settled for picking low-hanging fruit in the form of Malik and Ata-ur-Rehman rather than straining higher to take down the star players – Wasim, Waqar, Mushtaq and Inzamam. He even admitted in 2006 that he had had a 'soft corner' for them. One senior Pakistan cricket journalist summed up the report as 'a classic Pakistani attempt at inquiry, one which bathes in its ambiguity and smells fresh of cover-up afterwards.'

The late 90s might have been what Michael Atherton called the 'golden age of match-fixing' but it was obvious that the practice was still in rude health a decade later, and there were several obvious reasons for this. The first was that gambling and cricket had long gone hand-in-hand – between 1772 and 1781 the Hambledon club, the epicentre of the game in its early years, had been witness to an estimated £12,467 in side bets on matches – and that was not going to change. Like any sport in which betting ran parallel, it was open to corruption. What left it more vulnerable was the emergence of the internet at the end of the millennium.

As it had other industries based on information exchange, the web had revolutionised betting, allowing real-time transactions and opening up a myriad of different markets and offerings beyond simply the result. Mobile and smart phones naturally accelerated this transformation. Rashid Latif, a former Pakistan captain who had been one of Qayyum's key witnesses, summed up how the culture changed in the years following the report: 'Focusing on small events within games rather than entire games gained prominence when the heat of match fixing got to be too much for bookies. There are clever ways to manipulate this and maximise your profits if players are involved.' 'Small events' was essentially another term for the 'brackets' which Mazhar Majeed had described in such detail.

Cricket had also acted as an unwitting accomplice to its own undoing. From the late 90s, more and more limited-overs cricket was being played and broadcast. The emergence of Twenty20, from 2003, took this to another level, especially in Asia. On a numbers-basis alone, this proliferation enhanced the likelihood of wrongdoing. Yet it undeniably had an effect too on player ethics. Limited-overs matches were becoming ten-a-penny and, outside World Cups, few lingered long in the memory of the professionals or their fans. It was becoming easier for any cricketer below superstar level to rationalise that accepting a few thousand dollars to bat slower or send down the odd wide in one of these forgettable clashes hardly constituted the worst betrayal of himself, his team or his sport.

It was clear, then, to any dodgy punter or bookie that if you had a man on the inside there was serious money to be made very quickly. In India and Pakistan, there was an abundance of these malefactors because most forms of gambling were proscribed, and driving it underground had the same effect as prohibition had on drinking in interwar America. Ultimately, it did nothing to undermine popular demand for the 'product'. Periodic police crackdowns would be initiated but they were simply cutting off one head of the hydra until another grew in its place. The biggest of the black market cartels in Asia was that believed to be controlled by Indian Dawood Ibrahim, whose daughter had married the son of Javed Miandad in 2005. As well as being a great player, Miandad had also served as Pakistan coach in three separate periods from 1998, though had never been accused of impropriety related to his in-law.

If international law enforcement agencies couldn't properly eradicate the plague of corruption, then what chance did the ICC and its ACSU stand? In its defence, cricket's governing body had put money behind the unit, as the appointments of such senior policemen as Condon and then his successor Flanagan had indicated. The unit had then put together a thorough education programme to take out to players around the globe. Its corruption hotline was heavily publicised, meaning that no one caught in the ACSU's crosshairs could plead naivety or ignorance.

Condon and Flanagan had themselves hired well, recruiting some of the most dogged investigators from UK policing and globally. In 2007 Sawani, who had worked on the 2000 Indian match-fixing inquiry, was brought in as chief investigator and general manager. The following year, the ACSU claimed a high-profile scalp when West Indian Marlon Samuels was banned for disclosing team information to a known bookmaker before a one-day international. In 2009 Sawani and in-house lawyer Ian Higgins toughened up the player code of conduct detailing what was and wasn't permissible and lowering the threshold for reporting any kind of contact with ill-meaning parties. ACSU officers became more visible in and around the hotels and dressing rooms of international teams.

The ACSU had very obvious limitations, however. It was effectively a paralegal body that relied on the assistance of whistle-blowers, players and international law enforcement agencies. Getting the latter to share information within their own units, never mind with outside organisations, was notoriously difficult. Without ready access to police intelligence or the power to intercept phone calls and emails, or to subpoena bank records, its hands were tied.

Those limitations had been exposed in 2008 when one of Sawani's team, Alan Peacock, had warned Pakistani Danish Kaneria that Anu Bhatt, an Indian whom Kaneria knew socially, was 'highly inappropriate company' because of his links to illegal betting.

Peacock had been able to do little more, though. The following year, while playing county cricket, Kaneria introduced Bhatt to his Essex team-mate Mervyn Westfield. Soon after the Pakistan spot-fixing story broke in 2010, Westfield was charged with accepting a corrupt payment to underperform in an Essex match. He subsequently went to jail though Kaneria did not admit his role until 2018.

The Butt–Amir–Asif case was about to lay bare again the inherent difficulties of the ACSU's task. In May 2010 it had admitted that it was working with the PCB to find out what had gone wrong during the winter tour of Australia. The ACSU's interest had been piqued by remarks made by assistant coach Aqib Javed to the PCB's committee of inquiry. Asked if he saw anything dark at work in Kamran Akmal's mistakes that led to the Test defeat in Sydney earlier that year, Javed had said: 'I'm not sure but my suspicions are pretty high. They are high because of other things I know about the process, the people in the surroundings...There is a question mark, yes'. Akmal responded by threatening to sue him. 'I am fed up with these allegations. My family is disturbed. I go out and people hoot me and I am mentally disturbed. I want to clear this unwarranted stigma with my name,' he told Reuters.

Mindful perhaps of the threat of litigation, Sir Paul Condon, who would step down from his role two months later, noted tactfully that 'the investigations at the time suggested it was more about a dysfunctional team, rather than match-fixing. But it is a live inquiry.'

Soon after that, the ACSU 'hotline' account received an email from 'Kitty Kat' warning that the two Majeed brothers acting for several Pakistan players were trying to lure them into illicit acts. ACSU officers immediately replied asking to know more but it was not until a month later that one was received. A confidence-building process took place in subsequent exchanges. Further information about the identity of the informant – it was clearly someone who had had professional dealings with the Majeeds before falling out with them – and what exactly he knew was secured. Now came the crunch point.

The whistleblower, who had print-outs of Mazhar Majeed's incriminating BlackBerry messages, wanted a simple cash-for-information transaction. The ICC was not comfortable with the basic principle. Nor were the few texts which its informant had shared definitive proof of wrongdoing. When negotiations broke down, it seems that the same individual then contacted the *News of the World*.

With this information tap turned off, the ACSU senior officers in Dubai discussed their options. The idea of setting some kind of financial inducement-based trap for the agents or their players who were now in England was raised. Legal counsel advised though that this would not stand up in English law. In such circumstances, the only firm action they could take was to write to Butt and Kamran Akmal asking to see their phone records during the period of the Asia Cup in Sri Lanka in May. This they did on 21 August. No response was received from the Pakistan camp in the week that followed. On 28 August, the *News of the World* rolled off the printing presses.

* * *

For Haroon Lorgat, the most pressing concern was to resolve the case before the next World Cup, due to start in February 2011 in Asia. The tournament would operate under the 50-over-a-side format and there was genuine concern about its future. While Test matches retained their timeless appeal, the dash and pizazz of Twenty20 had left the original one-day form looking dated. It was imperative that the stench of corruption was not still wafting over the sport by the time the World Cup began. That meant not only ensuring that the PCB got its house in order – at the start of October it was given a deadline of 31 days to improve its methods of anti-corruption education – but also holding a full disciplinary hearing for the accused as soon as the ICC had its case and an independent judging panel assembled.

Though Majeed had appeared to implicate more than just the Pakistan captain and his two bowlers, and had referred to fixing matches before the Oval and Lord's Tests, the ICC confined their investigations to the two fixtures in London in August 2010. It was obvious that Majeed had been a braggart. Other than the agent's boasts, no evidence of fixing had been adduced against the others Majeed had claimed to represent – the Akmal brothers, Wahab Riaz, Imran Farhat. Wahab Riaz and Farhat would later threaten legal action against Majeed for impugning their reputations.

What was needed was a tight, focused inquiry. Sawani and Higgins would lead but they needed outside help. So it was that Jonathan Taylor, a lawyer in London with the international firm Bird & Bird, received a call from Higgins as soon as the story was out asking him to work with the ICC. Taylor, who specialised in sports law and had already been employed by the ICC, was in Portugal and was playing in the swimming pool with his young daughter at their villa when the call came through. He couldn't get hold of a copy of the *News of the World* that Sunday so ended up reading photocopied pages dispatched from England via fax.

Once back in London, Taylor spent September liaising with the Metropolitan Police, who were not happy that the suspension of the players had been effected before they themselves had decided whether to press charges. The Met even wrote to him asking him to desist from his inquiry. Taylor went to meet them and concluded that they were bluffing: they had no judicial power compelling him to stop or not to use the *News of the World* files in any 'prosecution', as they had requested. One of the officers later admitted that if it hadn't been for the paper and other media kicking up an almighty stink then the police would not have followed up the claims.

With the law at bay, Taylor's next task was the trio's appeal against their provisional suspension. Playing for Pakistan might not have generated the biggest pay packet in world cricket but it was the main source of income for Butt, Amir and Asif. Suspension, irrespective of the ultimate outcome of their hearing, cut that off. The final indignity came in October when they were informed that they would be denied training access to the PCB Academy in Lahore.

The date and location for the appeal were set for the end of October and Doha in Qatar. Usually, the ICC's base in Dubai would have acted as the venue but Asif was barred from entering the United Arab Emirates following his arrest in Dubai airport that June on suspicion of possessing drugs. A small amount of opium had been found in his wallet. Asif, who had in 2006 been found guilty of using the steroid nandrolone, claimed he had not been aware of its presence. On 22 October he announced that he was withdrawing from the process. 'I have chosen not to contest the provisional suspension at this time simply because I am content to await the main disciplinary hearing where my full case can be placed before the ICC,' the bowler said. That meant that the hearing could now be switched to Dubai.

Butt was still batting on the front foot. On 27 October he stated, 'I am pretty sure to be cleared. It has been annoying for me because these kind of allegations have not only brought defamation, but as well it is career-threatening. Such things do come in your life but you have to stand up and face them.

'Majeed is not somebody who is an agent for me because he has been there even before I was there [playing international cricket]. These are the people who deal with the marketing side of players and the promotional stuff and they also make money out of it. This is what is being done in the sporting arena around the world and this is not something that came up with Salman Butt. I hope the captaincy will come again some day. I cannot grab it. God gave me one chance and I hope I will get the other chance as well. I want to be remembered as a player who won games for Pakistan.'

On Saturday, 30 October the appeal began in the impersonal surroundings of the ICC's headquarters at Dubai Sports City. It would be heard by Michael Beloff QC. Educated at Eton and Oxford, the 68-year-old Beloff was one of the most esteemed lawyers in London. He was a friend of Tony Blair and his wife Cherie, and had been president of Oxford's Trinity College. He was also a popular figure at the Bar, as well liked socially as he was regarded professionally. Like Taylor, he was an expert in sports law and arbitration. He had even been at Lord's on the Saturday of the Test under scrutiny.

While Taylor was representing the ICC, Amir would be represented by Shahid Karim, who had defended Asif during his doping case in 2006. Butt's lawyer was Aftab Gul. The 64-year-old Gul was himself a former Pakistan Test player who had been hit on the head during the first Test of his country's 1971 series in England. 'Gul's all right,' noted BBC commentator Brian Johnson when he returned to action. 'The doctor inspected his head this morning and found nothing in it.'

Gul was also a political activist who had been detained as a student agitator – 'I am a founder member of the Pakistan People's Party. I am on the left and in thrall to Karl Marx,' he said when it was announced he was acting on Butt's behalf – and it was clear to Taylor early on that the activist in him was going to get the upper hand over the lawyer.

His delivery was theatrical and the basis of his excitable oratory was that there was simply no case against his client. The *News of the World*'s recordings proved nothing and their veracity could not be confirmed anyway. Tom Crone, who had played schoolboy rugby with Taylor's father at Wimbledon College, south-west London, was present on behalf of the paper to rebut this. Gul said that Butt denied that it was his voice on the other end when Majeed had put his mobile on speakerphone in Mazher Mahmood's presence.

Ironically, Gul then admitted that 'if this were a genuine conversation between someone who wished to involve themselves in the gambling conspiracy and a cricketer who was party to it … that conversation indicates that the cricketer is participating or intending to participate in the conspiracy. I will be frank with you – yes, if at the other end of the line there is a cricketer who has some grunt service [sic] who plays in the match and he says these things, then, yes, the conclusion can be drawn fairly that he is in with them.' Taylor was bemused and bewildered by his adversary's antics. At one point during proceedings, the Pakistani nodded off. Even Butt found this funny and recorded it on his phone camera.

After a day of argument and counter-argument, Beloff gave his judgment on 31 October. To no one's surprise, he stated that there were no grounds for lifting the suspension. The lawyers and the cricketers filed out of court to meet a media scrum. Responding to the ruling, Butt stated that the hearing had been a sham: 'They listened to us but it felt as if their decision had already been made from before. It was not based on a single piece of evidence. After a 12-hour hearing the only so-called evidence they had was the same *News of the World* article and the same video everyone has seen. It [the PCB distancing itself] wasn't expected. Nobody from the PCB has even called us so I don't know what is going on there. But I think now is the time for even the government to get involved as well as the PCB because it isn't just about three players. This is Pakistan being cornered.'

Amir mined an identical seam: 'Before leaving for Dubai we felt the case will be in our favour, but when he [Beloff] gave the decision it looked as if he had written the decision before. We went for the truth but this could be a conspiracy against Pakistan, to tarnish Pakistan's reputation.'

Less than a fortnight later, Gul announced that he would not go forward with Butt to the tribunal, which had been scheduled to start on 6 January 2011. It was not clear if he had been sacked or resigned, but he continued to bang a familiar drum: 'It is no use fighting this case because the ICC tribunal has already decided what to do. Having this hearing [in the new year] is all a drama, I don't think they are going to get justice at this hearing.' By way of an encore, he gave an interview to Sky Sports on 13 December in which he proclaimed, 'Corruption is rife in world cricket. I have so much evidence. I will tell you names which will make your hair stand on end.'

At the same time that Gul was withdrawing, Mazher Mahmood was making another intervention. On 14 November the *News of the World* published on its website an interview its star reporter had conducted with Pakistan wicketkeeper Zulqarnain Haider. A week earlier, Haider had quit the country's tour of Dubai and flown to Heathrow. At a press conference at Dilawar Chaudhry's restaurant in Southall, he said that he would be asking for asylum from the UK on the basis that his life was under threat from bookmakers.

His wife and two daughters, aged seven and four, were placed under police guard in Lahore.

'I don't want to trust anyone,' Haider explained to Mahmood when the two were alone. 'There's a big mafia all over the world of bookies to fix matches. I heard it was a very common thing now to approach players. When I knew I was selected for matches with South Africa, I went to my mother's graveside to be safe from that mafia of bad people. It [cricket] feels dangerous.' He had been understudy to Kamran Akmal in the summer against England and said of Mazhar Majeed, 'He was always there, having dinner, at the ground. He was close to Salman. The players asked if I wanted to go for dinner with Majeed. I didn't go.'

Pakistan sports minister Ijaz Hussain Jakhrani was short on sympathy. 'If he is such a weak and scared person he should not have played cricket in the first place, particularly not for the national team,' said Jakhrani, explaining that his government would not be supporting the application for asylum. 'This is no way for a member of the national team to behave or for even a professional cricketer to behave.'

* * *

The venue for the tribunal would be Qatar since Asif obviously had to be present and he was still *persona non grata* in Dubai. It would be held at the rooms within the commercial court and regulatory tribunal headquarters. The building had opened less than a month earlier, on 14 December 2010, and marked the Gulf state's attempt to rival London as a judicial hub for international dispute resolution. It lacked the grandeur of the high courts, however, located as it was inside the Qatar Financial Centre in downtown Doha, a high-rise area that exuded artificiality.

Joining Beloff on the bench were two other jurists the QC had been allowed to select. Aged 75, Albie Sachs had been one of the more famous anti-apartheid campaigners. Not only was he white but he had been imprisoned, exiled and, in Mozambique in 1988, had his left arm blown off and lost sight in his right eye after a car bomb explosion, perpetrated by the South African secret service. Six years later, he was appointed to the South African Constitutional Court by Nelson Mandela. Soon after, the country's cricket chief, Ali Bacher, asked if he would serve on the disciplinary appeals board of the International Cricket Council.

The other judge was Sharad Rao. Born and educated in Kenya, the 74-year-old had been called to the bar in London in 1959. He had subsequently worked on international disputes at The Hague and knew Beloff from their time together working for the Court of Arbitration in Sport. They, the ICC's own legal team and their witnesses were put up in the nearby W Hotel. Jonathan Taylor was back in his role as prosecutor-in-chief, joined by his Bird & Bird colleague Jamie Herbert.

For the accused, Shahid Karim was retained by Mohammad Amir. Butt's new legal team consisted of Ali Bajwa and Yasin Patel. Both were London-based and both cricket fans. Patel had come to the case through the great Pakistan spinner, Abdul Qadir, whose son he knew in England. A fortnight earlier, they had applied for the hearing to be stayed until such time as the Crown Prosecution Service had decided whether to press charges in the UK. The application was rejected by Beloff.

Asif's defence was also being mounted by an English lawyer and not any old brief. Alexander Cameron, 47, was not just a QC but he was also the older brother of the Conservative Party leader. David, three years his junior, would be elected Prime Minister four months later.

The tribunal would last from 6 to 11 January and Beloff opened it by reminding those present of the ICC's Anti-Corruption Code, articles 1.1.1 and 1.1.2, stating that 'all cricket matches are to be contested on a level playing field with the outcome to be determined solely by the respective merits of the competing teams ... [This is] the essential characteristic that gives sport its unique appeal ... Public confidence in the authenticity and integrity of that cricket match is vital. If that confidence is undermined, then the very essence of cricket, the characteristics that deliver its unique appeal, is shaken to the core.' The three cricketers were charged with contravening that code with their actions at The Oval as well as at Lord's.

Journalists would not be allowed to attend proceedings, though there were plenty present in Doha. Sachs was not wholly comfortable with this and pressed, to little avail, to be allowed time to converse with the media to stop the hearing looking so secretive. There was, however, one journalist with whom he would not have a problem conversing. Mazher Mahmood was also staying in the W Hotel and would be driven each day to court where his car would go into the exclusive, underground car park, allowing him to conceal his physical identity. The ICC had no power to compel Mazhar Majeed to attend, so, in his absence, Mahmood would be the star witness.

Jonathan Taylor would later compare Mahmood's testimony and documentation to a Christmas present which had been beautifully wrapped and then tied up in a neat bow. The recordings – video and audio – were damning of Majeed and his three players. Even Butt eventually stopped contesting their authenticity. On the stand, the journalist was very comfortable handling probing questions about his modus operandi because he had done it so many times before in courts in England.

Even so, his appearance and the evidence he had compiled was not alone going to be enough. After the *News of the World* man, the second most compelling witness was David Kendix. The 54-year-old Englishman was a trained actuary and cricket statistician who had been recruited by the ICC nine years earlier to calculate its international rankings. The question which he had been brought in to help resolve was the one that went to the heart of the case and was pithily coined by Sachs: were the no-balls fluke or fix?

Kendix told Taylor that the odds of anyone being able to predict the time at which three no-balls would be bowled without inside information were 1.5 million to one. Those odds, coupled with Mahmood's evidence, set a daunting challenge for the trio's legal teams, but they were not going to go down without a fight.

Ali Bajwa led for Butt. He began by focussing much of his attention on the 'invisible man' – Mazhar Majeed. Under questioning,

Butt explained that his agent was, in essence, a bullshitter. Some of his boasts to the *News of the World*'s undercover reporter – acting on behalf of footballer Rio Ferdinand, his friendship with various celebrities – were demonstrably false. As it pertained to this alleged crime, Bajwa argued, Majeed's mendacity resided in his claim to have the captain working the fix for him.

Bajwa insisted that the captain was not even critical to the plan. Amir and Asif were the established opening bowlers and, whatever the team, he said, the opening pair invariably sent down at least ten overs at the start of an innings. With Amir taking the first over, it was quite clear to anyone that he would have bowled the third (for the first no-ball) and Asif the tenth (for the second), irrespective of who was leading the team. The third no-ball on day two had then been privately arranged overnight between agent and Amir, Butt's team insisted.

Bowling coach Waqar Younis gave evidence by phone. He said that when the players had come off after the first day at Lord's had been curtailed by rain, he had shouted at Amir, 'What the hell was that?' referring to his huge no-ball. Butt, he revealed, then intervened, 'I told him to do it because the batsman was coming on the front foot. I told him to come forward and bowl him a bouncer.' In Qatar, Butt claimed that something had got lost in translation – the conversation was in Punjabi – and that his 'come forward' reference was to the batsman.

What about the phone calls where Butt could be heard assenting to Majeed's request to bat out a maiden at The Oval? Butt said it was just banter, a continuation of a joke the agent kept making that the reason Pakistan were performing so badly was because they were being bribed to do so. The captain just went along with the gag to humour him.

The problem with that was exposed by Jonathan Taylor, who cited the BlackBerry messages that the pair had exchanged during the World T20 in the Caribbean in May 2010. There was plenty that looked suspicious ('Ok, how about the other thing. One in 7th over and one in 8th ... This will only work if u score in first 2 overs and no wickets. Also even if we bat second innings it is same'), but no hint whatsoever of a running joke. It didn't end there. The ICC had written to Butt asking him to own up to all mobile phone numbers he used between 25 April and 16 August. He had failed to declare the two SIM card numbers he was using to communicate with Majeed.

There was also the evidence of the £50 notes, found in his possession, which could be traced back to the *News of the World*. Like Amir, who also faced the same problem, Butt claimed that it was money the agent had given them to attend the opening of a new branch in Tooting of his ice cream parlour chain. That was possible, of course, but was undermined by the testimony of Major Najam, head of security for the Pakistan Cricket Board, who appeared in person. Najam recalled how he had accompanied Butt up to his room at the Marriott Hotel in St John's Wood when the police were searching it. Najam said Butt was 'very distressed' and kept saying, 'I am fucked, I am screwed.'

The case against Asif was not as strong and in Alex Cameron he had the most persuasive advocate. In cross-examining Martin Vertigen, the ICC's information manager who had analysed the communications between the players and Majeed, Cameron was able to make the point that the agent enjoyed far fewer exchanges with Asif than with the other two. It was curious too, Cameron suggested, that when contacting Asif, Majeed did not use his dedicated 'fixing' mobile phone as he had done with the others. And while it was true that Majeed could be heard telling Mahmood that he had Asif in his pay, there was no recording of him discussing fixing with the bowler. Nor could any of the *News of the World* £50 notes be traced to him.

But how to explain the no-ball? Asif revealed that he had been told, 'run faster, do it' by his captain. When he had, as a result, overstepped the line, he had only done so by a small margin, nothing to compare with what Amir had done. If it was comparable with anything then it was the no-ball by Wahab Riaz in the following over and no one was asking questions about Riaz's probity.

But was the supposed command to run in faster a satisfactory explanation? This is where it got technical. David Kendix stated that Asif had bowled the no-ball at 80.2mph, which was only 0.8mph faster than his average over the six-over spell. In his career to that point, he had averaged a no-ball every 90 balls. At Lord's he delivered one on his 30th ball of the innings.

Shahid Karim for Mohammad Amir pursued a more legalistic line. He repeated his position set out at the suspension appeal sitting when he said that the ICC had not held an autonomous investigation. Breaches of confidentiality had followed. Having listened to and dismissed this reasoning in Dubai, Beloff sat through them again impatiently.

Beyond those specious arguments, the best that Amir and his representatives could come up with was a simple denial that he had bowled no-balls to order. So how had those no-balls come about? The first, he insisted, came down to the slippery conditions. No one disputed that the grass was damp and had he not, like Asif, asked for sawdust after that first no-ball to secure his footing? The second was an unfortunate by-product of his eagerness to force the batsman back with a bouncer.

In this, he had some support from umpire Tony Hill who had shared his take on it with the media a fortnight after the match: 'In our minds that was more a deliberate overstep to have a go at Trott, who had been batting so well. It all seemed to be one of those things that fast bowlers have been known to do to get an advantage.'

Leaving aside the timing of his no-balls at the exact moments that Majeed had predicted, Amir also had difficulty accounting for his exchanges with the agent. Why had they spoken so late (11.10pm) on the eve of a Test and then again at dawn on the day of the game? Simple, he said, the night-time call was just friends talking; the morning call was Amir ensuring his agent was taking care of tickets for his friends and transferring money to his family.

Then there was the text at the end of the first day at Lord's, which Majeed had accidentally sent to Mahmood (*Yaar after you finish your current over then 3 overs. Text back*). Immediately after the journalist had replied, 'wrong person', the agent had texted Amir, who himself responded almost instantaneously. Amir now said that he hadn't seen Majeed's message and wouldn't have understood it anyway if it had been in English. That he sent a text back within two minutes was, he claimed, pure coincidence. That text was just 'small talk', he testified.

These arguments went back and forth over six days, with periodic breaks for lunch and refreshment. The atmosphere among the protagonists was a curious, almost slightly surreal one. At the start, the three Pakistanis remained close, chatting together in the breaks. During one of these, they talked excitedly about Roger Federer, who was in town at the same time for a tennis tournament. If anything, the trio were almost too relaxed. Amir had turned up one day wearing a T-shirt with the slogan Legalise Cannabis; Butt wound up Jonathan Taylor with the lack of seriousness with which he treated his cross-examination; Asif, well, he was always laid back.

Butt's blasé demeanour was initially sustained by the informality with which all parties mixed during the intervals. Most of the lawyers already knew each other and were happy to swap trade gossip. They, along with the accused, ate lunch together in an adjoining room, each waiting in line for their turn to be served at the buffet. Someone even brought along a bat for Butt to sign. It was, observed Sachs, most convivial.

During one of the intervals, Mazher Mahmood found himself apart from the group standing next to Amir. He pressed the teenager to drop his claims of innocence. Plead guilty, he urged, and you'll get a lenient sentence. Mahmood caught sight of Butt looking darkly at the pair. Amir declined the opportunity to confess.

Butt's cheeriness ebbed over time. There was one point when he could be seen fiddling with his prayer beads, a sure sign that it was dawning on him that there was a very real chance he could lose his livelihood. Butt's wife was also in attendance and her elegant presence brought home to Albie Sachs the fact that the captain was from a more elevated class than his two bowlers. The longer the tribunal went on and the more their defence teams pursued an 'each-man-for-himself' strategy, the less the three cricketers were seen together outside the hearing.

On 10 January the ICC told the judges that all charges relating only to The Oval Test would be dropped, except for those involving Butt. The following day, closing arguments were concluded. Beloff signed off with a statement asserting that 'the tribunal has determined to continue its deliberations and hold a further hearing in Doha on 5 February of this year, at which its decisions will be handed down to the parties and any consequential matters will be dealt with.' In the meantime, the suspensions remained in place.

* * *

On 4 February, Mazher Mahmood was on the same flight out from Heathrow to Doha as Alex Cameron. Despite the lawyer's efforts to discredit him, Mahmood liked Cameron. The cross-examination was nothing personal and he had an affable, wry manner. That manner was going to be tested by the news that greeted them when they landed seven hours later in Qatar that Friday. The journalist turned on his phone to discover a statement from Simon Clements of the Crown Prosecution Service special crime division that he had 'authorised charges of conspiracy to obtain and accept corrupt payments and also conspiracy to cheat against Mohammad Amir, Mohammad Asif, Salman Butt and Mazhar Majeed.'

'Not looking too good for your boy, is it?' teased Mahmood.

The following day, they – Mahmood, Cameron and the other lawyers, the cricketers and Beloff – were back in the Financial Centre in Doha. Beloff read out the verdict that he, Sachs and Rao had deliberated over in the intervening 25 days. In fact, they hadn't needed that long to reach a verdict. All three concurred that the Pakistanis were guilty, including Butt in relation to a charge stemming from The Oval Test. The published judgement, which was concurrently being issued to the media, sketched out the following argument.

The judges agreed with everyone on Mazhar Majeed: 'The recordings show him to be plausible, quick-witted and ever ready to "big up" his prowess as a controller of the players. Moreover, he reveals himself to be venal to a degree, and capable of boastful exaggeration. Thus, he stated that he had opened Swiss bank accounts for his players, when in reality he appears to have preferred using envelopes with cash.'

Beyond that, they took a divergent view from the defence lawyers. 'As in so many things, however, the proof of the pudding had to be in the eating. The no-ball project was intended as a confidence-building exercise, to establish that he [Majeed] was indeed honest in his claims of successful corruption. We accordingly have to look to the objective facts to determine how much weight must be given to his claims, particularly when they involve the three players.' For all Majeed's bullshit, the circumstantial evidence of the 'extent of contact, social and commercial' between him and the trio left Beloff, Rao and Sachs 'satisfied that the relationships were, albeit in varying degrees, close'.

In the case of Butt, they noted that 'after the first day of the Lords Test ended early, [he] was in prompt and constant attempted contact with Mr Majeed. His reaction to the police search of his hotel room and the fact that notes found there corresponded with notes given by [Mahmood] to Mr Majeed was itself significant.' His claim that he had been in contact with his agent on the Saturday morning of The Oval match because he needed new white trousers was deemed 'implausible'. His refusal to inform the ICC of the two SIM cards he had used in the Caribbean 'suggested a certain sensitivity on Mr Butt's part which would have been unnecessary if he had simply been the victim of a tedious tease'.

Even if he had been going along with a lame running joke by his agent, as he claimed, Butt's 'non-disclosure to the ICC of the renewed and highly improper approach to him by Mr Majeed amounts to a breach of Article 2.4.2, if not of any other Article … The episode in Spring in St Lucia then appears to have been the overture to the main performance in summer in England … The success of the fix could not be ensured without his collaboration.'

The judges accepted that 'it has not been proved beyond reasonable doubt that Mr Butt is guilty of having agreed to take part in a spot-fixing agreement [at The Oval]. The ICC have, however, established beyond reasonable doubt that he failed to report to the ICC Mr Majeed's approach to him to bat a maiden over at a certain moment in the game. This failure constituted a violation of Article 2.4.2. b). With regard to the charge based on the alleged Lord's fix and revised Lord's fix agreement, we find that the ICC have proved beyond reasonable doubt that Mr Butt played a significant part in both establishing and securing the implementation of a spot-fixing agreement under which three balls would be bowled at pre-determined moments in the game.'

Attention then turned to Asif. His 'explanation that the cause of his no-ball was the instruction to "run faster, do it" by Mr Butt was not advanced until he delivered his response to the ICC opening brief', the judges wrote. 'The police interview with Mr Asif on 3 September 2010 naturally focussed on the circumstances of his no-ball and how it came to coincide with Mr Majeed's prediction. The Tribunal could identify four occasions during that interview when, if the cause of the no-ball were truly an instruction by Mr Butt to run up faster, Mr Asif had every opportunity to say so. He never did. The fact that he was never asked expressly whether Mr Butt had asked him to do something other than bowl a no-ball does not seem to us to diminish the force of his silence on the precise cause. Indeed far from suggesting a cause, he expressly described it as "an accident".

'This was moreover at a time when the incident would have been fresh in Mr Asif's memory and when he must have had the benefit of legal advice from the experienced lawyers who accompanied him to the police station to furnish to the police full information – at any rate of the kind that was in no way adverse to his interests. He would surely have told the police what he now tells the Tribunal if it were indeed the truth. The inference must be strong that his excuse is recent invention.

'The coincidence of prediction and the actual no-ball, the manifest confidence that Mr Majeed had that Mr Asif would perform as indicated, and the implausibility of the suggestion that somehow he was precipitated into bowling a no-ball by advice to have a faster run-up, are buttressed by the phone calls from Mr Majeed late at night in the middle of a Test Match and his subsequent failure to offer an innocent explanation on the many occasions on which he had an opportunity to do so.' Put it all together and 'the only conclusion we can come to is that he knew full well what was going on. We are convinced beyond reasonable doubt that, allowing himself to be sucked into an insidious and corrupt relationship with Mr Majeed, Mr Asif was a consensus agent in the no-ball fix, and violated Article 2.1.1 of the code.'

The case against the third man was much simpler: 'The essential and incontrovertible items of evidence against him are two and joined at the hip. First that Mr Majeed accurately predicted the exact moment in the game when Mr Amir would bowl two no-balls, a feat made all the more impressive given that the timing of the second had to be adjusted because of the premature ending of the first day's play at Lords. Second, he did bowl two no-balls at precisely those particular times.

'Nothing could detract from those items; and nothing was needed to enhance them. Absent some convincing explanation, the only conclusion that one can draw was that Mr Amir was party to the fix and a principal agent in its execution … There was nothing in the video evidence that supported Mr Amir's explanation for the first no-ball: his (and Mr Asif's) call for sawdust after their no-balls had the aspect of a charade. As to Mr Amir's explanation for the second no-ball, not all bouncers are no-balls and the fact that it was not bowled in the manner prophesied by Mr Majeed, a matter again emphasised by Mr Karim, distracts from the real issue – why were the no-balls bowled exactly when they were?

'We could see for ourselves the considerable extent by which Mr Amir's foot overstepped the popping crease on both occasions. As one commentator said, the no-balls were huge, further reducing the chance of their being pure coincidence … Mr Amir said nothing to disturb the conclusion which we have drawn from other evidence that the various calls passing between him and Mr Majeed at critical junctures related to the fix. We therefore conclude that Mr Amir was an active party to both the conclusion and the implementation of the Lords no-ball fix, in clear breach of Article 2.1.1.'

Getting to that point had been the easy bit for the panel. Where there was lengthier debate was over the appropriate punishment. In many ways, they were entering into new territory. The ICC decreed a mandatory five-year ban for anyone caught 'fixing' and seasoned cricket observers were clamouring for life bans. But spot-fixing was slightly different from match-fixing and the ICC had never had to deal with such a high-profile case where the prospect of the offenders receiving a custodial sentence was also very real.

Among the three, it was Sachs who pushed hardest for leniency. He was influenced by his experience working with South Africa's truth and reconciliation commission. Even if their defence had spurned the opportunity, it was important that there remained an incentive for the trio to own up to their crime and work with the authorities to clean up the game. He thought this particularly important in the case of Amir. The 18-year-old's lawyer Sharim had also pressed this, citing the dictum of the American legal scholar Kenneth Culp Davies that 'where law ends discretion begins'.

Beloff accepted that 'it is within our powers to suspend any additional period of ineligibility'. He also noted that 'the initiative for involvement in the fix came not from the players, but from Mr Majeed'. The term 'groomed' was used. The problem was that 'standing against all the players is that from the beginning to the end they have failed to acknowledge their guilt, and this in spite of overwhelming evidence of an objective nature establishing their involvement in the Lord's no-ball fix.'

For Butt, the judgement concluded, his 'offence is more serious than that of his team-mates [and] the minimum penalty of suspension for five years alone would not be appropriate. We consider that a further five years suspended on condition, inter alia, that he participates, starting as soon as possible, in programmes of public education and rehabilitation under the auspices of the PCB is here warranted. We envisage such programmes which the PCB may devise as having the potential to allow all three players to recover much of their honour and dignity, and be able to make valuable contributions to cricket in the future. We sense that a restorative process of that kind would be well received by the general cricket loving public, and the ICC.'

Of Asif, 'we consider that as a senior player [he] should have been more able than Mr Amir to resist temptation but was less responsible for what occurred than Mr Butt, who had the duties of a team captain. We impose a sanction similar in kind but less in degree than that imposed on Mr Butt i.e. the five-year minimum and an additional two years' suspension on like conditions.'

Finally they came to the 'kid': 'Mr Amir is the brightest new star in the international cricket firmament. This makes his particular case especially sad … The fundamental principle of equality before the law tells against allowing his talent, as distinct from his youth, as a mitigating factor. At the same time, however, we feel that a five-year ban is more than adequate to meet the circumstances of his case.'

Emerging from the Financial Center in Doha after the verdict had been delivered, Amir was mobbed by Pakistani expatriates who competed to touch him as if he had been acquitted. They were less supportive of Asif and Butt though that did not stop the crowd requesting photographs with and autographs of the pair.

* * *

For the *News of the World*, the timing of the judgement could not have been better. Early afternoon on a Saturday, the day they went to press – it was perfect timing for a Sunday newspaper, particularly one that owned the story. Reporter Matt Drake and a photographer had been dispatched to Doha to cover the reaction of the various parties, while Mahmood mingled among the ICC representatives and the legal team looking for background information on where the story would move next. Back in Wapping, *News of the World* editor Colin Myler set to work on the edition, waiting for his team's investigation to be validated by the decision of Beloff.

As far as Myler was concerned, natural justice, not to mention the publicity fanfare he intended to unleash, demanded life bans for all three. When news filtered through that the door for a return had been left open for them, he was furious. He wasn't the only one. David Bond of the BBC reported that 'the ICC lawyers simply cannot understand why the independent tribunal seemed to go soft on the players' punishments'.

By now, Taylor, Ian Higgins and another ICC lawyer, David Becker, were taking it all in back at the W Hotel where they were chatting over a pre-dinner drink in the bar. They spotted Alex Cameron amble in on his own and invited him to join them. Not long after that, Beloff appeared. The next thing they knew they were all heading up for dinner to the Spice Market restaurant on the first floor. Matt Drake spotted them dining together and reported back to the office. Myler was fired up even more. It was one thing for Beloff to decline to hand down the cricketing equivalent of a death sentence; it was another for him and his pals from the Bar to be joshing about proceedings over a slap-up meal (all on expenses no doubt).

Myler passed on his orders to James Mellor – Ian Edmondson had by now left the *Screws* – who passed them on to Drake. He was to 'doorstep' them at the table and ask them whether they thought it fit and proper for the 'bench', 'defence' and 'prosecution' to be fraternising so lavishly after such a controversial judgement. Drake was a little apprehensive about the assignment, not least because one was the Prime Minister's brother and he had found them all to be quite helpful in his dealings with them. Still, he had done worse in his time and orders were orders.

'Michael Beloff, is it really appropriate for you to be having dinner with Alex Cameron so soon after you have sat in judgment on his client?' It wasn't the opening salvo that Jonathan Taylor expected when he saw Drake, whom he knew, sidle up to the table. Nor could he understand why the photographer on the hack's shoulder was now focussing his lens on the party? Taylor was furious: 'Hold on a minute, there's nothing improper going on. I'm here, the ICC are here as well, there's no story. What the fuck are you doing?'

Drake could see he wasn't going to get very far and beat a hasty retreat, taking a copy of the menu with him so he could shock readers with details of the eye-watering amounts the group were spending on dinner. Within half an hour he had filed to the desk and waited for the call telling him that his work for the day was done.

The call duly came and it wasn't good. The enraged Taylor had been straight on to Mazher Mahmood. The ICC, he insisted, had never been anything less than a straight player with the *News of the World*. So why were they returning the favour in this way? Opposing lawyers, with much in common professionally and socially, getting together *after* a case was hardly unheard of or untoward. Mahmood liked Taylor and appreciated the point he was making. He phoned Wapping and told them to call off the dogs.

By the time he was informed by Mellor that his dinner intervention had all been for nothing, Drake needed a drink. Back down in the bar, one of the first people he bumped into was Alex Cameron. The table had broken up and Cameron was after a nightcap. The journalist wasn't going to apologise but he didn't want to part on bad terms. 'Can I buy you one?' he asked.

The Prime Minister's brother looked at him suspiciously and then relaxed. 'Go on, then,' he said before returning his gaze to the area behind the bar where the brandies were kept. Once he had alighted on his preferred tipple, he told the barman to make it a double. The pair chewed the fat amicably enough for half an hour before Cameron said his goodbyes, leaving Drake to pick up the tab. The *Screws* man needed a stiff one himself when he saw the bill. Cameron's brandy came in at £90 a shot. Try putting that through on expenses.

The following day, Drake flew back into Heathrow and headed for the terminal newsagent eager to see how the *Screws* had covered the Qatar denouement. He wasn't the only one there picking up the Sunday papers. As he scanned the titles on the shelves, he felt a tap on his shoulder. 'Thanks again for that drink,' said Alex Cameron with a wry smile and a wink.

CHAPTER SIX

'WE HAVE TWO DEFENDANTS EFFECTIVELY TURNING ON EACH OTHER WITH A VIEW TO WRIGGLE OUT OF WHAT EACH OTHER HAS DONE'

SOUTHWARK CROWN Court is located in the south-eastern part of central London, between London Bridge and Tower Bridge, just behind where HMS *Belfast* is moored. Most of the high-profile trials brought there have been initiated by the Serious Fraud Office. In January 2012 the trial of leading football manager Harry Redknapp, who had been charged with tax evasion, would be held there. Three months before that, it welcomed the world's media for cricket's 'trial of the century'.

The wheels of justice had moved slowly since the cricketers had first reported for police questioning at Maida Vale on 3 September 2010. On the surface of things, it seemed apparent that they were obviously guilty of something. But was it a criminal offence? Gambling was at the heart of spot-fixing but no one had defrauded the bookies because no bet had been placed on the no-balls. As we have seen, no bet could have been placed because no betting shop or broker would ever accept a wager on the timing of no-balls.

Eventually, the Crown Prosecution Service alighted on a section of the statute book which gave them the basis to proceed. Soon after they had been issued with their bans in Qatar, the 'Lord's three' received a summons to face a criminal hearing at Westminster on

17 March 2011. That summons alleged that 'between the 15th day of August 2010 and the 28th day of August 2010 you conspired together with Mazhar Majeed and with others unknown to obtain and accept from Mazher Mahmood for yourselves the sum of £150,000 as an inducement or reward for doing an act in relation to the affairs of the Pakistan Cricket Board, namely to bowl three no-balls during the fourth Test at Lords [sic]. Conspiracy to obtain and accept corrupt payment, contrary to s 1 (1) of the Criminal Law Act 1977.' In the meantime, on 26 February, Salman and Amir filed appeals with the Court of Arbitration for Sport in Lausanne, Switzerland, against their ban. On 1 March, so did Asif.

On the appointed date in London, the trio and Majeed went before Chief Magistrate Howard Riddle. Sally Walsh, representing the crown, argued against unconditional bail for any of them. Riddle demurred, however, 'It is mandatory on them to be present in court on each and every date hearing, and they can also be called on at short notice to attend such hearing.' Majeed was told that his passport would be kept by the police and he could not apply for a new one.

To compound Amir's humiliation, on 8 April the cricket 'bible', *Wisden*, announced that its latest edition would only be honouring four 'cricketers of the year', rather than the usual five. It was clear that the young bowler would have been the fifth for his deeds during the summer of 2010 but what had transpired after that had rendered his inclusion impossible.

The next judicial hearing date was set for 20 May, though none were required to attend and at which the trial date was set for 4 October. Another preliminary hearing would take place in the meantime in July at which the accused could attend in person or via videoconferencing.

The case was then transformed on 16 September. It was on this date that lawyers for Majeed and Amir announced that their clients would be pleading guilty. It meant that defence plans would have to be ripped up for the other two, who were now set to face trial without their co-accused. It was a huge shift in proceedings and would not have come about without Amir trusting in the judgement of his legal team. Since March, this had been headed up by human rights lawyers Gareth Peirce and Sajda Malik of Birnberg Peirce and Partners in London. Between them they had done what those close to him, the ICC and the PCB, who had no prior warning of his confession, had failed to achieve in the year preceding: make him face the truth and admit his crime.

This had not happened overnight and the guilty plea had itself been driven by legalistic as well as moral considerations. Peirce had analysed the evidence and if ever there was a case of entrapment this was it. She also knew though that English criminal law would only view this as mitigation rather than as an actual defence. The guilty plea was the right call judicially and ethically.

This was the background to the trial which began on the scheduled date in October when the jury of six men and six women was sworn in in Court Four in front of Mr Justice Cooke. The 62-year-old judge, also known as Sir Jeremy Cooke, warned the jury that the process could take up to five weeks and that they should infer nothing from the absence from court of Majeed and Amir, whose guilty pleas the media were not allowed to report. An Urdu interpreter was also present to translate for Asif.

Representing the Crown was Aftab Jaferjee QC. Of Sri Lankan heritage, Jaferjee was the first member of any ethnic minority to be appointed a treasury counsel and had been called to the Bar in 1980. *The Times* had ranked him in one of its lists of top-ten criminal barristers at/under the age of 50.

Appearing for Asif and Butt were two equally eminent silks. For Asif, Alexander Milne had been called to the Bar a year later than Jaferjee and had served as counsel on the epic Bloody Sunday inquiry into the army shooting of civilians in Northern Ireland in 1972. Butt's brief was Ali Bajwa, who had acted for him in Doha. Bajwa had only taken silk that year, one of the youngest barristers to do so. He was also a cricket fan. The defendants had been able to call on such esteemed advocates thanks to Britain's means-tested legal aid system. Although they were foreign nationals, they could apply to the state to pay towards the costs of their defence as the charges had been brought by an English court.

Aftab Jafferjee told the courtroom, 'This case reveals a depressing tale of rampant corruption at the heart of international cricket...By the time the last Test match at Lord's took place, each of them were well at it – the two bowlers being orchestrated by their captain, and the captain's agent, Majeed, to bowl three no-balls at a pre-arranged point in the game. The bowlers were willing participants so that they could all profit – those lower down the ladder probably profiting less than those at the top. The activity of these four men not only contaminated the games which took place and were watched by millions in this country but it represents a betrayal by them of their own team, their own board of cricket, and most damaging of all a betrayal of the sport of cricket itself – and all for greed.'

The jury should understand that beneath the surface of international competition lurked an underworld of 'influential but shadowy figures' in Dubai, Mumbai, Karachi and London and a black market where 'simply breathtaking' sums of money were gambled – up to $50bn in the Indian subcontinent in one year. Sadly it would be near 'impossible for anyone hearing the details to watch future games of cricket without a sense of disquiet'.

The central planks of the prosecution were not going to be much different from those nailed down by Jonathan Taylor in Doha: the *News of the World*'s audio and video evidence of Majeed, the mobile phone communications between him and the players, the no-balls delivered and the marked notes subsequently found in their possession. Some of the witnesses would be the same, others would be new.

The video footage of Majeed spoke for itself. The defence did not try to dispute its authenticity and its accuracy, though it would try to depict its lead character as a fabulist. The mobile phone records and texts, many of them originally deleted but later retrieved by a Canadian mobile data specialist, were also advanced as exhibits. Jafferjee wanted to avoid information overload so was careful not to bombard the jury with too many of these. Rather he wanted them to note the 'frenetic activity' between the four within a couple of hours of play being abandoned on day one of the match, when the first two no-balls had been completed. 'It is an irresistible inference, say the prosecution, that between these four men, what is being sorted out is that third no-ball,' Jafferjee stated. 'How will that now take place? The credibility staked – as well as money exchanged – is high. An arrangement for the next day is still not finalised.

'Why do we say that? Because when the journalist calls Majeed, it is plain that things are not finalised. More texts have to follow between them. Furthermore, that triangulation of calls has to be repeated, involving the three players and Majeed.'

The big evidential change from Doha was the involvement of the Metropolitan Police, which had handed charge of the investigation, 'Operation Seawell', to Chief Superintendent Matthew Horne. Horne's team were able to assist the prosecution's cause by filling in some of the gaps around the money and the players' demeanour under questioning.

Jafferjee took the court back to the evening of 28 August 2010 when police descended on the Marriott Hotel, Regent's Park, an hour or two after close of play at Lord's and about the same time before the *News of the World* would go public with its story. Backed up by search and seizure warrants, around half a dozen police officers in gloves and white overalls were on the scene to perform formal searches of the rooms. Butt was in his room, No. 714, when they called. One unnamed player present on the scene, not quoted in court, would later say that, 'It seemed like Salman would try and jump out of the window, so one officer had to guard the window and keep an eye on Salman while the others searched the rooms.'

Once inside, the police would find around £40,000 in cash in eight different denominations, as well as four mobile phones. A sum of £2,500, made up of notes marked by the paper, was included in that. The officers would eventually discover the notes as part of a sum of £14,003 found in an attaché case locked inside a suitcase. Butt had said his wife had flown back to Pakistan with the key to unlock it. In Asif's room, they uncovered £8,000 in cash, held in eight envelopes tucked inside two rucksacks, though none of the notes were from the marked batch. Amir had more than £9,000 sitting in a safe. Thirty of the £50 notes within could be traced back to the *News of the World*.

Under formal police questioning on 3 September 2010, they were asked how they had come by such large cash totals and what they had intended to do with them. Butt said he had brought some from home and some of it had come from Majeed, as an advance for agreeing to open *Afters*, his ice cream parlour in Tooting. He was intending to spend some of it himself – he liked the luxuries of life, he had to admit – while much of the rest would be passed on to his sisters for wedding shopping. Asif and Amir claimed that they had accrued their individual sums mainly through the daily allowance given to them by the PCB of £114 and again spoke of shopping expenditure.

Butt was asked by detectives if the money was actually payment for fixing. 'I don't think anyone can influence me to cheat my country,' he said indignantly. 'There's no way I'd ever do that in my life. There's no individual in the world who can tell me to do that and no way I can tell Mohammad Asif or Mohammad Amir to do that.'

Still, £40,000 in US, Canadian and Australian dollars, South African rand and Indian dirham was a lot of money to have on tour, not to mention the mobiles … Butt explained that this was cash handed to him by adoring expats: 'Especially in England there's lots of Pakistan community [sic], they take us out to dinner and they do not want us to pay. It's wonderful money, we are some of the best-paid sports people in Pakistan. People in the team don't think I've cheated. No one's said that. We know if we don't play well we get slammed with tomatoes and eggs. We hate losing because we get so hated when we lose.'

After the money came the deed. Making a re-appearance to talk about the probability of three no-balls being bowled at pre-determined moments was David Kendix, the ICC statistician who had given evidence in Qatar. Again, his figure of 1 in 1.5 million was rolled out. Alexander Milne managed to get Kendix to confirm that the sixth ball of the tenth over of the innings – when Asif sent down the second deliberate no-ball – was his quickest delivery of the over. The purpose of this was to imply that his client's overstepping of the line was due to him running in faster than usual as opposed to anything more sinister.

Sky Sports statistician Benedict Bermange backed up Kendix's evidence. Pakistan, he had worked out, bowled 23 per cent more no-balls than any other Test nation, but he also said that Asif's incidence of no-balls was low compared with his peers and would have been even lower had he not committed 40 per cent of them in one match against South Africa. Again, Milne looked for some sort of concession to aid Asif. Pointing to one of the images of Asif's no-ball, he asked if Bermange agreed that the front foot was only over the line by a small amount. Bermange did and noted that it was in stark contrast to that of Amir at the moment of his critical deliveries: 'I have attended 50 Test matches within my current position and these two [Amir's no-balls] were the largest no-balls in terms of the front foot being over the crease that I have seen.'

* * *

On 10 October, Mazher Mahmood was called to give evidence. Much had happened in his world since his last meeting with Majeed on 25 August 2010. In March 2011 Mahmood had been unanimously named news reporter of the year at the UK Press Awards. The cricket story had also won scoop of the year, the judges citing it as 'the definition of a scoop for its jaw-dropping impact'. Colin Myler accepted the reporter award on behalf of Majeed who, as was customary with these things, had stayed away to preserve the secrecy of his identity.

Trouble was waiting around the corner, however. On 7 July 2011, in their new headquarters in Wapping, just across the road from the old 'Fortress', Rebekah Brooks and Colin Myler took the lift down to the floor where the *News of the World* was housed and broke the news that the edition staff were currently working on would be the last one.

In the months before, the company line that phone-hacking had been confined to one 'rogue reporter' – former royal correspondent Clive Goodman using private detective Glenn Mulcaire – had collapsed in the face of revelations by *The Guardian* and its dogged reporter Nick Davies. The gravest charge News International found itself handling was the report that *News of the World* journalists had tried to hack the phone of Milly Dowler, a 13-year-old who had gone missing in 2002 before being found brutally murdered. Hacking celebrities' phones had been one thing but, for company proprietor Rupert Murdoch, hacking the mobile of a teenager while the police were conducting a frantic search for her had rendered the *Screws* toxic.

Mahmood was not in the office when Brooks and Myler stunned his colleagues. However, he was soon told that he was one of the journalists for whom management were hoping to find another role in the company. Not everyone viewed his continued employment in journalism as a good thing. On 13 July Mazhar Majeed tweeted: 'NOTW – corrupt, dirty, underhand and jobless. M Mahmood would rape his daughter for a story. We know what u have done and your day is coming.' Two months later, he pitched up at the *Sunday Times*, producing news investigations, albeit of a less lurid nature. His debut appearance on 18 September exposed 'the illicit trade in fake medical reports and death certificates sold by corrupt foreign doctors to unscrupulous holidaymakers seeking to make false insurance claims.'

His prominence at the tainted *News of the World* offered a chink in the Crown's case. It would not have escaped the attention of any member of the jury that many of its executives had been arrested since its demise. These included former editors Andy Coulson and Rebekah Brooks and former executive editor Neil Wallis. Ian Edmondson, who had been involved in the early stages of the Pakistan investigation, had been suspended from the paper at the end of 2010 and arrested the following April.

Jafferjee had pre-empted all this when he told the jury that, whatever their view of the paper, its endeavours had exposed 'matters of national and international concern'. He continued: 'Were this investigation not to have been permitted, this activity of fixing would almost certainly have continued, unabated and unaccountable, and beyond the reach of the law.'

As in previous trials, Mahmood was allowed to give evidence behind a screen to preserve the secrecy of his identity, the judge clearing the court before his arrival. Once proceedings got under way, some in the press gallery were able to crane their necks and catch a glimpse of his features. He was an old hand at these courtroom appearances and, like a batsman facing a fast bowler, knew that a few bouncers were coming his way.

Acting for Asif, Alexander Milne wasted no time digging one in short. 'The *News of the World* has experienced several problems,' he pointed out. 'Do you know of [convicted phone hacker] Glenn Mulcaire?' Mahmood replied, 'I have read about him but I have never met him, never spoken to him.' Milne cited an interview he had given to *Press Gazette* in May 2008. Of Clive Goodman's conviction, the interviewer had written, 'Mahmood insists it was an isolated incident, but admits it was a blow for the *NoW* and gave more fuel to the paper's critics. He says: "It's sad that an incident like that can overshadow all the good work we do."'

That isolated incident remark did not look very clever now, but Mahmood played a straight bat: 'Are you suggesting I was aware it wasn't an isolated incident? I had no idea at all in my 20 years. I had no knowledge of phone hacking. I read about the arrest of Goodman in the papers. I never met Glenn Mulcaire. I had no knowledge of that in my 20 years at the paper. I hope that the guys who were responsible for that go down.'

Nor, despite rejoicing in the title of investigations editor, could he be held accountable for the activities of fellow hacks. 'I had no idea what other reporters on the paper were doing, I was not responsible for other reporters,' he said. 'My job was researching, and reporting and exposing criminal and moral wrongdoing. I had nothing to do with phone hacking or the illegal interception of voicemails.'

'It is in the context of phone hacking that you received information relating to Mr Majeed,' Milne insisted. After all, how else could the data from Majeed's BlackBerry have come into his possession? 'This story has nothing to do with phone hacking. One, you're assuming it's downloaded from the telephone without the knowledge of the person, and second this is nothing to do with hacking at all,' Mahmood hit back. It was very simple, he explained: a source, who would have to remain confidential, had originally tipped him off about Pakistanis involved in fixing. Later, that same source had come by print-outs of the messages which he had forwarded on to himself as well as to the International Cricket Council. 'There was no hacking involved, you are barking down the wrong tree.'

He also applied the public interest argument. However his source had come by these messages was almost irrelevant because it was evident from them 'that these guys had been involved in criminality and had been involved for a long time'. No less a figure than company lawyer Tom Crone had told him it 'was completely within the law' to use the messages obtained from the BlackBerry. He did admit that the source had been paid after questioning.

Milne tried to use some of the more outlandish boasts of Majeed, whom he dubbed a 'snake-oil salesman', to undermine the Crown's case. The agent had boasted of being on good terms with Brad Pitt and Roger Federer but 'we haven't had so far any comment from Mr Federer or Mr Pitt as to the extent of their friendship with him. Did you believe that?'

'Anything's possible,' said Mahmood flatly before accepting that some of Majeed's boasts had to be 'taken with a pinch of salt'. Even so, 'Some of the things he said were completely true.' Having been dealing with criminals on a regular basis for 20 years, he had viewed Majeed oxymoronically as an 'honest villain'.

Milne also had a googly up his sleeve. He wanted to know if the journalist had, in the days after the *News of the World* had come out at the end of August, posed as a Mr Imran Skeikh who, through a law firm called Malik & Malik, had tried to arrange a meeting with his client at a central London restaurant. He was also asked if he had pretended to be a solicitor to meet Asif at the offices of

Hill Mathieson & Partners estate agents in Primrose Hill, north London. Unsurprisingly, Mahmood denied both charges: 'That would be a criminal offence, I would be in the dock. It would be ludicrous for me to meet him. I'm the guy who has received death threats after this story ... the last thing I would want to do is meet a cricketer from Pakistan.'

Milne also questioned whether he had met with Asif back in his own country between September 2010 and January 2011. 'If he is saying that, he is not only a match fixer, he is a liar,' Mahmood said, and he would be happy to produce his passport to prove it. He had been to Pakistan but this was to pursue leads into the killing of Al Qaida leader Osama bin Laden after his death in May 2011. Milne then drew laughs by noting, 'He [bin Laden] hasn't featured in this case so far, but it's early days.'

The idea that Mahmood might want to influence witnesses was not so outlandish, Milne implied, by reminding him of his meeting with the Pakistan batsman Yasir Hameed at a hotel in Nottingham the day after the Lord's Test. As we have seen, Mahmood had lured him into the meeting by pretending to be a potential sponsor, Abid Khan, with a £50,000 deal. Hameed had then been scathing about this subterfuge when his accusations against team-mates had appeared in print. Again, Mahmood played a straight bat. He had acted simply as a journalist pursuing 'information relevant to the investigation'.

He was in the witness box for around ten hours. In that time, the defence had landed few blows but its questioning had not been completely wasted. Milne had reminded the jury that the witness had plied his trade in a working environment where criminality – hacking – had been commonplace. More specifically, he had underlined that deceit was an integral part of Mahmood's modus operandi as an undercover reporter. If he lied when he donned the robes of the Fake Sheikh or the suit of 'Mohsin Khan' or any other of his aliases, who's to say he wasn't lying now?

Nor had Mahmood been able to prove beyond doubt that the messages had not been acquired illegally. That the source had also been paid did not exactly paint him or her in an honourable light and was a reminder of the grubby nature of 'chequebook journalism'. And how was anyone to know if the source was actually real? The journalist's refusal to name that source could just be a front. It wasn't much but it was something. It would, however, take a lot more from his client and Salman Butt when they took the stand to turn around this struggling innings.

* * *

The first thing the few journalists who had also been at Doha noticed was that the accused were no longer fraternising. During breaks, they could be found taking a walk outside, having lunch in the court canteen or chatting with their legal teams – but seldom, if ever, together. Asif liked to pop out for a cigarette, and before he did so would ask one of the journalists in attendance if they could pick him up a bottle of orange juice (freshly squeezed) for when he came back. His preferred lunch was chips and beans. He occasionally nodded off in the dock and did his reputation for unreliability no harm by arriving two hours late on one day. Milne mentioned his absence to the jury but offered no explanation.

He was dressed much smarter than he had been in Qatar, usually a suit. Butt, meanwhile, was described by one journalist who covered most of the trial as 'happily self-sufficient. He cut a relaxed figure and by the end of the [first] week was snappily dressed in velvet jacket, Armani jeans and sneakers.' Whether that composed mien was just a front would become clear when he went into the dock on 17 October. Ali Bajwa QC said his client did not dispute that there had been a conspiracy to bowl no-balls, but it really had nothing to do with him. The guilty men here were the absent men, Mohammad Amir and Majeed.

On the subject of the latter, Butt, speaking in English for most of the time, said that he had resisted pressure from his agent to get involved in spot-fixing. This included texts which police had recovered from the World T20 in the Caribbean in which Majeed had instructed the Pakistan captain to deliberately lose wickets in their group stage match against South Africa (Butt was out for 2, Pakistan won by 10 runs).

He said he had turned him down, telling him, 'You must understand these kinds of things we have to report. He [Majeed] said, "I am just checking if you are doing something dodgy or not." He said he was trying to test me with something non-serious. Anyone in my place would have had suspicions about it. I had known him for years and he had never done this before.' Of course, he should have reported the approach to the authorities, but that would have ended their working relationship and that had been going well.

Of the audio recorded by Mazher Mahmood at Majeed's house when he had spoken over the phone of playing out a maiden at The Oval, Butt insisted he was just humouring him. 'Never in my life have I intended to do anything like that,' he told his counsel. 'I play in a certain way. I do what is required to the best of my ability.'

The following day it fell to Jafferjee to see how his claims stood up to some hostile cross-examination. Why, he asked, had he transferred $181,000 from his bank account to his mother on the day he attended police questioning? Butt played the loyal son card. He did not know how long he would have to remain in England for and wanted to ensure that she was financially secure in his absence. The timing was just coincidence. 'It might have happened on the day of the interview, but it was not aimed to happen on the day of the interview,' he said.

On the texts from Majeed during the 2010 World T20, Butt said he had been too trusting of a friend. 'I misjudged him. I thought I knew him well. I took his word and trusted him. I never thought there would be another side to him.' Jafferjee said simply, 'You are lying to the jury.' Butt replied, 'That's what you think.'

But what about the money found in his hotel room? Butt repeated that the envelope of £2,500 handed to him on the evening of 26 August was for a future appearance at Majeed's ice cream parlour in south London. He referred too to a contract with Adidas, which paid well, and another to display a sticker with Majeed's company logo on his bat. These were the reasons why he was flush with cash and had bought four designer watches, including a Rolex, Bulgari and Tag Heuer worth £25,000 in total, though these were more investments than adornments, he said.

Butt made it all sound plausible but there was one thing he couldn't answer adequately. When police searched his room on 28 August he maintained he could not open the suitcase in which the money had eventually been discovered because his wife had taken the keys with her back to Pakistan. It was not in dispute that his wife had returned to Lahore *before* the cash had been given to him, so if he didn't have the keys, how could the money have made its way inside? The answer was obvious, said Jafferjee, 'You had a lot to fear from what was to be found in that suitcase and were playing a stalling game.'

Butt was poised during most of these exchanges but there was definitely an antagonistic undercurrent in his back-and-forth with Jafferjee. On the odd occasion, he became flippant, such as when the prosecutor asked him about the potential of cheating to destroy the game of cricket. Butt brought up the example of WWF (the World Wrestling Federation) – 'Everybody knows it's fixed but it still has a lot of following and viewing.' It was the kind of throwaway comment that did him no good.

After Butt, it was the turn of Asif. A portent of how his defence would be run had been provided by his brief's own examination of the captain. Alexander Milne had asked Butt about his instruction in Punjabi to the bowler before the second of the three no-balls. According to Milne, that order was 'Run faster, fucker, you're running too slow.' Butt looked genuinely baffled at the suggestion.

Yet this was the line that his co-defendant stuck to when he appeared in the witness box. Asif's no-ball, his counsel seemed to be setting out, was down to two factors. The first were the exhortations of his skipper. 'He said to me all the time, "Come on, you look sleepy, haven't you slept."' It was after the fifth ball that Butt had issued the 'run faster, fucker' command. 'It is not friendly. It is unusual for the captain to say something like this to me, the ranking bowler,' Asif said. 'You cannot say that to me in this position.'

Milne also told the jury that this, combined with having two leg-before appeals turned down in the same over, had disrupted Asif's rhythm and led to him working up such a head of steam that he transgressed on the sixth ball. It was the combustion rather than conspiracy theory of history.

Butt shook his head as he heard this, sometimes he laughed too. His lawyer Ali Bajwa denounced it as a 'desperate invention'. They had all watched the video replay of the over in question and, in fact, there had only been one leg-before appeal. And why was it that he had mentioned none of this in his original police interview? Was this really 'the best you could think of?' Bajwa asked rhetorically. Whether Bajwa had helped his client was not clear, but he had certainly assisted the Crown in dismantling the other cricketer's defence.

The man for the prosecution made a more subtle but equally valid point: 'You know full well the role of your captain in fixing games,' Jafferjee said, 'and that is why you came close to blaming him for your no-ball. You appreciate that if you tell the jury he told you to bowl a new no-ball you are coming as close as you can to admitting your guilt. You have been sucked into the web of corruption and there were two people who were equally responsible for sucking you in, Mazhar Majeed and Salman Butt.' To Asif's claim that he really didn't know Majeed and had no formal contract with him, Jafferjee could simply point to the record of phone calls and messages between the two.

In summing up for the prosecution, Jafferjee reassured the jury that the saga was 'nothing to do with being blinded with the technicalities of cricket. It is no different to a fraudster manipulating markets and saying "you do not understand the market". You the jury do understand deceit, greed and corrupt practice by some on the inside who are lucky enough, through talent, who have the opportunity to exploit it.'

He then listed 13 facts that mapped out a trail of guilt leading to the men in the dock. 'In this case we have two defendants effectively turning on each other with a view to wriggle out of what each other has done. The sad truth in this case is that there are decent things to be said of everybody – perhaps not Majeed. But none of this could have happened without these four people involved. Butt, Asif and Amir were involved. And all for what? Money. More money.'

With Amir not present to give evidence, Bajwa rounded on him in his summing-up for Butt. 'This isn't some naive and wholly innocent 19-year-old,' he told the jury. There was evidence of suspicious texts sent to Pakistan over a week before the Lord's match, and another sent to a number in Pakistan after his hotel room had been searched – 'Amir here. Don't call my phone. ICC police have taken my phone. Are you able to delete those calls you made to me? If you can, do it OK. Don't reply.' Such an individual was obviously knee deep in the underworld of cricket corruption, Bajwa maintained. If anyone was giving him orders to bowl no-balls, it wasn't his captain.

Speaking for almost an hour and a half, Milne reminded the jury again that his client's no-ball had been marginal, no way near the overstep of Amir. The point he really wanted to ram home, however, was the notion that in crimes of corruption they should 'follow the money'. The only notes handed over by the *News of the World* had been in the possession of Butt and Amir. 'It's up to you members of the jury what conclusions you draw from that, but none of that money went to Mr Asif. If Majeed was that keen to pay Mr Asif he would have found a way. If you follow the money, you will find that it does not lead to Mr Asif.'

Majeed might have described himself as the accused's agent, but they were never close: 'Asif was never in Majeed's company. The only times they spent together was on a tennis court in the West Indies [during the Twenty20 World Cup] and twice in London hotel foyers during the tour. There are no photos, no signed contracts between them and there were never any dinners. Majeed never spoke to Mr Asif in the 36 hours leading up to that meeting at the Copthorne Tara Hotel when Majeed received the £140,000. However, there were 65 forms of contact between Butt and Majeed and Amir and Majeed. That equates to contact every 34 minutes in that period. Butt and

Amir were in very, very regular contact with Majeed. Mr Asif? Not a word. Not a whisper. Not a meeting.'

From the bench Mr Justice Cooke spoke for a day. 'You can proceed on the basis that Majeed and Amir were involved because all parties agree that this was the case,' he advised the jurors. What they had to determine was whether the two men who stood before them were 'knowingly involved' in the conspiracy. Perhaps his most significant point concerned a discrepancy in Asif's evidence. When interviewed in September last year, he simply said that his no-ball was accidental and 'no one had pressurised him to do so'. Now he was saying that Butt had told him to 'run faster, fucker'. 'Could Asif reasonably have been expected to tell officers of this account?' the judge asked them to consider.

On Thursday, 27 October the jury was sent away to reach a decision. The judge said he wanted it to be unanimous. A decision was not immediately forthcoming and at 3.24pm on 31 October Mr Justice Cooke sent them home for the day, saying he would now accept a verdict on which at least ten of them agreed. On 1 November, they had reached that verdict.

* * *

Salman Butt was found guilty on a 10-2 majority verdict of the charge of accepting corrupt payments. He and Asif were found guilty unanimously of conspiracy to cheat at gambling. The jury had been held up on whether Asif had accepted corrupt payments – the absence of marked *News of the World* notes in his possession probably giving them pause for thought – but they eventually came to another 10-2 majority of guilty. At this point, the judge was allowed to inform the court that Amir had already pleaded guilty to the same charges. Neither of those in the dock gave much away. Less than half an hour before, Asif had been sitting next to a couple of journalists, playing games on a friend's iPad. Butt must have thought of his second child, a boy, born earlier that day in Lahore.

Outside, Aftab Jafferjee gave much of the credit to Mazher Mahmood. 'It was due to the efforts of a journalist with the *News of the World* that this pernicious and criminal activity was exposed,' he said. 'Here the role of undercover reporting was to expose matters of national and international concern. Were this investigation not to have been permitted, this activity of fixing would almost certainly have continued, unabated and unaccountable, and beyond the reach of the law.'

There was also a bizarre moment when a gentleman by the name of Salman Ahmed turned up to tell the media that he was really Asif's manager and had also been working with Butt. 'Obviously there is not much room any more to do any business so it looks like it is the end of the contract effectively. I had never even heard of Mazhar Majeed or Azhar Majeed until all this fixing stuff came up. I found it really amazing that Majeed was claiming to be his manager yet he never did anything for him. It was my company that assisted Asif getting paid by the Delhi Daredevils and when he had other troubles to deal with. Since I realised some time ago that Pakistan players don't have agent values, I don't expect any of them to stay loyal to any one agent.'

Back in Islamabad, Yawar Saeed, the tour manager in 2010, described it as 'a sad day for all of us and I'm very sad that this beautiful game of cricket has had to see this day. I feel very sad because I tried my level best to tell them to keep away from notorious people. They should have understood that and they committed a blunder, and when you commit a blunder, you are punished.'

Sentencing would naturally follow but that could not happen without the playing out of what turned out to be a trial within a trial. On 2 November the two Pakistanis were joined in court by their former team-mate Amir and Mazhar Majeed, who had already pleaded guilty to charges of conspiracy to cheat and conspiracy to obtain and accept corrupt payments. This trial within a trial effectively became another blame game when Mark Miliken-Smith QC stepped up to argue on behalf of Majeed, who would be described by Mike Atherton in *The Times* in derisory terms – 'sitting in his ill-fitting suit, unshaven, twitching like Inspector Dreyfus, Mazhar Majeed during the past two days in the dock looked like exactly what he is: a small-time crook from Croydon, South London.'

Miliken-Smith wasted no time casting Butt as the ringleader. He harked back to the dinner between player and agent in London in the summer of 2009. 'Butt raised the topic [of fixing] and he did so not as an offer but in frustration. Butt saw others were at it. He compared his own lack of wealth with others playing in the Pakistan team, where wealth is represented by the number of houses they had in Pakistan. Butt was asking, "How could X or Y have so many houses when he did not, when he came from a wealthier background and had the same contract as these players?"'

At a subsequent meeting involving the pair and another Pakistan player who could not be named, Majeed 'was given a number for the bookie Sanjay, whom the players had met in the Indian Premier League in 2008, and they said he was a good contact and someone they knew.' Asif, he alleged, was already doing his own thing, but the players wanted to keep him within their own operation. That led Miliken-Smith on to the distribution of the *News of the World*'s money: 'Amir was to receive £2,500, £10,000 to Butt and £65,000 to Asif. I can explain why. The larger amount was paid to a certain player in order to ensure that player remained loyal to those in the dressing room rather than to be tempted by others.'

This line of attack was denounced by Ali Bajwa as 'derogatory mitigation'. 'These accusations Mr Butt denies. Those relating to Sanjay in India, this is false. There were many assertions made and we take issue with them.' Alexander Milne raised similar objections on behalf of Asif and the judge indicated that he would not bear these claims in mind when sentencing. But Miliken-Smith wasn't done. 'He [Majeed] must be sentenced but he was never a recruiter. An outsider would never be trusted and wouldn't have the influence. He did not have the natural contacts. This is not about blaming others but about answering explicitly and implicitly what has been said and setting the record straight.'

All of this might have carried more weight had the police not recovered more incriminating texts from his client's phones, including two to 'Raj' in India on 29 July 2010 when Pakistan were playing England at Nottingham ('It is hard to do this but they will try. Two edges gave away eight runs in first over and If they do it they will want to be paid') and another ('Boss, you can see they have done it') the following day to a number in the UK.

Amir, meanwhile, was the model of contrition. 'First and foremost, I want to apologise to Pakistan and to everyone that cricket is important to,' he said in a statement. 'I do know how much damage this has done to the game, which I love as well, more than anything else in the world. I did decide many months ago that I wanted to admit that I did throw two no-balls at the Lord's Test last summer, but I know this was very late. I want to apologise for not saying it before. I didn't find the courage to do it before and I know very well it made everything more difficult.

'I don't want to blame anyone else. I didn't want money and I didn't bowl the no-balls because of money. I got trapped but, in the end, it was my own stupidity. I apologise to everyone that I did what I did and that I didn't accept responsibility earlier. I want to apologise to my family as well for the distress I have caused them in this past year. I want to apologise to Pakistan and to everyone that cricket is important to. I do know how much damage this has done to the game.'

Yet there was more to Amir's case than an innocent teenager caught between a manipulative agent and greedy captain. Mr Justice Cooke alluded to evidence that he was also involved in a plot to fix The Oval Test. He was therefore minded not to accept his plea that his no-balls at Lord's were his 'first and only involvement' in this kind of criminal activity.

His lawyer Henry Blaxland QC admitted that his client had made contact with a suspected illegal bookmaker but no fix had resulted from those communications. He could also produce character references for his client from cricket greats Imran Khan and Michael Holding.

Making the plea of mitigation for Butt, Bajwa observed, 'He has gone from a national hero to being a figure of contempt. He has lost almost everything. There is only his liberty and his family left to lose. What purpose would a custodial sentence serve?'

It was a desperate plea which inevitably fell on deaf ears. 'It is the insidious effect of your actions on professional cricket and the followers of it which make the offences so serious,' began the judge on 3 November in his sentencing remarks addressed at first to all four. 'The image and integrity of what was once a game, but is now a business, is damaged in the eyes of all, including the many youngsters who regarded three of you as heroes and would have given their eye teeth to play at the levels and with the skill that you had.'

Starting with Majeed, he said, 'Your position as manager to half a dozen members of the Pakistan team and your close friendship with Salman Butt meant that you and he together were in a position to influence other players in the team as you did. Whereas the defendant players present have already been the subject of an ICC arbitration and have suffered bans which significantly affect their cricket-playing careers and their future earnings, which I will bear in mind when I come to sentence them, you stand alone as a non-player, who decided, according to an email exchange with your brother in February 2010, to make as much money as you could from the game of cricket – by corrupting those involved. If you had not pleaded guilty the sentence would have been four years on each count. In the light of your plea, the sentence on each count, to run concurrently, is one of two years and eight months.'

Butt was next. 'It is clear to me that you were the orchestrator of this activity, as you had to be, as captain, in arranging for these bowlers to be bowling the overs which were identified in advance to Majeed and which he identified to the *News of the World* journalist. I consider that you were responsible for involving Amir in the corruption – an 18-year-old from a poverty-stricken village background, very different to your own privileged one, who, whilst a very talented bowler, would be inclined to do what his senior players and particularly his captain told him, especially when told there was money in it for him and this was part of the common culture. For an impressionable youngster, not long in the team, to stand out against the blandishments of his captain would have been hard. It appears that the corruption may have been more widespread than the defendants here before me, and may have permeated the team in earlier days, though I have seen no direct evidence of that. If that is the case, you, as captain, perpetuated such an atmosphere of corruption and would be responsible for it.

'I take fully into account the ICC ban and the effect it has on you, which in itself is a considerable punishment for a man in your position. You do not have the benefit of a plea but the effect of the ban on you is such that I can reduce the sentence I would otherwise have imposed to 30 months' imprisonment.'

Then came Asif. 'There is no evidence of any prior involvement on your part in such activities but it is clear that Majeed had every confidence in you playing your part when identifying the no-ball that you would bowl on 26 August. It is hard to see how this could be an isolated occurrence for you either. There will be concurrent sentences of one year's imprisonment on each count.'

Finally, he addressed Amir. 'You have referred, in material presented to the court, to threats to yourself and your family, saying that there are significant limits to what you can say in public. The reality of those threats and the strength of the underworld influences who control unlawful betting abroad is shown by the supporting evidence in the bundle of documents, including materials from the anti-corruption and security unit of the ICC. Compared with others, you were unsophisticated, uneducated and impressionable. You were only 18 at the time and readily leant on by others. I am clear that you bear less responsibility than your captain who influenced you in the manner to which I have earlier referred.

'But you agreed to do this for money and £1,500 of *News of the World* marked money was found in your possession. Moreover the fact remains that there is evidence, in the shape of texts and telephone calls with a Pakistani number, of your involvement in discussions about fixing brackets at The Oval during the period of the indictment, though there is no evidence that such fixing actually occurred. If you had not pleaded guilty you would have received concurrent sentences of nine months' imprisonment on each offence. As you did plead, the sentence will be six months in each case.'

The four were each handed legal bills for costs towards the prosecution, ranging from £8,120 for Asif to £56,554 for Majeed. Cooke explained that there would be 'no orders for compensation as I consider that the *News of the World* got what it bargained for when paying the £150,000 in question'. This last point was a reference to the rather startling revelation that of the £150,000 the paper had shelled out, officers had only been able to recover £45,700.

In Pakistan, effigies of the three were burnt in the streets and relatives interviewed. Through her tears, Amir's mother Nasim Akhtar told reporters who had travelled to the village of Changa Bangyaal that 'my son is innocent and he did the no-ball at the asking of the captain. I spoke to him two days ago and he asked me to pray for his acquittal ... I'm ill after this case, suffering from several diseases and I may not be here [when he gets out].' Her son Mohammad Ijaz said of his brother: 'He should not have been sentenced after his confession. We were under the impression that he will be released after the imposition of a fine.'

In Lahore, Butt's father Zulfiqar said his son had been set up: 'Our own friends conspired against us. I will do my best to prove that my son has been implicated and made a scapegoat.' The player's sister Khadija added, 'His mistake was to be at the wrong place with the wrong people. This is his only mistake.' Asif's father Hasan Deen, a dairy farmer, objected to the custodial sentence. 'It is human beings after all who go to jail,' he said. 'He hasn't committed a murder. We haven't made any great money from cricket. I know Asif will return home one day.'

In England, there was agreement that the prison terms handed down were the least that the four deserved, though there was sympathy for the youngest. It was led by Mike Atherton. Writing in *The Times*, Atherton began by providing more detail of the credible threats to his family which the judge had referred to. 'The day after Mohammad Amir pleaded guilty for the first time, a member of his family was approached in a mosque in Lahore.

THE THIN WHITE LINE

The message was a simple one: tell Amir to watch his step and watch what he says.'

'As Imran Khan suggested in a strong character reference,' he continued, 'it took immense courage to admit his guilt at all, given that such an admission is unprecedented in Pakistani cricket ... There are those who rejoice at the sight of cricketers being hauled to jail. Here, there is only sadness and the hope that, for Amir, redemption can be found.'

* * *

Amir was taken away to Feltham Young Offenders Institution (YOI) in Middlesex. The place housed just under 800 inmates, all of them under 21. Eleven years earlier young British Pakistani inmate Zahid Mubarek had been murdered in his cell in a racially motivated attack by 20-year-old Robert Stewart. Soon after, its deputy governor had resigned over what he complained were its 'Dickensian conditions'. A subsequent government inquiry into the death of Mubarek also made strong criticisms of the regime there and a report from the Hounslow Racial Equality Council in 2004 claimed racism was 'widespread'.

After a visit on 12 September 2011, HM Chief Inspectorate of Prisons highlighted the challenges of 'the lack of information about new arrivals, which made it difficult to carry out initial assessments to keep them safe [and] the introduction of some young people to gangs and a violent culture in prison, which they had not previously experienced.' It was into this environment that the 19-year-old cricketer was condemned to spend his first nights behind bars in a foreign country.

Butt and Asif at least had each other for company where they were going, but that was the only consolation. They would initially be held at HM Prison Wandsworth, which took in Category B prisoners ('Those who pose a risk to the public but may not require maximum security, but for whom escape still needs to be made very difficult'). In August the chief inspector of prisons had described its conditions as 'demeaning, unsafe and fell below what could be classed as decent ... black and minority ethnic prisoners were disadvantaged in significant areas of the prison'.

The drill on arrival was simple: strip (behind a screen) and then, clad in just a towel, be searched, weighed and measured. A doctor's check and urine sample would follow before they were handed their bedding for the night.

It wasn't long before a familiar face showed itself. As part of his social outreach programme, the Southall caterer Dilawar Chaudhry delivered halal food and other specialities for Muslims in prison, and in early November his duties took him to Wandsworth where he had about 450 parcels of sweets and some religious texts to hand out. After unpacking them in the gym and getting ready to leave, the prison chaplain asked if he wished to see his 'friends'. He didn't know who he was talking about until the chaplain mentioned the names of the Pakistanis.

Butt was in no mood to meet visitors so it was only Asif who came out to see him. Dressed in his prison uniform of grey jogging bottoms and sweatshirt and orange bib, the fast bowler was not looking for a confessor, insisting on his innocence and wondering what cruel hand of fate had condemned him to this existence. Chaudhry's response offered no consolation: 'The people who run this prison must be idiots, mustn't they, to have so many innocent people behind bars ... because I've never met a prisoner who admitted he was guilty.'

CHAPTER 7

'I WANTED TO TELL THE TRUTH BUT I DIDN'T HAVE COURAGE'

IT WAS only a short journey from Lord's in north-west London to Mike Atherton's home on the Middlesex–Hertfordshire border, but it had been a long road for Mohammad Amir to get to the place he was now in.

Released from Portland Young Offenders Institution, where he had been transferred after Feltham, just under three weeks earlier, on 1 February 2012, he now sat in front of Atherton ready to tell his story fully for the first time.

It was to be a very different yarn from the one he had been spinning for at least the first six months of the affair. On 6 September 2010, little more than a week after the damning edition of the *News of the World* had appeared, his brother, Mohammad Naveed, told the media, '[He] has told the family he will swear on the Koran he did not do these things. There is no way these allegations are true ... He said because he was winning man of the match awards, somebody is trying to destroy him.'

Aunt Tahira pitched in too – 'That boy grew up in my arms. I know him and I know this scandal has political roots'; and cousin Mahbood was of the same opinion – 'This story has been planted to defame Pakistan by slandering a national hero.' And so it continued, through to his appeal against suspension from international cricket in Dubai in October 2010 and his defence in the ICC tribunal in Doha in early 2011.

There had been private entreaties to come clean. When Shahid Afridi flew into England to lead his country in the limited-overs series which followed the Lord's game, he took Amir aside and asked him if he was involved. He quietly admitted that he was but could not bring himself to say so publicly. In late 2010 the Pakistan Cricket Board contacted his lawyer, Shahid Karim, offering a deal. If he admitted his guilt, he could expect leniency in his punishment from the ICC. 'Ijaz [Butt] practically pleaded with him for two hours, begging him to think of himself and the country; to come clean and make up for his mistake,' said one close to the negotiations. 'But Amir was adamant that he hadn't done it. He kept insisting that he hadn't done anything so why should he admit to it.'

His adherence to these denials would face a tougher test when the Crown Prosecution Service announced in February 2011 that it would be pressing charges. If he was convicted but had pleaded guilty, it could be the difference between prison and a non-custodial sentence. This was *really* serious. Fortunately, he finally had people around him to bring some moral and legal clarity to his predicament.

Educated at Cheltenham Ladies' College, Oxford, and the London School of Economics, Gareth Peirce had impeccable establishment credentials but had dedicated her career as a solicitor to eradicating its worst judicial mistakes. A solicitor, Peirce had become notable for her work in helping to overturn the wrongful convictions of the men sent to jail for the IRA pub bombings in Guildford and Birmingham in the 70s. Her tireless efforts on behalf of Gerry Conlon of the Guildford Four would lead to her being played on screen by Emma Thompson in the film *In the Name of the Father.*

A cricket-loving member of the legal fraternity in London could see that Amir was in need of proper help and had connected Peirce, along with her colleague Sajda Malik at Birnberg Peirce and Partners, with the young man. They were there for him from the first pre-trial hearing through to the trial and beyond.

From spring through to autumn 2011, Amir spent more time than the two other cricketers in England, staying with friends and working with his defence team. Bizarrely, in June 2011 it was reported that he had played a village match for Addington in Surrey, hitting 60 and taking four wickets in his nine overs. This technical breach of his ban prompted a warning from the ICC.

Amir began to put his trust in Peirce and Malik, who was also able to translate for him, and they grew to like him. Peirce herself knew little about cricket but found herself fascinated as the player explained the arts of his fast-bowling craft. She had also received a cricketing education from Atherton and another former England captain and Cambridge graduate, Mike Brearley. Both were sympathetic to his plight.

Atherton had argued for leniency for Amir in his *Times* column the day after sentencing, and had talked with Peirce about the case at her offices in Camden, north London. She had met Brearley, who was married to an Indian lady, and had a deep interest in and affection for cricket in Asia, at an event put on by the Institute of Psychoanalysis – Brearley was a practising psychoanalyst. Again, he offered to help Amir's defence in any way possible.

When the truth could be denied no longer, Amir decided it was time to acknowledge it. Though ashamed of what he had done, he took a certain pride in his statement of guilt submitted three weeks before the trial. Not only did he admit his crime but he 'owned' it too. He had not blamed or 'ratted' on his team-mates or anyone else, though the threats made to his family might have dictated this. He owed a debt too to Peirce for securing character references from his country's greatest player Imran Khan and fast-bowling legend Michael Holding (he of the 'Wow!' commentary).

After release, he met Peirce and Malik in London to offer his thanks and did the same to Brearley and Atherton. The idea of a TV interview with the latter was discussed and agreed. There would be two pre-conditions. It would need to be in Urdu and, though Atherton was working for Sky Sports, would have to be made available to Pakistani broadcasters at the same time as it was screened in the UK. No money was asked for, nor was it offered. With that confirmed, they sat down in Atherton's house on 20 February 2012 to talk. It was a cold day and Peirce, on behalf of the interviewee, asked the host to turn up the heating. Warming to the surroundings and his interrogator, Amir finally began to talk.

* * *

Like a lot of stories involving fixing, it started in Dubai. It was November 2009 and Pakistan were in the United Arab Emirates for a limited-overs series with New Zealand. Amir, who had turned 17 that April, had played only seven ODIs up until then but made his name in the third game of the tour when he scored an unbeaten 73 off 81 balls to take his team to within a whisker of what would have been a remarkable win. His innings was the highest score for a No. 10 batsman in one-day internationals.

It was in the days after that knock that Butt introduced him to a man called Ali. He was just one of many expats in the Gulf state who wanted to be the new star's friend. Ali said that if he ever needed anything in Dubai he only had to say the word. Ali also went back to Pakistan on a regular basis. If Amir would share his contact details then, again, he would be honoured to look after him back in his own country. Amir was flattered, gave him his mobile number and, sure enough, they later met in Lahore.

It was two days before the second Test against England at Edgbaston, at 9.38pm on 4 August, that Ali contacted him again. The first conversation lasted 48 seconds. There would be four more chats over the next three weeks, including one on 7 August when Ali wanted to know if Butt had spoken with him; and another in the early hours of 17 August, the day before The Oval Test, when Ali asked for his bank details. Amir queried why he needed them but Ali told him he would find out later. Later that day, between 9.45pm and 10.15pm as he ate dinner alone in Kensington, Amir would send a series of texts to Ali. They read, 'yes; yes what; for how much; but what needs to be done; it would be too much friend; so in the first 3 bowl whatever you like and in the last 2 do 8 runs.'

Butt had indeed spoken to him. In fact, he had raised the issue of fixing twice with him before Lord's. The first time he had done so in a jocular fashion (this was exactly how Hansie Cronje had raised the suggestion with his team-mates so that if any player took serious offence it could be brushed off as a bad joke). Sure enough, Amir said, 'No, bro', and they both smiled and went their separate ways. On the second occasion, the captain was more serious and so was Amir's response, almost to the point of what would have been considered rude within the hierarchy of the Pakistan dressing room. 'Bro this is forbidden. Leave it. I am not going to do it.'

This was awkward for Amir, and not just because it was his skipper he was talking to. They had first met when Butt had broken into the senior team and Amir was just a junior at the national academy. Despite his elevated status, Butt was always generous with his time and kit with the juniors, including Amir. Soon they were team-mates for the National Bank side. Their relationship, as the younger man saw it, was like that of brothers. He therefore unburdened himself to Butt about his exchanges with Ali.

He did so on the morning of the first day of The Oval Test, 18 August, as they were going through fielding practice, saying Ali had been 'bugging' him. Butt smiled, that was just like Ali, but he offered little more by way of help or advice. Amir had little time to think about it anyway because what followed in south London would be the best days of his career to date. Match figures of 6-101, batting when the winning runs were brought up and a man of the match award in the country's first away victory against England for nine years – to think he had only celebrated his 18th birthday four months earlier.

Fast forward exactly a week, the day before the Lord's Test. Amir was in his room at the team hotel, the Marriott near Regent's Park. He had just come out of his morning shower when his phone rang. It was Mazhar Majeed. Could he come to the car park for a chat? Of course he could. Amir liked Majeed. They had first met during the World T20 in England the previous summer and the bowler had taken him on as his agent. Majeed was funny, not in a crude manner but in a relaxed, sophisticated man-of-the-world way. He had introduced his players to his wife too, who wore a hijab and liked to say her prayers. How could he not trust him?

In the lift he bumped into Butt who, he discovered, was also heading out. Majeed was there in his Aston Martin. Amir sat in the front next to him. Majeed spoke first, 'Oh bro, you've got yourself in big trouble, you're trapped, and your career is at stake.' The man in the passenger's seat was lost for words so the agent filled him in. Majeed had been tipped off that his calls and texts with Ali had been picked up by the ICC. Amir protested that he had done nothing. That, his agent stressed, was the point. He was duty bound to report any dodgy approach to the governing body. Failure to do so left him open to a charge and a ban. 'You're trapped; your name's being mentioned, and the case is now open.'

Trouble could be averted though. The contact who had tipped Majeed off was a friend – 'You're lucky that he's the one who is in charge of this case.' Majeed explained how he had pleaded with him: 'Bro, put an end to this case, shut this file. Whatever you need me to do, I'll do it. Whatever needs to be done, I'll do it. I'll do anything. But Amir's name should not be mentioned.' It appeared to have worked, but now it was time for the bowler to return the favour. 'Do two no-balls for me,' said Majeed flatly.

In retrospect, Amir realised how stupid he had been in his reaction to this request. First, Majeed had told him that the ICC had opened a file on him in relation to match-fixing. Then, in the next breath, he was asking him to engage in corruption. There was a dissonance there. He was in such a panic, however, that logic and sense deserted him. The best reply he could muster was: 'I don't do this kind of thing, nor do I know how to go about it. I don't know how to bowl no-balls. My front foot is always behind the line. I very rarely delivered no-balls throughout my entire career.'

Majeed was not giving up. 'No, no, just go to the ground and practise.' Butt would be there to help, he assured him. By sheer co-incidence (or maybe not), it was at this point that the captain opened the back door and climbed in. If the teenager was hoping his 'brother' would tell his agent to back off, then he was misguided. In fact, if he hoped Butt would say anything really, he was wrong. Instead, Butt perched his elbows on to the two front seats and listened as Majeed continued to apply the pressure. His only words were to reinforce the message of 'bowl two no-balls', before Amir got up and left. Butt remained in the car. At no point during the conversation was there talk of money.

Soon after, the Pakistan team arrived for pre-match training at Lord's. It was raining so they had to use the indoor facilities. In a quiet moment, Butt asked, 'Are you going to do it or not?' Amir said he was too scared but his skipper kept pressing, 'Don't worry; nothing's going to happen, bro.'

When the moment came around in the early afternoon of the next day, third ball of the third over, Amir's stomach was churning. On the one hand, he was about to cheat knowingly. On the other, he had been told that this was the only way to avoid being exposed as a cheat. He was unaware that Asif would do the same a few overs later.

Majeed was back at the team hotel that night and he could not have been happier. 'You're my little brother,' he said as if Amir had just been 'made' and was joining the same mafia family. He then handed him £1,500 in an envelope and told him to do some shopping. Amir didn't have to ask if it was related to the no-ball earlier on because he knew. He put the money in the safe and never touched it again.

His ordeal was not yet over. There was the little matter of another no-ball to come. When the due delivery came around on the morning of day two at Lord's, Butt was in his ear: 'You remember, don't you?' Yes, he remembered. What he also remembered at the time was the visit he had made to Lord's three years earlier with the under-19 team. Taking in the ground and all its glory, he had promised a team-mate that he would play here one day and give a performance worthy of the setting. He had done that with his opening spell that morning and now it would be tarnished by what he was about to do.

There was an awkward moment later at lunchtime. Amir was untying his shoelaces when Waqar Younis turned on him. Where on earth had that giant no-ball come from, the bowling coach wanted to know. Before he could muster some sort of excuse, Butt had intervened: 'I told him to go forward and bowl a bouncer.' At the ICC tribunal, this exchange was said to have happened after they had come off for rain at the end of the first day. Whichever day it was really didn't matter because with Butt's words Amir had effectively been joined at the hip to his captain in the conspiracy.

When the officers descended on the team hotel on the evening of 28 August, Amir's first thought was that they were from the ICC's ACSU outfit and there to question him about his correspondence with Ali, whom he quickly texted asking him to delete any record of calls and texts between the two. By chance he had bumped into Majeed's brother, Azhar, in the lobby but he did not connect the arrival of the police with what his agent had asked him to do. He knew nothing of the man who had paid Majeed £150,000 and he had certainly never heard of the *News of the World*. It wasn't until the paper was on general sale the next morning that he finally understood what he was accused of. The next few days were a cumulative nightmare of stomach cramps, difficult calls to and from family and desperate attempts to shut out the world.

* * *

On the evening of Saturday, 25 February Amir flew out of Heathrow, arriving at Lahore airport at 4.35am local time the following day. From there, a white car took him to his home in the Defence Housing Authority suburb. Neither he nor his family would speak to the media, who had assembled outside.

Back in London, Atherton was working with Sky's production team, editing the interview to get it ready for broadcast. With the Urdu translation – he himself had an earpiece relaying what Amir was saying in English as he said it – this wasn't going to be an overnight job. It was in fact not until 9pm on 19 March that it was aired for the first time in the UK. The PCB had been charged with ensuring Pakistan media could access the footage that same day. Characteristically, there was some sort of communication breakdown which meant few journalists or broadcasters in the country were aware of the interview until Sky had shown it.

From many, the cricketer earned praise and sympathy. Not everyone was impressed, however. Salman Butt's father, Zulfiqar, said, 'Amir on record said before the ICC tribunal that Butt did not ask him to bowl no-balls and then before the UK court last year he said the same, so was he lying then or now? I definitely think he is lying now ... Amir's latest interview suggests that he wants to revive his career and that's why he is accusing my son. We have gone through hell and Amir is trying to put more trouble on us.' He also claimed that the authorities had denied Butt's youngest son – born the same day as he was sentenced on 3 November – a visa to travel with his mother to be presented to his father. 'We hope our bad days are over sooner than later,' said Zulfiqar.

A more interesting note was struck by a 'former Pakistan captain' writing on condition of anonymity in *Dawn*, the country's oldest English-language newspaper. This individual noted that 'in his first five Test matches, Amir did not bowl a single no-ball. Then, all of a sudden, in his seventh outing – in Australia – he over-stepped a staggering 13 times ... Between the above mentioned Australia Test and the Lord's outing, he again remained steady and went over the popping crease only five times in six Test matches.' The connection between these outliers and his admission of contact with 'Ali' could not be clearer: 'No points for guessing why Ali and Mazhar Majeed could blackmail Amir on something which had previously happened between them on the Australian trip ... I was amongst Amir's biggest supporters until the latest interview was televised. I have no hesitation in admitting that now my viewpoint has changed drastically. Sorry, but he is just trying to prove his innocence by distorting the facts.'

As he worked his way through the transcript of their interview, Atherton too had a few reservations, especially over the 'Ali' link. In *The Times* the day after broadcast, he admitted that the texts to Ali on 17 August, especially the message that read 'So in the first three bowl whatever you like and in the last two do 8 runs?' looked 'damning'. Whatever interpretation you chose to put on that, Atherton wrote, 'none can escape the fact that Amir engaged in text conversation about fixing, so breaking the ICC code of conduct by not reporting this approach.'

Yet he also noted that most of the traffic between the two had come from the other man. Between 4 and 16 August, he revealed, Ali tried to speak to Amir on 12 occasions, and only once, on 7 August, did Amir pick up the phone and talk. After the 'So in the first three ...' text on 17 August, there were another seven messages from Ali that night alone, and one mobile call. Amir did not respond to any of these but Ali did not give up so easily. Over the next ten days he bombarded Amir with nine texts and 33 phone calls. Amir responded only three times, once with a text ('yes, what') and two short calls on 18 and 21 August. Atherton told this in Amir's defence but, he conceded, 'unless Ali is found and speaks – which is not very likely – we shall never know [what he wanted]'.

Atherton also wanted to stress the importance in Amir's life of Asif Bajwa, who had run the cricket academy in Rawalpindi where he had spent his formative years. If Butt was like a brother then he was like a father, as indicated by a touching text sent to Bajwa before the last day's play at The Oval: 'Ok, sir, god willing I will try my best. Tomorrow morning I was calling you but it looked as if you were busy. I will call you after the match. I am going to the ground now.' Unfortunately, with Pakistan 'on the road' for most of the calendar year, Bajwa's influence inevitably waned as that of Butt waxed.

Soon after his interview with Atherton, Amir was in front of the cameras again. This time he was with Colin Gibson of the ICC in the Meridien Hotel at Dubai airport. The meeting had been set up by the governing body as part of the youngster's 'rehabilitation'. Gibson was there to help him record a video warning other young players of the dangers of being sucked in by fixers, bookmakers and other nefarious characters. The film was to form part of a presentation given by the ICC's anti-corruption unit.

Perhaps unsurprisingly, Amir wasn't comfortable at first and he was given a night to sleep on it. When he returned, his delivery and his message, recalled Gibson, were exemplary. 'Prison is a bad place for everyone,' he said. 'Don't make the mistakes which I did. I was stupid I didn't tell anybody because I didn't have courage … If someone comes to you go straight to team management and ICC team.

'I took six wickets but I did something very bad … My life is changed, my life is ruined because of two no-balls. I always knew this was cheating cricket, but I was under pressure. But I accept my mistake … When I was in the ICC hearing, I knew I was totally embarrassed. I wanted to tell the truth but I didn't have courage … When the police put me in handcuffs I was literally crying.'

* * * *

Life might have been slowly getting better for Amir, but the other two were reaching their nadir. Asif and Butt had launched appeals against their sentences soon after they were issued and also put in applications to serve their time back in Pakistan because of fears for their safety inside in England. These were declined though they were at least transferred for the rest of their sentence to the HM Prison Canterbury in Kent (Category C), sharing a cell for the first couple of months.

In April 2012, the *Daily Mirror* reported that the pair had been made 'gym orderlies'. A prison 'source' was quoted as saying, 'There has never been so much talk at the prison about how to bowl a googly or achieve reverse swing. The pair became quite popular because they kindly passed on a few secrets of their trade. But at times it has seemed more like they were in the nets at Lord's, rather than a gym in a tough prison.

'The lads really took to their gym orderly jobs and seemed quite happy. It is a fairly privileged position and better than something like working in the laundry and mopping the landings. I guess it made sense to get two international sports stars to work in the gym. The cricket tutorials were so popular, there was a waiting list – both of inmates and staff. There could be a few decent amateur cricketers trying out their new skills this summer.'

Asif was freed on 3 May. He had served six months. 'I look forward to meeting him and helping him in his legal fight to restore what was an otherwise brilliant reputation he once had,' said his lawyer Ravi Sukul somewhat optimistically. Later that month, Butt's wife and his elder son were permitted to visit him. On 21 June, seven months into his sentence, he was granted his freedom through the early removal scheme. That came with it a ten-year ban from visiting the UK.

Around 200 fans, including his father Zulfiqar, were there at Lahore's international airport when, wearing a green shirt and jeans, Butt arrived home. 'I am happy and relieved,' he told the media. 'I want two to three days with my family and once I do that I will hold a detailed press conference to answer all questions to clear my name from spot-fixing. I am thankful to all those who helped me in my difficult times and I hope that my tough days are over. I am desperate to see my second son who I have not seen since his birth.'

A week later he spoke in more detail and with more defiance. 'If you look at the evidence you can judge that I didn't get justice,' Butt said in his first television interview. 'I had to make a sacrifice because I didn't take anyone's name, it didn't suit me. It's not about me or anyone else, it's about Pakistan. I would like Pakistani courts, the Supreme Court, to hold an open trial and I am sure they will clear me. I don't accept anything against me. If you look at the evidence against me, I had no links to spot-fixing. Who did and who planned it [I don't know], but certainly I didn't do that. I played for my country and respected that [honour].'

Of the money found by the police in his hotel room, he stuck to his story. 'Yes there were £4,500 and that was my money. I had to inaugurate an ice cream parlour and got £2,500 [from Majeed] in advance. I didn't know that he had paid me notes which were marked. That was my money and that's why I got them back [when released] and I have receipt of all that.' He later confirmed that he would be going to the Court of Arbitration for Sport (CAS) in Switzerland to challenge his ban which, with five years suspended, amounted to ten years.

On 16 April 2013 CAS announced it had rejected his and Asif's appeals. Dave Richardson of the ICC said, 'The time has now come for them to stop misleading the members of the public, especially the supporters of the Pakistan cricket team, and to publicly accept their parts in this corrupt conspiracy.'

He would have to wait some time for that because at another press conference, two months after the CAS decision, the former Pakistan captain delivered an apology that stopped well short of an admission of guilt. 'I apologise to the nation and all the fans who have been hurt by the spot-fixing case. I admit the ICC tribunal decision and warn the future players to avoid the pitfalls of corruption because this is bad for the country and for the fans.'

Asif's apology, delivered in August of the same year, was more contrite, though again he made no mention of his criminal conviction despite his appeal being rejected by the High Court in London in June 2013: 'I accept the punishment from the ICC tribunal in 2011. I apologise for my actions that have brought disrespect to my beloved country, to the millions of fans in Pakistan and in the world. When I look back at the events of my career, I feel very sorry,' he said.

'I request to all the players who want to represent their countries that they must keep away from all sorts of corruption. I am ready to help any player who wants to avoid such pitfalls. I will duly cooperate with the ICC, its anti-corruption unit and with the PCB in fighting the corruption in the game. I have suffered a lot because of my wrongdoings. Now on the independence day of my country, I promise that once my ban finishes I will try to repair the damage I have done.'

In fact, it would not be until 2015, nearly five years after their crime, that either would truly come clean. Guilt finally kicking in? Possibly, but it did not escape anyone's attention that the suspended terms of their bans were due to start that September and could not be dropped until they had fully co-operated with the authorities.

The ICC had made it clear through the PCB that full confessions were the minimum requirement.

Sure enough, in February 2015, according to reports in Pakistan, Butt had, in a meeting in Lahore with PCB chief, Shaharyar Khan, 'made a full confession that he knew and was involved in the spot-fixing that took place in the fourth Test against England at Lord's and that he had instructed Amir and Asif to bowl the no-balls. Butt also expressed his complete regret and said he was willing to cooperate totally with the ICC. Butt has had a change of heart after he approached the PCB to also plead his case with the ICC anti-corruption unit to review his ban under the revised anti-corruption laws under which Mohammad Amir has got a relaxation to play domestic cricket before his five-year ban ends in September this year.'

On 2 September 2015, the ICC formally lifted the suspended sentences against the pair after they had committed to PCB rehabilitation courses. Asif, it emerged, had spent some of his time in exile staying with friends and playing cricket in Norway. He cited Nelson Mandela as an inspiration while he had been in prison and spoke of his hope to be back at Lord's the following year when Pakistan were due to tour England. He wasn't the only one of the trio targeting that date with destiny.

* * *

It was around 11.30am on 15 July 2016 when Mohammad Amir made his way down from the visitors' dressing room in the Lord's pavilion, through the famous Long Room and out to the middle at Lord's. It was early on the second day of the first Test against England and the wicket of Wahab Riaz had brought him to the crease with Pakistan on 310/8. He had last made that walk on 29 August 2010, the day of his public shaming in the *News of the World*. There had been the walk out to bat in Pakistan's second innings and the walk back soon after his dismissal for a five-ball duck. On each occasion, silence greeted him. Then, once the match had concluded, there had been the walk from the dressing room to the Long Room, where he was declared Pakistan's man of the series.

Muted applause would have been a generous description of the reaction to that announcement.

This time, he was greeted by mild applause. No more, but probably no less than usually accompanied an opposition tailender coming to the crease. Critically, there had been no booing. That was a victory of sorts for the player, his defendants and, many felt, cricket itself. He would face his first delivery from Stuart Broad, who had scored his only Test century in the 2010 Test. Amir didn't know too much about it as the ball caught the inside edge of his bat, missed the stumps and ran away for four. It was another victory for the player. Broad got his man four overs later, as Amir was caught in the slips for 12, bringing the Pakistan innings to an end on 339.

That was only the first part of the ordeal. What about when he came on to bowl? That was why he had been selected and it was an act committed while bowling six years ago which had brought dishonour on him, his country and the sport. He didn't have much time to think about it between his dismissal and the start of England's innings because his captain Misbah-ul-Haq asked him to open the bowling. Misbah's opposite number Alastair Cook was facing. It wasn't the greatest over Amir had ever sent down, six runs coming off it, and the announcement of his name on the tannoy had produced a polite as opposed to warm response from spectators. Again, though, it was a step on the path back to cricketing acceptance.

The first significant step on that path had been laid down by the PCB, which had realised that its own integrity as much as his depended on his return to the game. Showing a duty of care from which it had fallen well short in years gone, the board had hired a psychologist to meet with him as far back as 2012. Slowly, in the years that followed, facilities and coaching were made available as Amir looked to re-discover the talent that had helped him become the youngest bowler to take 50 Test wickets in his last appearance for his country.

Credit too to the ICC. On 29 January 2015 a statement confirmed that it had brought an end to his playing ban nearly eight months early: 'Sir Ronnie Flanagan, with the prior approval of the ICC board and the Pakistan Cricket Board, has exercised his discretion to allow Mohammad Amir to return to domestic cricket played under the auspices of the Pakistan Cricket Board with immediate effect.' It had reached the decision on the basis of Amir having met its four key criteria. He had 'co-operated with the ACSU by fully disclosing his part in the matters that led to his disqualification; admitted his guilt and showed remorse; co-operated with the unit's on-going investigations; helped alert fellow cricketers to the dangers of fixing by recording messages for education sessions.'

He was back. On 11 May he took a wicket with his second ball in his comeback game for Rawalpindi Rams, dismissing Abbottabad Falcons's opening batsman for a duck, in Pakistan's Twenty20 cup. He picked up another soon after as Rawalpindi won by six wickets. By the end of the year he was playing in Bangladesh's leading T20 competition. In late November, in his first match outside Pakistan in five years, he took 4-30 in Chittagong Vikings' defeat against Rangpur Riders. The signals coming out of the PCB around this time were that they considered him ready in mind and body for international cricket. A week before Christmas, he was named in a 26-man fitness camp ahead of the tour to New Zealand the following month. Finally, on 2 January, he was picked in the squad for that tour.

Not everyone considered this a good news story, including the captain for that tour. Azhar Ali, along with Mohammad Hafeez, had refused to attend the first part of the training camp in protest at Amir's inclusion. Hafeez had even rejected a contract with Chittagong if it meant playing alongside a known cheat. 'I am not against any individuals,' he explained. 'It is about the image of Pakistan cricket.' Ali then offered to resign over Amir's inclusion in the squad for New Zealand. That offer was rejected by the PCB and somehow Ali, Hafeez and Amir (the delicate matter of him being granted a visa having been resolved at diplomatic levels) were all on the plane together heading south in the new year of 2016.

His comeback match was the first T20 in Auckland on 15 January, probably as low-key a fixture as you can get in international cricket. Some sections of the home crowd booed him but Pakistan won the match and 1-31 in his allotted four overs represented a decent night's work. There was an unedifying moment in the third and final T20, though, when the stadium announcer in Wellington, Mark McLeod, chose to play the sound of a cash till ringing on the PA system as the 23-year-old got ready to bowl. David White, the chief executive of New Zealand Cricket, apologised, saying, 'I think it was inappropriate and disrespectful, and has the effect of trivialising one of the biggest issues facing cricket at the moment.'

From there it was back to the Pakistan Super League where he took a hat-trick for Karachi Kings before he returned to the international treadmill for the Asia Cup in Bangladesh and the World T20 in India in the spring. The appointment which held the most significance would be in the summer of 2016. That was when Pakistan were scheduled to conduct their first tour of England since the disaster of 2010. Every major Test nation had been at least once to England in the intervening time and it was hard not to conclude that Pakistan's absence from the rostrum of visitors was related to the bad blood which had flowed six years before. There were to be four Tests, followed by five ODIs and a solitary T20. On 5 June Amir was named in the tour party. Neither Butt nor Asif even came close to consideration. Two weeks later, the squad arrived in England.

It was a very different group who arrived that month to the one that had gone before them. Of those selected alongside Amir, only Wahab Riaz and Azhar Ali remained from the XI who had turned out at Lord's in 2010. The more profound change was in the leadership group. Coach Mickey Arthur was like Bob Woolmer, a seasoned campaigner who, also like Woolmer, had coached South Africa before Pakistan. Taking over from Ali as captain was the 42-year-old Misbah-ul-Haq, who brought a lot more gravitas and dignity to the role than Butt. Misbah had also publicly defended Amir's return to the national team six months earlier. The tour manager was Intikhab Alam. The 74-year-old had played 47 Tests for his country, been its coach and manager when they won the World Cup in 1992, and was respected in international cricket circles for his diplomacy.

The first game of the tour was against Somerset in Taunton. While there, he did another Sky Sports interview with Atherton. 'Life was very tough and there were times I thought I might not be able to play again,' said Amir. 'I didn't pick up a ball for three years. It was very depressing for me, because as a professional, it's very difficult when you can't use the facilities, play cricket, you can't even touch the ball, so what are you going to do then? They are terrible memories, but now they are helping me because I've learned a lot and I want to be a better human being, and a better-behaved cricketer.

'I am still learning. Nobody can be Mr Perfect. But the past is the past and I'm looking forward now. I want to be the best cricketer I can be for my country. If I work hard, the main aim for me is to be the world's best bowler. It's very special for me to be representing my country again and at the same place which it ended; same team, same crowd. I think for me it's a miracle, but dreams come true.

'Lord's is a very special place, I have good and bad memories but now I hope to make more good memories for the future. I want to put my name on the honours board, like in 2010. Everybody has the right to their own opinion, and the crowd has the right to say some things, but my aim is to do well and behave. If I perform, hopefully they will forgive me and they will shout for me one day.'

As proof that he was in a good place, he took 3-36 in the first innings against Somerset in a match which the tourists nearly won. Nor had he been booed, as Alastair Cook implied might happen before the series. 'I'm sure there will be a reaction, and that is right,' the England captain said. 'It is part and parcel: when you do something like that there are more consequences than just the punishment. That is something for him to cope with, whatever comes his way.

'Whether I agreed or disagreed with the punishment, [Amir] got it, served his time and he is absolutely right to come back. What he did wasn't good but he served his punishment then. The ICC haven't made any big statements, but if I was in charge, if you got caught once that would be it – one strike and you're out.'

Like Cook, Graeme Swann thought Amir should have been banned for life. Unlike Cook, he was now retired which meant he did not have to be tactful when he put his thoughts down in print five days before the first Test. 'Mohammad Amir will walk out on the green and glorious turf at Lord's on Thursday – and it will make me feel sick,' Swann wrote in a newspaper column on 9 July. 'This is a man who crushed the morality of the game. And yet he is being allowed back to play at the Home of Cricket. Amir should have been banned for life for his part in the corruption scandal of 2010. If you want to protect the integrity of the game, help cricket grow and inspire youngsters, there can be no place for corrupt players. You must have proper deterrents.'

By way of a counterbalance, on the morning of the Test Mike Atherton wrote an open letter to *Times* readers attending Lord's. 'I hope to persuade you that Amir deserves his chance to play again (in a moral rather than a legal sense, about which there can be no debate) and to move on with his life; that a polite, respectful welcome would be the most fitting reaction.' Atherton got his wish.

The match at Lord's got better for the away team as it progressed. Amir only took one wicket on that second day, but it was an important one, Cook out for 81, as England reached 253/7 at the close. That evening, as was traditional in their capacity as Lord's hosts, the MCC held a drinks reception for the visiting team in the pavilion. Mike Brearley had been president of the MCC from 2007–08 and was there that evening to meet the tourists. Amir spotted him, sought him out and the pair renewed acquaintances. Brearley was proud that the home crowd had treated the Pakistani with civility. 'Its understated sense of fair play was both a relief and a reassurance,' he wrote at the time.

England were quickly bowled all out the following morning, and although Pakistan managed only 215 in their second innings a target of 283 always looked beyond the reach of the home side. At around 6pm on Sunday, 17 July, on one of those perfect summer's evenings in which Lord's specialises, Amir bowled Jake Ball to seal the win by 75 runs. The wicket gave him match figures of 3-104 which, given all the attention that preceded his game, were respectable. The sun had shone for most of the four days and never did it shine brighter than at the end when the victors performed celebratory press-ups on the outfield in front of their team balcony. It was an acknowledgment of the virtues of fitness which had been drilled into them at a pre-tour army boot camp. Even the home fans smiled at the gesture.

Of Amir's winning wicket, Misbah said, 'That was a special moment. That could be the start of his new life. I hope that he will perform like that and be a really good man now: a good cricketer, a good human being. He's so lucky that he got another chance and I think it's a new life for him.'

Somewhat predictably, Pakistan were well beaten in the two Tests that followed Lord's, including at Old Trafford where the odd cry of 'no-ball!' could be heard from the crowd when Amir ran in to bowl. But the team of 2016 were made of stronger stuff than the side of six years earlier who had succumbed so meekly in their series decider. In the fourth and final Test at The Oval, where Amir had been named man of the match on his last visit, they won by ten wickets to draw the series. Amir did nothing sensational but that wasn't really the point. He had played all four Tests, taking 12 wickets at an average of just over 40, a far worse return that he had managed on his previous tour of England. This time, however, he could walk off with his head held high. He had cheated no one.

CHAPTER 8

'THERE'S A DIFFERENCE BETWEEN ENTRAPPING A CRIMINAL AND SETTING UP AN INNOCENT PERSON'

THE SUMMER of 2016 had restored the fortunes of Mohammad Amir. The months that followed would send those of Mazher Mahmood to an all-time low. Like many of the tawdriest scandals, the origins of his downfall began in Las Vegas. It was here, back in March 2013, that Tulisa Contostavlos flew first class from Los Angeles with her assistant Gareth Varey to meet with a Bollywood producer.

Born in London to an Irish mother and Cypriot father, Tulisa's upbringing had not been conventional. Her father, who had briefly been part of the Seventies pop band Mungo Jerry, had left home when she was young; her mother was bipolar and had been sectioned under the Mental Health Act. Their daughter self-harmed and took drugs, but that didn't stop her making it big in the late 2000s with the hip-hop band N-Dubz. She had then enjoyed solo success. In 2011 Simon Cowell appointed her one of his fellow judges on ITV's Saturday night hit *The X Factor*. She bought a five-bedroom mansion in Hertfordshire worth £6m and was seeing Premier League footballer Danny Simpson. Times were good.

They didn't stay that way for long. In March 2012 a former boyfriend, Justin Edwards, posted a six-minute sex video of the pair on the internet. Though she managed to get an injunction to stop its distribution, the emotional and reputational damage was done.

In February 2013 it was reported that she had been dropped from *The X Factor* panel.

Now 24, and her relationship with Simpson rapidly deteriorating, she had gone to California to reset her career and break into the US entertainment industry. Her head was quickly turned by someone claiming to work for the 21st Century Fox TV and film studio who followed her on Twitter and put her in touch with a Bollywood producer, Samir Khan. He was keen to discuss her plans to move into acting. It was not long before that producer was agreeing to pick up the tab to bring her and her entourage to Vegas for a few days where they could meet face-to-face. This could be the pick-me-up she needed.

Samir Khan clearly wasn't short of money. Stretched limos picked up her and Varey from the airport and brought them to a five-star hotel, where two of the finest suites would accommodate them. As they all sat down to enjoy his lavish hospitality, the nature of the offer became clear. They – Khan was accompanied by a woman called Nish and another man of Asian appearance – were interested in Tulisa for the role in a film starring Leonardo DiCaprio. Khan didn't pretend that he alone would be financing the movie, but he was lucky to be able to call on the help of the investors who had backed Danny Boyle's Oscar-winning film set in India, *Slumdog Millionaire*. Was Tulisa interested? *Was the Pope Catholic?*

She was not some dizzy airhead, however. Her road to pop stardom had been far from easy and she wasn't afraid to knuckle down and work to whatever brief she was given to land the role. So she was careful not to overdo the hospitality and pushed for more information on what the role demanded. What kind of character did the producers have in mind? Could they reveal who she was up against? Keira Knightley's name was mentioned and she assumed that meant they were looking for someone posh. Not at all, was the reply, they were after an actress with a 'street' persona. Well, that was good news because she knew all about that. When her time on *The X Factor* was brought up, she said she 'wanted to get away from that'. At one point Khan's aide, 'Nish', had to make a call to Cameron Diaz.

After Vegas, the singer and friends were flown back first class to London, where further meetings were arranged, culminating in a night out on 10 May. Yet again, no expense appeared too much for their host. The evening began at Nobu, the Robert de Niro-owned restaurant in Mayfair which was renowned as a celebrity hangout (it was in Nobu's now infamous broom cupboard that tennis star Boris Becker had conceived a child in the most fleeting of encounters). From there, they adjourned to the nearby and equally starry Metropolitan Hotel.

Accompanying Samir Khan that night again was Nish, whose role seemed to be a combination of executive assistant and casting consultant. Tulisa liked Nish. She was friendly and maternal and seemed to be rooting for her to get the role. At one point, she told her, 'I read your book [her autobiography, *Honest: My Story so Far*], everything you've been through with your mother is so sad, you deserve this. I'm the one who brought you to the attention of these guys because my daughter is a big fan of yours.'

The way the drinks kept coming – the moment Tulisa had finished one, another instantly appeared in front of her – it was hard not to be friendly. Despite that, they were fast approaching crunch time. More than once, she had been told that every meeting with Khan was an audition in itself. Like the great method actors, she had to be in character all the time if she was to make the part truly her own. Nish had also stressed this to Varey. 'I really want the bad girl, and they're going to give it to Keira Knightley,' she told him.

Late in the evening, as 10 May became 11 May, Nish followed Tulisa to the bathroom to ram home what was at stake. There was a major acting role, £3m and a Hollywood breakthrough up for grabs but 'you've just got to go in now and do whatever they want – be the bad girl, the ghetto girl'. Before they returned to the bar, she looked her in the eye and said, 'Tulisa, I want you to have this so badly, trust me.'

The subject of drugs had been raised on a recurrent basis by Khan and his people. She had already admitted to them that she had smoked weed – a matter of public record anyway – and that one of her ex-boyfriends, Adam Bailey, had been a dealer. Now, emboldened by the drink and the prospect of a big payday, she played on her knowledge of the drugs world to deliver the performance required. She had sold crack as a teenager, she told them. She joked that in the showbiz circles she moved in narcotics were referred to as 'sweets'. White sweets were cocaine, green sweets cannabis. 'Half my phone book sells [cocaine],' she told them. This clearly got Khan interested, so first she texted Bailey. 'Call me ASAP need help.' Then she went into the smoking area at the back of the hotel and called him. 'Get me some sweets, white sweets,' was the message.

Khan said he would be leaving for the Cannes film festival shortly but would be back in London towards the end of the month and looked forward to seeing her again and continuing their conversation about 'sweets'. When the evening finally came to an end, he offered the use of his car and chauffeur to take her, Varey and her friend Michelle McKenna back to Hertfordshire.

That conversation came around again on 21 May. Khan was due back in the capital a couple of days later and Tulisa offered to help arrange a boys' night out for him. Various exclusive clubs were mentioned – Whisky Mist, Mahiki and Stringfellow's – but they settled on a strip club called White's, which was run by Bailey. 'What about white sweets?' asked Khan. 'Yes, definitely on the day. I can definitely sort it. I just need to make some more calls,' she assured him. At 5.28pm the next day she texted, 'Let me know wen u land so I can sort u out! Love Tulisa xxx.'

They spoke two and a half hours later when she revealed that she had just split up with Danny Simpson and apologised for 'pecking your head about man problems'. After telling her that she was better off without the footballer ('he's an idiot'), Samir Khan again raised the issue of the white sweets and she assured him that she would forward on the number of the man who would be able to sort him out. 'Call when you want your white sweets and he'll sort you out immediately … Just say, "Hi it's Tulisa's friend, I'm calling about the white sweets."'

That man was not Adam Bailey but Michael Coombs, a friend also known as the rapper Mike GLC. He was, as promised, soon in touch with Samir Khan. Asked what amount of white sweets he could provide, Coombes said, 'I only really deal in halves.' Half an ounce (14g) of cocaine would cost £800. That would be OK. Khan said he would even pick up the cost of Coombs's taxi ride to the Dorchester where the drop was to be made the following day. At the appointed time on 23 May, Coombs arrived at his hotel suite, was invited in and both parties proceeded with the transaction. With £860 in his pocket, he headed straight back out.

Samir Khan was, of course, Mazher Mahmood, now of *The Sun on Sunday*, the successor to the *News of the World*, which had launched in February 2012. The room at the Dorchester had naturally been kitted out with recording devices, just as all the previous meetings with Tulisa in Vegas and London had been taped. Mahmood was soon packing up and heading for a lab in Stafford to ensure the contents of the bag Coombs had handed him matched what was promised. Tests would confirm that it was 37% pure cocaine. It just remained for Samir Khan to inform Tulisa that their plans for that evening would have to be postponed.

On 1 June 2013 her PR Simon Jones took a call from Mahmood. 'Oh great! How can I help you?' he asked. There was nothing great about the reporter's reply: 'I just want you to know that your client is going to be on the front page tomorrow for selling me cocaine.' Jones had been around the pop industry long enough not to be shocked by such a claim but he was baffled as to who he could be referring to. He was even more confused when Mahmood told him it was Tulisa. 'Tulisa Contostavlos? Tulisa sold you some cocaine?' he said stunned. 'I can't get into it any further, but we've already gone to the police, so I'd expect you to be hearing from them shortly,' explained Mahmood. Jones said he would call him back the moment he had spoken to the singer.

He couldn't get through to her so he ended up calling Varey, who was as much a confidant and friend of the star as an assistant. Varey had had his suspicions about the 'movie people' and instantly made the association between them and *The Sun*. Both felt sick and that was before they had to break the news to Tulisa.

The *Sun on Sunday*'s 'world exclusive' was every bit as damaging as they could have feared. *Tulisa's Cocaine Deal Shame*, shouted the front page. On the inside spread, Mahmood reported that 'the singer and former *X Factor* judge was taped telling undercover *Sun* reporters at London's posh Nobu restaurant: "Half my phone book sells it. Of course I can get it for you. Half the guys I know are drug dealers. One's a massive cocaine dealer. He's my best friend. He's a gangster – he's my gangster." The 24-year-old N-Dubz star's shock admission came before she set up an £800 cocaine deal and contrasts vividly with her carefully crafted public image.'

On 4 June she and Coombs were arrested. On 9 December, the pair were charged: the pop star with 'being concerned in the supply of class A drugs'; Coombs simply with 'supply of class A drugs'. Her solicitor told the media that his client would be pleading not guilty. 'In due course Tulisa will give a full answer to these allegations in court,' said Ben Rose. 'This case is not simply about drug supply,' he went on. 'It is about the limits which we set on the conduct of journalists.'

* * *

The trial did not begin until 14 July 2014. Like that of the spot-fixers, it would be heard at Southwark Crown Court. The first major development was for Judge Alistair McCreath to accept Coombs's guilty plea but advise that he would have to wait until the case of his co-defendant had been heard before sentencing could be passed.

The following day, Timothy Cray sketched out the thrust of the prosecution. It boiled down to this: 'In a sentence, we say the defendant was instrumental in arranging the supply of cocaine carried out in the Dorchester early on that Thursday morning. This was a *Sun* newspaper sting and she fell for it. But we say she then went on to supply the cocaine for real. It certainly made for a good newspaper story, as the defendant has been a member of a pop group, a judge on a TV talent show and is well known in the world of entertainment. You will have to decide whether the investigation also revealed evidence of criminal conduct.'

On the surface, it looked like a clear case of criminal conduct. But was it entrapment? How much pressure had Mahmood applied to persuade the defendant to set up the drugs deal? Was she merely acting out a role that Samir Khan had asked her to play? Did the fact that she had been plied with drink and that a £3m carrot was being dangled in front of her excuse her behaviour? She was, after all, an adult and could have walked away at any point.

The jury heard some of the audio footage from the night at the Metropolitan Hotel where Tulisa was heard saying, 'A lot of my boy mates were selling crack cocaine. Because I was young and pretty, no one suspected me. They'd give me the drugs and I would take a cut.' Cray asked of the jurors, 'The simple question is, is she exaggerating her links to the drugs supply or not? She says she is, but we say there is enough evidence to say that she knows exactly what she is doing.'

On 16 July Tulisa's friend and assistant Gareth Varey took the stand. Varey regularly popped up in the footage recorded in Las Vegas and London. 'If she was to do the film and nothing else … it would be her call, but she would want three [million pounds],' he could be heard telling the film producers in one of the negotiations. Soon after Mahmood's report had appeared, Varey had sent a late-night email to one of *The Sun*'s investigative team saying, 'I'm going to kill you bitch.' He subsequently accepted a police caution.

His most memorable contribution to the trial, though, would have nothing to do with the charge at all. At one point in the recordings, Samir Khan had asked Varey if the rumours about the music impresario Simon Cowell being gay were true. 'Yes,' said Varey, who was himself gay. He had not himself slept with Cowell but 'I know people who have.' The comment certainly caught the attention of those in the press gallery, not least because the privilege of court reporting meant they now could publish without fear of litigation what had been a showbiz whisper for many years.

By the end of the day, Cowell's solicitors had written to newspaper editors to inform them that this was untrue and released a statement complaining that 'the issue was the false suggestion made by Mr Varey that Simon – who is renowned for his honesty and candidness – had thus not been truthful in the public arena and this is what we have been obliged to clarify.' Varey would later apologise for his remark. 'This is not true,' he said. 'I do not know why I said it, but assume it is because I was so drunk and felt that I was giving Mahmood the type of information he was seeking. I am very sorry for this.'

With that little sideshow done and dusted, attention naturally turned to the chief prosecution witness. Mahmood had heard all the counter-arguments of defence lawyers in countless cases before, so when he gave evidence, as usual behind a screen, he wasn't unduly perturbed by the ordeal of cross-examination. Jeremy Dein for the defence claimed Mahmood's relentless insistence that he was looking for a 'bad girl' was the cause of a crime being committed. The witness had a good response: 'I said I wanted her to play a bad girl. I didn't say I wanted a bad girl to play the part.'

He then came on to another accusation which previous Mahmood victims had raised – he had spiked Tulisa's drink. She would later say that 'even though I was very drunk, for some reason I felt as if I was buzzing, on a high. Not pissed and slurry.' Again, Mahmood batted this away as 'outrageous' and 'utter nonsense'.

With these jabs parried, Dein got to the nub of the matter, and that was that ever since they had first met in Las Vegas the journalist was 'desperate to incriminate' the accused in a drug deal. Mahmood said there was no desperation: 'My attitude was: if she's at it, she's at it; if she's not, let's go home. You cannot manipulate someone into supplying cocaine.'

With that salacious sub-plot kicked into touch, the court should have been hearing the testimony of Alan Smith, who had driven Tulisa and her friends home after the night out in London. This was the same Alan Smith, now aged 65, who had acted as Mohsin Khan's driver for the appointment with Mazhar Majeed at the Bombay Brasserie in August 2010. But it was at this point that the trial took a dramatic turn. It suddenly became another trial within a trial but this time the individual on the hook would be Mahmood.

It all came down to this: a pre-trial hearing had taken place in June when a three-day application to stay proceedings was argued. The defence maintained that 'evidence of Mr Mahmood's misconduct in past cases demonstrated a propensity to manipulate evidence, to contrive incriminating but ultimately fictional narratives and to present a distorted version of events.'

Jeremy Dein had stated that Mahmood had a 'long and chequered history' which included 'inventing informers and for creating factual scenarios which are not true'. He called one of these informers, Florim Gashi, to give evidence via videolink – Gashi was now living in Croatia. Gashi, a Kosovan asylum-seeker, said that he had been roped in as an accomplice and agent provocateur for several Mahmood 'investigations' during his time in the UK: 'Everything was pre-planned from Maz and basically I was involved in assisting him, helping him make up stories for his newspaper.' The most high-profile of these, Gashi admitted, was a front-page exclusive in 2002 which claimed that the paper had, through Mahmood, smashed a plot to kidnap ex-Spice Girl Victoria Beckham. 'There was nothing genuine in regards to kidnapping Victoria Beckham. This plan originated from Mazher Mahmood and I assisted him to my best to make this story happen.'

Under questioning at that hearing, Mahmood naturally defended his conduct then and as it related now to Tulisa. He was specifically asked if he had 'asked, found out or discussed' with his driver Alan Smith what was said by Tulisa's party as they were chauffeured back to Hertfordshire from the hotel, and he said he had not. He had also denied discussing a statement Smith had been obliged to make about the journey for the pre-trial hearing. Dein's wife had attended one day of the hearing and warned her husband that he had his work cut out with this particular witness. The way Mahmood presented himself in the box he appeared to think he was invincible.

On 3 July the application to stay the proceedings had been rejected by Judge McCreath in a 20-page ruling which essentially

ICC chief Haroon Lorgat, left, and Ronnie Flanagan, chair of the Anti-Corruption and Security Unit (ACSU), try to get on top of the scandal five days after it had broken

Pakistan's one-day captain Shahid Afridi, who had reported his suspicions of Majeed to PCB officials three months earlier, arrives back at Karachi airport after the acrimonious limited-overs series with England in September 2010

Alex Cameron, QC, represented Mohammad Asif at the ICC tribunal in Qatar in January 2011. Cameron's younger brother, David, would be elected Prime Minister four months later

From left: The ICC's independent judging panel of Sharad Rao, Albie Sachs and Michael Beloff arrive at the Doha Financial Centre Tower in Qatar in January 2011

The News of the World team celebrate a successful night at the UK Press Awards in April 2011, including Mazher Mahmood winning scoop of the year. Editor Colin Myler is pictured centre, associate news editor Neil McLeod raises a glass behind him, while lawyer Tom Crone and sport editor Paul McCarthy (with glass of red wine) are standing far left

Less than 12 months after the spot-fixing investigation, Colin Myler holds up the last ever edition of the News of the World outside the News International headquarters in east London on 9 July 2011

News of the World lawyer Tom Crone is heckled by former Grange Hill actor John Alford after appearing at the Leveson Inquiry in December 2011. Alford had gone to prison after a Mazher Mahmood exposé

Mohammad Amir makes his first appearance at Southwark Crown Court, London, on 2 November 2011, having pleaded guilty two months earlier

Mazhar Majeed, who also pleaded guilty, arrives for sentencing at Southwark Crown Court, London, on 3 November 2011. He would receive a custodial sentence of two years and eight months

Salman Butt struggles to get through the media scrum as he arrives at Southwark Crown Court. Butt pleaded not guilty and was handed a 30-month prison term

Mohammad Asif arrives for sentencing at Southwark Crown Court, London, on 3 November 2011. He too pleaded not guilty and received a 12-month custodial sentence.

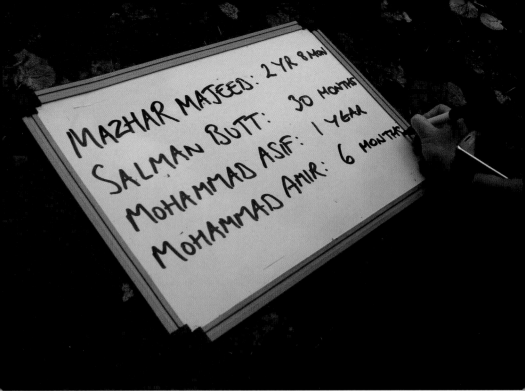

The sentences of each of the four are written down outside the court for the benefit of the attendant media

Back in Pakistan, Amir's tearful mother Nasim Akhtar and his older brother Mohammad Ijaz react to the 19-year-old's prison sentence

Protesters in Pakistan burn effigies of Butt and Asif

Mohammad Amir celebrates the wicket of England's Jake Ball on his return to Test cricket and Lord's in July 2016. The wicket brought Pakistan a 75-run victory

Pop star Tulisa Contostavlos and her assistant Gareth Varey arrive at Southwark Crown Court in July 2014 where the former faced a charge of being concerned with the supply of cocaine after another Mazher exposé

Mazher Mahmood covers his face and is flanked by private security guards as he arrives at the Old Bailey in to face a charge of conspiracy to pervert the course of justice in October 2016.

Alan Smith acted as Mahmood's driver in his spot-fixing and Tulisa investigations. Here he arrives at the Old Bailey trial as a co-defendant. He was given a 12-month suspended sentence

Mazher Mahmood in police custody after being arrested for conspiracy to pervert the course of justice. He was convicted in 2016 and sentenced to 15 months in prison

John Alford outside the Old Bailey during Mahmood's trial with his file on the journalist. To this day, he maintains that he was fitted up by the News of the World reporter and wrongly convicted

stated that previous instances of alleged malpractice by the journalist could not be cited as relevant to this particular episode. Past practice didn't matter now because, a fortnight later, Dein had an ace up his sleeve, and it was Smith.

In his original statement, the driver had reported overhearing Tulisa express her disapproval of drugs. She had told her fellow passengers that one of her relatives had had a drug problem and that was why she disliked the whole subject. Under the duty of disclosure, Smith's draft statement was handed over to the defence, as was a handwritten, anonymous note questioning whether the line about her antipathy to drugs was correct. When a final, signed version of Smith's statement was submitted, the crucial passage had been removed.

Interviewed by the defence team, Smith had now admitted that he had emailed his draft statement to Mahmood, and that after discussion they had agreed to excise the part about her anti-drugs remarks. As he detailed this, he appeared to have little idea that he had potentially incriminated himself and his boss and undermined the prosecution's case: if the pop star had admitted in private that she didn't like being involved in drugs then the defence's claim that she had been entrapped appeared to have some substance.

Dein had held this back until the end of his cross-examination. He had been irritated that the judge had struck off his earlier attempt to have the case dropped; he had been annoyed by the deference that the court had shown Mahmood who had entered via the same entrance as the judge; and he had been irked that the mysterious 'Nish', one of the reporter's acolytes, had not been called by the prosecution. All those frustrations were about to be forgotten because when he began to let the witness know about Smith's latest admission, Mahmood's aura of invincibility evaporated. The combative cockiness which had riled Dein at the hearing and impressed his wife was gone.

Mahmood did his best to stick to what he said were the salient facts of the present case – 'the information was that she [Tulisa] supplies drugs to her friends. She supplied drugs to me – simple'

– but he was fighting a losing battle. The judge was aghast and appalled by the development. Counsel were called to his rooms at the end of the day with the prosecution asked to consider whether it wished to continue. It was more a recommendation than a request.

They were all back on 21 July for the inevitable denouement. The abuse of application process was re-opened with Dein telling the judge, 'There may be a number of reasons for the change in Mr Mahmood's evidence but the reasons for the change are secondary to what the evidence reveals about Mr Mahmood's honesty and his ability to manipulate the court's process.' The Crown wasn't arguing and the judge concluded that the integrity of the court demanded that proceedings against Contostavlos be stayed. Of Coombs, Judge McCreath said that the 'clock had been put back' and he could vacate his guilty plea.

Of Mahmood, he was damning. 'It should not be forgotten that Mr Mahmood is the sole progenitor of this case; the sole investigator; the sole prosecution witness; a man who has exercised his journalistic privilege to create a situation in which the identities of others involved in the investigation are unknown to the defence (or the prosecution or even to me); someone who appears to have gone to considerable lengths to get Ms Contostavlos to agree to involve herself in criminal conduct, certainly to far greater lengths than would have been regarded as appropriate had he been a police investigator.

'None of that, taken on its own or taken together, was sufficient to allow me as a matter of law to halt this case. But there now must be added to the mix two very important factors. First, there are strong grounds for believing that Mr Mahmood told me lies when he gave evidence to me on 27 June. Secondly, there are also strong grounds for believing that the underlying purpose of these lies was to conceal the fact that he had been manipulating the evidence in this case by getting Mr Smith to change his account.

'Had I known of that when I gave my decision at the end of last month, then I have no doubt at all that my decision would have been very different indeed. And that is why I have now said, armed with the knowledge that I now have, that this case cannot go any further.'

If that wasn't bad enough, there was a hint of something worse to come in his closing remark: 'My view of the evidence cannot bind any other court which may (or may not) be called to consider this matter in a different context.' The clear implication was that Mahmood could face a perjury charge. He was immediately suspended from work by *The Sun*, which opened an internal inquiry.

Four days after she had left the court with her name cleared, the pop star spoke to a journalist from *The Guardian*. She said that *The Sun* had targeted her at a time of maximum vulnerability and automatically assumed that because she was in the entertainment industry she must be into drugs. She credited Mahmood and his team for having done their homework with their suggestion that she could star alongside Leonardo DiCaprio – 'He was my childhood crush. I'd admitted it in interviews, so they knew.' They had also done their research on Varey because she thought they had gone down the Bollywood line after learning that he had worked as a dancer in India: 'I think they'd studied the people he'd worked with, the movies he'd worked on, the places he'd been to – because that's what they based it all on.'

'The way they laughed with me and pretended – I didn't think people could be that evil ... If I was a drug dealer or a bad person, I can understand that. But there's a difference between entrapping a criminal and setting up an innocent person.'

* * *

Mahmood was now fighting a war on two fronts. First, there was the likelihood that a charge of perjury would be brought. While he had had plenty of experience of the criminal justice system he had never had it turned on himself. Then there was the reputational damage to him and his employers, News UK, who had put him on paid leave. It was only a month earlier that his former boss, Andy Coulson, had been sentenced to 18 months in prison for conspiracy to hack phones.

The hits kept coming. In September the Crown Prosecution Service (CPS) had decided to offer no evidence against Dr Majeed Ridha and pharmacist Murtaza Gulamhusein, both of whom were accused of illegally supplying an abortion drug. The prosecution emanated from one of the first articles Mahmood had written in his brief stint at the *Sunday Times* in September 2012. Around the same time, drugs charges were also dropped against Leon 'Starino' Anderson and Ashley Gordon, charges based on allegations in *The Sun on Sunday*. *Press Gazette* reported that 'Mahmood was said to have received the drugs at the Metropolitan Hotel in London's Old Park Lane on 10 May last year [2013] in a "dry run" for his sting against Tulisa Contostavlos.' That would have been the same day that he enjoyed his night out with Tulisa at the same venue.

In front of Judge McCreath at Southwark Crown Court again, Quinn Hawkins for the prosecution said, 'As My Lord knows, having presided over the Contostavlos case, the position is that Mazher Mahmood gave evidence on two occasions in that case which tended to contradict itself. The position is that the Crown can no longer rely on Mr Mahmood as a witness of truth in this case, and for that reason, I offer no evidence against Mr Gordon on behalf of the Crown.'

In media circles, it was open season on Mahmood, with every major investigation he had worked on now being pored over for signs of sharp or illegal practice. The BBC's *Panorama* had a documentary on him ready to go in November of that year, which his lawyers wanted dropped on the grounds that it could prejudice any future judicial process. The same lawyers had already tried and failed with a high court appeal to stop his identity from being made public in the programme. In a statement issued shortly before the broadcast, he argued that it be dropped in the interest of justice, which would have had his critics guffawing.

'The BBC proposes to broadcast, it would appear whatever the evidence shows, a programme designed to condemn my career as an investigatory journalist. They are doing so while there is an active investigation being carried out by the Metropolitan Police into the collapse of the Contostavlos trial. I am cooperating fully with the police inquiry and have not been arrested. However, because a decision will be taken shortly on whether any proceeding should be brought, the BBC has been asked by the attorney-general of England and Wales to consider delaying the broadcast to wait on any decision to prosecute, so as not to prejudice any proceedings should they be brought.

'They are ignoring this and seem hell bent on broadcasting, whatever effect it may have. This is deeply irresponsible and not in the public interest or in the interests of justice, but unfortunately in line with the attitude they are taking around their programme in general.'

The documentary was aired and went back over the Beckham kidnapping story with Florim Gashi and also interviewed former Page Three model Emma Morgan, who, like Tulisa, had been stung by a drugs deal set up with a man called 'Billy'. 'I'd like to apologise to Emma for my part in stitching her up,' said Billy, who claimed he had been paid by Mahmood to act out a part in a script that the journalist had written, directed and produced all by himself. 'The only real criminal was Mazher Mahmood. He gave me the money to buy the cocaine.'

It was no surprise when the Crown Prosecution Service (CPS) announced the following month that it was reviewing 25 cases in which convictions had been secured using evidence provided by the undercover reporter. An investigation into 13 men accused by Mahmood in *The Sun on Sunday* of a conspiracy to 'spot-fix' football matches had also been halted.

While the CPS pondered its next move in these cases and that of Mahmood himself, Siobhain Egan was mounting her own charge. The solicitor was representing all those victims who believed they had been stitched up by what she regarded as an unholy trinity of the crafty Mahmood, publicity-driven police officers and a credulous CPS. She had had first-hand experience of this when defending one of the men charged with conspiracy to kidnap Victoria Beckham in 2002.

That the arrest of five Albanian and Romanians by officers from the Met's serious and organised crime branch had been choreographed by Mahmood and the *News of the World* already offended her legal sensibilities. She had then been both baffled and enraged that that case had ever made it to court because at first glance it was apparent that her local nursery would have provided a more likely kidnapping gang. She had driven out to look at the Beckhams' house with someone who knew the premises but even they ended up getting lost. There was no way five lowly immigrants had the nous and wherewithal to locate and scope it out without input from someone familiar with the Beckhams' situation. She was sure that Mahmood had driven them out there and demanded to see his phone records to confirm her suspicions that he had orchestrated the whole plot. She never got to see them because the CPS dropped the prosecution on the grounds that one of Mahmood's informants, Gashi, in the operation had admitted he had been paid £10,000 by the *News of the World*.

Now Egan was going back over similar cases and offering to represent those who believed they had been subject to a miscarriage of justice with a view to overturning their convictions through the Criminal Cases Review Commission. One of them was John Alford, a young actor, briefly famous for his appearances in *Grange Hill* and *London's Burning*, who had been convicted of supplying drugs to Mahmood and who would repeatedly claim that he had been set up and his life ruined. Another was Mazhar Majeed.

While Egan had been busy working through her caseload, the Crown Prosecution Service had finally reached a decision. On 29 September 2015 it confirmed that it would be bringing charges. In a statement prepared by his solicitors, Mahmood said he was 'deeply disappointed that, after a totally unjustified delay, the [CPS] have today informed me that they have decided to charge me with conspiracy to pervert the course of justice. I deny the offence. I will vigorously contest it at court. In the meantime I have nothing further to say.'

On 25 February 2016 Mahmood and Alan Smith, who had also been charged, appeared at a preliminary hearing at the Old Bailey. Both men, on unconditional bail, entered a plea of not guilty. A trial date was set for 19 September.

* * *

The jury was sworn in at the Old Bailey on the scheduled date, which was just over a week after Mohammad Amir had flown back to Pakistan from the summer tour of England. This time, Mahmood would not be granted the privilege of concealment. There would be no screen for him to hide behind. Instead, he would appear in the dock on view to all, like the many he had given evidence against in the past. Outside, at least, he could arrive at the 'Bailey' each day with a hoodie drawn tightly over his face, stopping press photographers from getting a shot of his distinguishing features. He was always flanked by security paid for by News UK. On several days, John Alford was there waiting to heckle him and to publicise his own grievance. As his home address, Mahmood gave the court a residence in Purley in Surrey which was only a few miles from where Mazhar Majeed lived.

The process was always going to be a reprise of the evidence presented at the Tulisa trial, which seemed stacked against Mahmood. As indicated by his not guilty plea, however, he was not going to go down without a fight. He maintained his point that she had agreed to help 'Samir Khan' procure drugs and then done just that. In this, she had been a willing participant. It is a stance he maintains to this day.

'In effect, the hearing in June 2014 put Mr Mahmood and his journalistic process on trial,' said Sarah Forshaw QC, staking out the prosecution case. 'He liked to call himself the king of sting, he boasted in a book he had written of the number of convictions that he personally was responsible for. He knew that if it could be shown that he had acted improperly as an agent provocateur, inducing Miss Contostavlos to do something she would not otherwise do, his own credibility and standing and the prospect of conviction in the case might both be severely damaged. This is a case about an agreement made between these two individuals to tamper with evidence in a criminal trial.

'Miss Contostavlos had expressed her disapproval of hard drugs to his own driver, that was the bit of the statement that was altered.

Mr Smith had told the police officer making the statement that he remembered that while driving Miss Contostavlos ... that she had spoken about someone in her family being dependent on cocaine.

'He [Mahmood] deliberately misled the court – not only had he discussed it [Smith's statement] but he had been sent a copy of the statement. There is no doubt that Smith did change his statement. The change would undoubtedly have disadvantaged Miss Contostavlos's case. It would have deprived her of supporting evidence from Mahmood's own right-hand man that she made an anti-drugs comment at a time when untainted by any influence or pressure.

'Mr Mahmood may be the master of subterfuge and deception. But on this occasion it is he, together with his employee, who are exposed.'

Now it was the turn of Contostavlos to give evidence against him. In a statement read out in court, she acknowledged that on the night out at the Metropolitan, she, Varey and Michelle McKenna 'consumed a considerable amount of alcoholic drinks provided by Mr Mahmood. By the time we left the hotel, I was drunk. I would describe my state as hyper drunk, as opposed to sleepy drunk. I was therefore aware of my surroundings.' (The hyper drunk reference looked like an implication that her drink had been spiked.) Though her memory of what was said in the car was 'quite vague', she did remember 'snippets and bullet points', including an argument with Varey and a 'fairly intense' conversation about a relative's 'hard drugs use'.

Then came the police witness. DS Andrew Nicklin was charged with taking Smith's statement for the pre-trial hearing on 23 June 2014 when the driver had said that the singer 'seemed really negative about cocaine and expressed her disapproval of drugs'. Asked about his reaction when, the following day, Smith indicated that he wished to remove that part, Nicklin said, 'I was surprised. There was no doubt about the statement earlier and it was the most significant part of his statement.' The reason he thought there was no doubt about the statement earlier was because he had read it back to him at the time and 'I remember him saying yes, yes, yes, repeatedly.'

Like Majeed and his co-conspirators before him, Mahmood would have to account for what looked like damning telecommunications evidence. Forshaw said that email and phone data showed that in six minutes after Smith had logged on to his email account after being sent the draft statement, there had been eight text messages between the defendants, as well as a six-second call from Smith to Mahmood.

Further calls and texts followed and it was subsequent to these that Smith got back to Nicklin to make the alteration. Mahmood and Smith were in contact right up until the following morning when Nicklin emailed through the new statement. What was written in the correspondence could not be discerned because the emails and texts had been destroyed and, unlike those of the cricketers and their agent, could not be retrieved.

It was hard to see how Mahmood was going to talk his way out of this one – and, in fact, he wasn't going to try. Both he and Smith exercised their right not to give evidence. The next best thing was a statement he gave to officers at Charing Cross police station in September 2014 when asked to report for questioning. The statement read: 'The operation against Tulisa Contostavlos was properly planned and lawfully undertaken. Her co-defendant pleaded guilty and indeed has stated recently that he was amongst a number of people she contacted to buy drugs. In my view she had been involved in the unlawful supply of drugs and supplied me drugs in the circumstances where she was under no pressure to do so. As such I had no need to invent, suppress or manipulate evidence and did not do so.

'I believe the court was looking for an excuse to drop the case and seized upon an apparent discrepancy without proper analysis. By the end of my evidence I had no support from prosecution counsel and was subject to cross-examination from the judge.'

These were not unreasonable points. It was what he also told the officers under questioning that stretched credibility: 'I was thoroughly confused. I was doing my best to answer the questions but was steamrollered into answers. It felt like all sides were trying to discredit me and it was a difficult and uncomfortable experience.' This was hardly the ace witness for the prosecution who had condemned so many villains to time behind bars.

In summing up the case for the prosecution, Forshaw drew the jury's attention to the refusal of the defendants to take the stand. 'The conspiracy to pervert the course of justice is now a conspiracy of silence,' she said. 'You may think if they were innocent men with nothing to hide, wouldn't they be shouting it from the rooftops?'

Representing Mahmood, John Kelsey-Fry QC, who had also defended one of his former colleagues, Clive Goodman, highlighted the fact that the first Smith statement had been made more than a year after the relevant night. 'It's obvious that there would be every reason for Mr Smith to have an insecure recollection about what was said by whom and it would be quite wrong of him not to say so,' the lawyer said. 'When Mr Smith got to see the draft witness statement he was concerned about whether it was right and whether he could be sure of who said what.' That was why he had then contacted his co-defendant.

But, his barrister insisted, Mahmood 'repeatedly' insisted that 'he did not discuss Smith's evidence with him and he repeatedly insists he could not discuss Smith's evidence … Witnesses should not discuss their evidence amongst themselves [but] if Mr Smith is concerned about the accuracy of the statement, advising Mr Smith to contact the police would be absolutely the right thing to do.' Besides, why would Mahmood feel the need to pressure Smith into making the alteration, Kelsey-Fry asked, since it was already evident that he 'had gathered irrefutable evidence that Mrs Contostavlos had supplied cocaine and that was all that mattered'?

It wasn't the worst line of defence but it was always going to be a struggle to convince the jury. On 5 October that jury returned guilty verdicts against Mahmood and Smith. Judge Gerald Gordon adjourned sentencing until 21 October, allowing the pair to remain out on bail in the meantime. In that period, Mahmood spent time putting his affairs in order and mentally preparing himself for time inside. Conversations with Andy Coulson, the former *News of the World* editor who had begun his stretch at HM Prison Belmarsh, helped in this latter regard.

When the court returned, Kelsey-Fry, in mitigation, painted an almost pitiful picture of his client who was divorced from his wife and saw his 14-year-old son every other week as part of the custody agreement. Mahmood was, he said, a 'very frightened man' whose 'career is over. He has brought catastrophe upon himself and a lifetime's work will be for ever tarnished.' Those words had little effect on the bench. Before passing sentence, Judge Gordon told Mahmood, 'It was your idea, you were the intended beneficiary and you made use of a loyal person, partly an employee, in order to achieve your purpose. The motive was to preserve and enhance your reputation, you wanted another scalp and Ms Contostavlos's conviction would have achieved that. You saw a problem, and you were prepared for the court to be deceived.' He was handed a 15-month prison term. Smith was given 12 months, suspended for two years.

As he was taken away, there were cries from the gallery of 'enjoy it' and 'it's your turn now, Mazher'. This latter remark was attributed to former world heavyweight champion Herbie Hide, another who had been caught up in a *News of the World* drugs sting. In the press reports, there was mention of Hide and others bringing civil actions which could end up costing News UK £800m.

How had it come to this? Those who had worked with him at the *Screws* insisted that Mahmood had suffered an aberration. Whatever you might say about his particular brand of journalism, he had always grasped the legal technicalities. Pressurising Smith to alter his statement was not only unethical, it was also foolhardy – there was always a strong chance that this would come out. His detractors argued that far from this intervention being the exception it was in fact the norm. He had got away with it because he had been trusted and indulged too often by editors, the police, prosecution lawyers who all had an interest in convicting those he accused. Over time, the critics said, he had got complacent, considered himself bomb-proof.

There was one thing his critics and former colleagues did agree on: *The Sun on Sunday* lacked the resources and clout of its forerunner and that weakened his hand. Unlike the *News of the World,* which was a stand-alone title with a colossal budget and revenue, it was essentially a seventh-day extension of *The Sun.* To reclaim many of the readers who gave up buying a Sunday newspaper when the *Screws* was closed, it had to make waves with less money and with shorter lead times. In the past, his defenders argued, Mahmood would have just walked away from the Tulisa investigation when he sensed she wouldn't play ball. In 2013, with so much time and money already committed, he had to keep pushing and pushing to get her to say yes. From there, he was locked into securing a conviction – whatever it took.

As he passed his time in jail, there was at least one crumb of comfort for Mahmood. Not one of the appellants to the Criminal Cases Review Commission had their sentences overturned. That included Mazhar Majeed.

AFTERWORD

THERE IS one remaining mystery around the Pakistan case which has never been resolved. Who tipped off the *News of the World*? The names of various ex-Pakistan internationals have been muttered over the years, but with little proof or conviction. In the summer of 2019 Shahid Afridi, who had once employed Majeed as his agent, was at least able to shed light on how his incriminating texts had come into the public domain.

In his autobiography, *Game Changer*, Afridi revealed that it was during or shortly after the Asia Cup in June 2010 that he first saw them in transcript form. 'At one of the Sri Lankan beaches,' he explains, 'one of Majeed's young sons dropped his father's mobile phone in the water and it stopped working. When Majeed went back to England, he took his phone for repair to a mobile fix-it shop. In a random coincidence, the shop owner turned out to be a friend of a friend of mine (this may sound like too much of a coincidence but the Pakistani community in England is quite closely connected).

'While fixing the phone, the owner, who was asked to retrieve the messages, came across Majeed's messages to the players of the Pakistan team. It was that leak from him to my friend and a few others that looped me in on the scam. It was that leak which probably tipped off the reporting team from the *News of the World*.'

Afridi claims that when he received the messages he alerted Waqar Younis, who was the team's bowling coach. However, at that point, Younis, like himself, was inclined to give the players the benefit of the doubt – 'Something that wasn't as bad as it looked, just a dodgy conversation between [them] and Majeed.' Neither escalated the matter to their bosses at the Pakistan Cricket Board.

Afridi goes on to write that during the World T20 in the West Indies a couple of months before, Abdul Razzaq, one of the more experienced players, had told him that the three cricketers who would be found guilty at Southwark Crown Court 'weren't up to any good'. He claims that he told Razzaq that 'he was imagining things, secretly hoping that their shady behaviour was just a sign of their youth and inexperience'.

There was another revealing exchange with Razzaq from the tour of Sri Lanka which had stuck with Afridi. Butt had returned to the dressing room after falling for a duck against the hosts in the ninth ball of the innings ('he went neither forward or back and groped blindly outside the line', said *Cricinfo's* live online commentary of his dismissal). Razzaq implied that all was not as it seemed. Afridi still didn't want to believe the worst but he couldn't put his team-mate's 'strange look' out of his mind.

So when he noticed Majeed hanging around the team when they arrived in England to play Australia in July 2010, Afridi, captain for the series, decided to take action. He claims that he formally asked team manager Yawar Saeed to ensure the agent was allowed nowhere near the squad. Saeed initially refused – Majeed had more than a handful of the players on his books – so Afridi showed him the texts. Still, Saeed was in denial, saying he really didn't see what he could do.

'Frankly I don't think the management gave a damn,' Afrid, concluded. 'It still was nobody's problem. That's why nobody wanted to tackle it or go to bat for it. Typical obfuscation and delay tactics; the Pakistani management's head was in the sand. Maybe the management was scared of the consequences. Maybe they were invested in these players as their favourites and future captains. Or maybe they didn't have any respect for their country or the game.'

By now, he says, the transcript had leaked out to others within the Pakistan cricket community. That almost certainly included the same individual who had contacted Mazher Mahmood at the beginning of 2010 and was then back in touch with him and the ICC in the summer of that year with something solid to go on.

* * *

Mohammad Amir went to jail for activities on his debut tour of England so it was ironic that the fates should conspire to see him return to the country for four consecutive summers from 2016. After the warm welcome of that first year back, his finest hour came in 2017 when Pakistan won the ICC Champions Trophy, a one-day tournament.

After beating hosts England in the semi-finals, Pakistan headed to The Oval for a showdown with arch-rivals India, who had thrashed them in the group stage. They won by 180 runs, Amir finishing with impressive figures of 3-16 in six overs. He had the fifth-best economy rate in the competition as a whole. Later that summer, he joined Essex on a temporary contract, where he found himself playing with Alastair Cook, one of his opponents during the 2010 Test. Cook found him to be a decent man. They didn't talk much about the case but what few conversations they had, combined with the evidence of Amir's general conduct at the county, compelled Cook to change his original conviction that the Pakistani should have been banned from the game for life.

A year later, Amir performed creditably in another drawn Test series with England, his seven wickets in the two matches coming in at just over 20 apiece. Before the match at Lord's, he gave an interview in which he revealed that 'not only once, on many occasions I thought I would never come back on a cricket field. Five years is a long time. But my family and friends supported me a lot. My lawyers, Gareth and Sajida, always kept me motivated. But, yes, there were many moments when I thought I would not play cricket again … A man should always be working hard. Being a Muslim, I have always believed that if you are working hard you are rewarded with great results.'

In 2019, aged 27 and nearly ten years after his one-day debut, he played in his first World Cup. Pakistan surprised everyone by accounting for the hosts and eventual champions, England, in their second game. They then surprised no one by following that up with a series of mediocre performances and a group stage exit. Soon after the World Cup, he announced that he had quit the long format of the game to concentrate on limited-overs cricket. He had played his last Test in January of that year in Sri Lanka and in 36 matches had collected 119 wickets at an average of just over 30.

At the time of writing, his most recent ODI appearance had been against Sri Lanka on his country's return to home soil in October 2019. He was last seen playing for Karachi Kings in the Pakistan Super League (PSL) before coronavirus brought a suspension to that competition in the spring of 2020. He should have been back in England in the summer of 2020 but announced in June that he would not travel because he wished to attend the birth of his second child.

His former captain Salman Butt had wasted no time reminding the world of his batting credentials, hitting a century in his first innings back in the country's one-day cup in January 2016. He and Mohammad Asif were part of the Water and Power Development Authority (Wapda) team who took on the Federally Administered Tribal Areas that day. Butt made 135 off 143 balls. 'A hundred on return is something I will remember,' he said, 'and I am satisfied with my batting and will hope to continue the same form in the remaining matches.' Of the recent selection of Amir for the forthcoming tour of New Zealand, he said that it would 'without doubt strengthen Pakistan's bowling ... so I wish him the best.'

Over the next couple of seasons, he would prove a prolific run-scorer in domestic cricket. In November 2017 he and his former Pakistan team-mate Kamran Akmal put on 209 for Lahore Whites in the National Cup. It was a T20 world record for an opening partnership, and the third highest in history. In February 2019 the Lahore Qalanders announced that they were drafting in Butt to replace their injured all-rounder Mohammad Hafeez for the final stages of the PSL.

His appointment was noted in a column by Mike Atherton in *The Times*. 'It is a depressing state of affairs to think that Butt will now be sharing a dressing room with two young bowlers who are, potentially, the future of Pakistan,' Atherton lamented. 'Actually, it is a depressing thought that Butt will be sharing a dressing room with any young cricketer again, such was his malign influence when he held the highest post a sportsman can enjoy ... Butt may need cricket again, but cricket doesn't need him.'

Butt scored only 22 in two innings but he was retained by the Qalanders for 2020. 'I have been playing cricket continuously and [I am] in good form,' he said on hearing the news in August 2019. 'My domestic track record clearly indicates my fitness and performances. My job is to perform, which I have been successfully doing, while [the] rest is on the PCB and selectors [on] what they decide about me.' At the time of writing the PCB selectors were still of the opinion that he was surplus to their requirements.

Mohammad Asif was 33 when he was cleared to play at the same time as Butt. Appearing in that return fixture for Wapda in early 2016, he took 2-22 in six overs in their 142-run win. 'The last five years were the toughest for me and for my family but I am happy that that period is over now and I am back on the field,' he said at the time.

Later that year, he became the last of the trio to make his first-class return when he finished with match figures of 4-70 in Wapda's victory by an innings and 100 runs against Islamabad. In October 2017, after Pakistan's defeat to Sri Lanka in the United Arab Emirates, a columnist for *The Nation* in Pakistan wondered why 'when tainted M Aamir [sic] can represent the country without major contribution with only exception of Champions Trophy final, then why not Salman Butt and M Asif could make a strong comeback, as both have been performing exceptionally in domestic cricket. The PCB chief should wake up and take strong action and provide justice to the genuine players to save Pakistan cricket.'

But the extended break was always going to have a more detrimental effect on a bowler the wrong side of 30 than a batsman like Butt, and Asif's successes were only fitful after the ban. In March 2019 he effectively confirmed his retirement when he said that he planned 'on taking [a] coaching course arranged by the Pakistan Cricket Board as I seriously want to pursue this field'. Amir's decision to retire from Tests at the age of 27 left him unimpressed. 'I curse the PCB for how they rescued his career,' he said in May 2020. 'It was his obligation to help Pakistan cricket in a tough situation and he should have stayed, especially when they had helped him return.'

Just how grievous Asif's absence was for Pakistan and cricket in general was underlined by an observation made that same year by Hashim Amla, the South African who had been ranked No. 1 batsman in the world in 2013: 'Mohammad Asif is the best one [I have faced]. [I know] he got banned for fixing but, at that stage, he was the best fast bowler I've ever faced. He was not quick, 135kph maybe, but his accuracy was phenomenal. We played him in South Africa and even in Pakistan in 2007. [If] he landed in the first stump I didn't know if it was nipping away or nipping in ... He tested your defence really, to the maximum. Funnily enough, as the years have gone by, meeting other cricketers from home, the world over, just loosely chatting ... so many of the guys feel exactly the same thing. They said Mohammad Asif was a magician of the ball in a way.'

It was a judgement confirmed in April 2020 by Kevin Pietersen, also one of the greatest batsmen of the era, who tweeted of Asif: 'I think there's plenty batters around the world that were happy he got banned! He was the best I faced! I had no idea against him!'

Of the final convicted fixer, less was heard. Like Asif and Butt, Mazhar Majeed had initially been incarcerated at HM Prison Wandsworth before a transfer to Ford Open Prison in West Sussex. It was there, *The Sun* reported in January 2012, that he was picking up '£9.50 a week for cleaning as a privileged con. He also gets his own cell with Freeview TV. A source said: "He's over the moon. He could have been given harder jobs."'

Around the same time, it was announced that the football club he owned, Croydon Athletic FC, was folding after playing their last league game on 3 December 2011. The club was found to have made irregular payments to players in the 2009/10 season, fined £7,500 by the Football Association and docked ten league points. The implosion of the club had been accelerated by the death, in October 2010, of its 44-year-old chairman David Le Cluse. The day after celebrating his daughter's ninth birthday, he had shot himself in a lock-up two miles from his home in Carshalton, Surrey. The previous month, Le Cluse had confirmed that Croydon were being investigated by HM Revenues and Customs as a follow-up to Majeed's arrest.

When the club resigned from their league in January 2012, Le Cluse's successor Chris Roots told the local press, 'As I've said to a lot of people, if we could have carried on we should have done, even if it meant putting youngsters out to field some sort of side. But it became clear that we could not carry on without financial support from the owner. It wasn't until Majeed was off the scene that we were able to look at the books and we found the debts were more than £100,000. That was crippling.' In Majeed's enforced absence, his sister-in-law Jenna Manji was meant to be running the business side of the club. Unsurprisingly, she was not willing to cover the debts. Outside investors were but Manji wanted a fee for the company which owned Croydon. There was one problem with this – it had no tangible assets.

In May 2012 Majeed's appeal against his conviction on what was effectively a legal technicality was dismissed. Justice Igor Judge explained that he and two other judges were upholding the convictions because 'the respective offences of conspiracy against Majeed and cheating against [Mervyn] Westfield were properly prosecuted ... Cricket is widely televised, not only in the country where the match is being played, but throughout the cricket-playing world. The prizes for successful gambling can be very great and the scope for corruption is therefore considerable. For the health, indeed the survival of the game as a truly competitive sport, it must be eradicated.'

He served less than half of his 30-month sentence but by November 2015 was once again a guest of Her Majesty. At Croydon crown court, he pleaded guilty to tax fraud and was handed a two-year prison sentence. HMRC had found that between 2006 and 2011 he had deliberately under-declared £259,000 of income from the sales of his property portfolio. Alan Tully, assistant director of its fraud investigation service, said 'Majeed was a very wealthy businessman who tried to wriggle out of paying his fair share. He selfishly stole money that should have been used to fund vital public services and he now must pay the price for his dishonesty.'

Sixteen months later, at liberty again, Majeed was, according to the *Daily Mail*, 'advising boxer David Haye in the build-up to his grudge fight against Tony Bellew a week tomorrow … A spokesperson said, "Mazhar Majeed is not employed, nor has a formal role, with David Haye or with his company. He is, however, a friend and trusted adviser."'

Approached to be interviewed for this book, Majeed first requested that the author sign a preliminary non-disclosure agreement before meeting. Soon after that, he decided that there could be no interview: 'I have realised that you work for the same people who owned *NOTW* so I'm afraid it's a thanks but no thanks.' He still lives on the outskirts of Croydon, the home where he bragged to Mahmood on the Saturday of The Oval Test about past matches he had helped to fix and about the Swiss bank accounts through which he channelled money for his players.

His wife Sheliza Manji remains a director of *Afters*, the ice cream parlour chain he set up in south London. It was *Afters* in Tooting which Butt claimed had paid him the cash found in his hotel room near Lord's in reward for attending a promotional event there. Her sister, Jenna, also a director of one of several Majeed-run companies, all now wound up, also declined requests to be interviewed for this book. His relationship with his brother Azhar can now be described as distant at best.

* * *

Mazher Mahmood was released from jail in February 2017. Like Andy Coulson, he spent his first few nights inside at HM Prison

Belmarsh, which he found to be every bit as horrific as he feared. Belmarsh was used to hold Category A prisoners – those considered the most dangerous – and that included some of the country's most high-profile terrorists. From there he was moved to Ford Open, where Majeed had served his time. 'People talk about it as a holiday camp, but in many respects it is even better,' George Best had said of his time locked up – if that is the right term – there. It was certainly more agreeable than Belmarsh and Mahmood found he was well looked after by its community of Asian inmates.

With everything that had gone before with him and the *News of the World*, a journalistic comeback was never on the cards when his liberty was restored. That did not mean that he had severed all ties with the Street of Shame. News UK had promised to 'vigorously defend' any civil claims brought against it in relation to Mahmood's activities and that drew him back into the orbit of its legal department. That was now headed by Angus McLeod, who had completed a hat-trick of having acted for Majeed, Mahmood in the Tulisa case and Rebekah Brooks when she was acquitted of conspiracy to hack voicemails, conspiracy to pay public officials and conspiracy to pervert the course of justice in 2014. Mahmood's responsibility was to advise which of the claimants were trying it on and those who might at least have a *prima facie* case.

Those claimants, originally led by Mark Lewis who had represented many of the phone-hacking victims, certainly hadn't been backward about coming forward. Most prominent in the plaintiff list was Sarah Ferguson, the Duchess of York, who was angling for a settlement for reputational damage and lost income caused by the 2010 'cash for access' story when Mahmood had recorded her offering to introduce him – 'I can open any door you want' – to Prince Andrew in exchange for £500,000.

Papers filed by her lawyers in 2018 alleged that 'Mahmood and NGN [the former parent company for the *News of the World* and *The Sun*] conspired together to use unlawful means to cause loss to the Duchess by inducing her to make various statements which Mahmood covertly recorded and then edited and used as the basis for a story [which] was calculated to and did cause serious embarrassment, humiliation, distress and reputational damage to the Duchess … The Duchess's ability to generate income from a variety of businesses was seriously damaged.' For this, she was reported to be asking for £40m in compensation.

Also taking legal action against News UK was the Duchess's former lover, John Bryant. Papers submitted by the lawyers for the American, most famous for having been photographed sucking Ferguson's toes in 1992 when she was still married to Prince Andrew, alleged that 'the vile conduct giving rise to this lawsuit includes a failed entrapment scheme, unlawful recordings and a malicious libel.' The entrapment part was the undercover reporter, posing as a potential investor in a casino, 'asking him to supply prostitutes and drugs'.

In April 2019 Ferguson's claim was dropped. In a document filed at the High Court, both parties agreed 'the claimant discontinues all of her claims against the defendants'. The Duchess was reported to have spent half a millions pounds in legal fees. To date, New UK has not settled with Bryant or any other claimant with a specific grievance against Mahmood.

The Fergie case wasn't the only ghost from Mahmood's former life to re-appear. In January 2019 his old adversary John Alford admitted resisting arrest at Highbury Corner magistrates' court. The details of the case were depressingly inane – he was accused of hurling a dustbin at a bin lorry and smashing its windscreen before two police officers grappled with him. As he struggled with the officers, Alford shouted, 'In cahoots with the *News of the World*. In cahoots with Mazher Mahmood … You're all corrupt bastards. Has Rupert Murdoch sent you in to kill me? My name is John Alford, I'm fighting Rupert Murdoch and corrupt police officers.'

In September of the same year, Mahmood made a brief re-appearance in media circles when the *Mail on Sunday* published video stills of Prince Andrew at the New York apartment of convicted sex offender and financier Jeffrey Epstein in the early part of the decade. Mahmood had reported on the connections back in 2011, before the

News of the World was shut down. His exclusive, 'Prince Andy and the Paedo', had even earned praise from Roy Greenslade at the time: 'I can't remember the last time I praised a story by the *News of the World*'s investigations editor Mazher Mahmood. But he certainly deserves a pat on the back for today's royal scoop.'

When interest was re-ignited eight years later following Epstein's prison suicide as he faced further charges, it is believed that Mahmood brokered the deal between the paper and his contact, who had recorded the original surveillance footage of the royal and the American. He lives today in the United Kingdom, though has also spent time working in the United Arab Emirates since his release.

Editor Colin Myler was kept on by News International after the closure of the *News of the World* in July 2011. There were still loose ends to be tied up and most of them involved phone-hacking. When awkward questions, many of them in Parliament, began to be asked about who at corporate level had known what, Rupert Murdoch's son and company chief executive, James, blamed Myler and lawyer Tom Crone for not being honest with him.

Murdoch told Parliament's culture, media and sport committee that when he had signed off on a payment of £700,000 for football executive Gordon Taylor, whose phone had been hacked, he had done so only because the pair had told him it was legally necessary. In fact, the reason the payment was so high was because Taylor's lawyers had seen an internal email which gave the lie to the party line that phone-hacking was confined to one 'rogue reporter' (Clive Goodman) on the paper. Myler and Crone denied that they had concealed this from Murdoch.

In January 2012 Myler returned to New York as editor of the *Daily News*, a post he held until early 2016. In a farewell interview with *The Guardian*, he was asked about a profile that had appeared in *New York* magazine soon after his appointment in which he was described as having 'shopkeeper's features'. 'What does that mean?' he complained to the interviewer. 'I think this was the guy that spent three months trying to find stuff out about me. He wouldn't have lasted long in my newsroom.' Myler's closing observation on his 47 years in journalism was: 'Nothing beats the definition of a good story. An exclusive story is what it is. You don't have to explain it.' He now divides his time between London, Kent and California.

Of his *News of the World* colleagues, Neil McLeod left the paper shortly before its closure to follow the well-trodden journalistic path into PR, landing a role at Phil Hall Associates. Hall is himself a former *News of the World* editor whose agency advises celebrities on how to handle the kind of tabloid revelations in which he once specialised. In November 2014 former executive news editor Ian Edmondson was sentenced to eight months in prison after being found guilty of phone-hacking-related charges. He spent Christmas in Brixton prison and separated from his wife. He too now works in PR.

James Mellor went with Mahmood from the *News of the World* to a job on the *Sunday Times* news desk. He left in 2016 for a position at the Barnardo's charity but was back in journalism in 2018 to work at the *Mail on Sunday* as news editor. Matt Drake and Phil Whiteside, who collected and then took the bag of £140,000 destined for Majeed to the Copthorne Tara Hotel in Kensington, have held jobs in print and broadcast media since leaving Wapping.

Legal manager Tom Crone was on holiday when the *News of the World* closure was announced. On the Sunday it appeared for the final time, he received a call from chief operating officer Susan Panuccio asking him to meet with her the following morning. 'Is this it?' he asked. She didn't answer the question but the polite vagueness of her reply made it clear that it was.

He then booked a table for lunch that Monday at one of his favourite restaurants in Leadenhall Market. Sure enough, the meeting with Panuccio was merely to go through the legal formalities and the terms of his pay-off from a place where he had worked for 26 years. As he left Wapping and walked through St Katharine's Dock en route to his lunch appointment, it suddenly occurred to him that at 59 he was effectively retired. When that sank in, he did a little jump and click of his heels.

If he thought he could enjoy a blissful retirement, he was wrong. On 30 August 2012 he was arrested on suspicion of conspiring to intercept communications and was taken to a local police station for questioning. It was not until October 2014 that the Crown Prosecution Service announced he would not face charges. His troubles were still not over. In 2016 he faced a Bar Standards Board tribunal which focussed on his ordering of the surveillance of two solicitors engaged in litigation against the *Screws* for phone-hacking. If found guilty of professional misconduct, he would have been disbarred – not a practical problem since his working days were behind him, but a huge personal humiliation. Crone was unanimously cleared. He still lives in Wimbledon.

* * *

But what of cricket itself? The hope that the exposure, disgrace and incarceration of the three Pakistanis, combined with a beefed-up anti-corruption unit, would act as a deterrent proved wildly optimistic. A report from January 2012 covering the first year of the ICC's anti-corruption and security unit (ACSU), under Sir Ronnie Flanagan, revealed that the unit had followed up 281 lines of inquiry, uncovering at least 11 'hard' approaches to players or officials to cheat in some way. The first figure was a sharp increase on the total of 158 intelligence reports in the previous year. Overall, the ACSU had identified more than 100 individuals across the world who were 'actively involved in, or closely associated with, actual or planned corruption attempts'. Most of them were Indian, messages on their mobile phones offering a trail of wrongdoing.

The report also shed light on the nature of the approaches. In addition to the usual, straightforward cash offers – an agent offered £200,000 by an illegal Indian bookie initialised as 'VG' to set up fixing – the report had photographs of a couple ('DP' and 'NM') who had 'attempted to approach players' at the Royal Garden Hotel in Kensington during the World T20 in England in 2009. 'NM' was pictured in a bikini and 'ACSU inquiries ascertained that NM was clearly using her charms – the honey trap – in an attempt to corrupt players.' She was spotted again at the 2011 World Cup in India when her approach to one cricketer was reported to the ACSU.

Ten months after the Lord's Test, the stench of fixing, particularly around Asian teams, still lingered long enough to befoul even the cleanest of victories, as Graeme Swann found out. At Cardiff, in May 2011, England had bowled Sri Lanka out for 82 on the final afternoon for a shock win, the England spinner taking four cheap wickets.His pride at this extraordinary victory had been rapidly eroded by contacts within the game suggesting that the opposition must have been up to something to fold so precipitously. Despite his insistence that he would have known if batsmen weren't trying or contriving to give their wickets away, he could tell that his friends and acquaintances were unconvinced.

In June 2012 India's cricket board, the BCCI, banned five domestic players who had been caught up in an undercover TV sting, though no fixing had actually ensued. Three months later, Sheriful Haque became the first Bangladesh player to be banned for spot-fixing.

In November 2015, five years after Butt, Amir and Asif had stood trial there, Southwark Crown Court witnessed another extraordinary prosecution involving cricketers. New Zealander Lou Vincent, 36, had already admitted 18 breaches of regulations including fixing the outcome of a county championship match in England, but he had also said that his 'role model', compatriot and captain Chris Cairns had drawn him into the conspiracy while they were both playing for the Chandigarh Lions in India.

Role model was no exaggeration because, for almost a decade, Cairns, whose father had also played for his country, was its best and most high-profile player. Cairns did not face charges as a result of Vincent's accusations and subsequently sued when IPL chairman Lalit Modi made, via Twitter, what he complained was 'an unequivocal allegation' that he was a fixer. He won but the New Zealander then found himself in Southwark on perjury charges stemming from his evidence in the libel trial, with Vincent as the star witness. Cairns was found not guilty but the proceedings left another huge stain on the game.

In 2019 Sanath Jayasuriya, one of the stars of Sri Lanka's shock 1996 World Cup triumph, was banned for failing to co-operate with the anti-corruption unit (ACU, as it was now known). Jayasuriya had twice served as chairman of selectors of the national team from 2013–17. Even in February 2020, just a few weeks before the Pakistan Super League was shut down due to Covid-19, Umar Akmal, brother of Kamran, was suspended under Article 4.7.1 of the PCB anti-corruption code. Reports alleged that he had failed to notify the board of an approach by a bookie.

This was the same Umar Akmal who had, in December 2010, raged against the slurs Mazhar Majeed had uttered about him in conversation with the *News of the World*'s undercover reporter: 'I can't even think of being involved in such practices. I don't know why he has taken my name, he is a liar.' On 28 April 2020 Umar was banned for three years for two breaches of Pakistan's anti-corruption code. Of those whom Majeed claimed he acted for, he is the only cricketer beyond the 'Lord's Three' to have suffered this fate. Beyond those four, none of the others with whom he implied he had had dealings, have faced similar accusations and all deny impropriety, blaming the agent for making false claims about them.

The week before Akmal was charged, Nasir Jamshed, who had represented Pakistan between 2008 and 2013, was sentenced to a 17-month prison term for his role in spot-fixing T20 matches in the Bangladesh Premier League in 2016. Jamshed had already been banned for ten years from cricket after being found guilty under the game's anti-corruption code for activities during the 2017 Pakistan Super League. Also implicated in that scandal were fellow cricketers Sharjeel Khan and Khalid Latif, who were handed five-year bans; Mohammad Irfan and Shahzaib Hasan who were given much shorter suspensions; while Mohammad Nawaz received only a two-month suspension for failure to report an approach by bookmakers. Like Nasir Jamshed, they had all played international cricket in the previous decade.

It did not reflect well on the PCB that it waived the last half of Sharjeel's ban after he had issued an apology for 'irresponsible conduct that brought embarrassment to everyone', but actually stopped short of admitting his guilt. Nor had the board learnt some of the more practical lessons about trying to ward off the money men, as broadcaster Ejaz Wasim said in November 2018: 'Cricket in Pakistan is still not professional, there are no professional anti-match-fixing personnel on the Pakistan Cricket Board. At the Asia Cup in the United Arab Emirates [in September], I didn't see a single Indian player in the lobby of the hotel that they were staying in but saw many Pakistani players with no security. They were walking around, in malls and restaurants without permission and no one is checking. It is so easy for them to be approached by anyone who may make offers.'

The main problem though for the PCB, their fellow national bodies and the ICC was that they were all playing an endless game of catch-up. As the years went by, another T20 competition would spring up, often in some part of the world where betting regulations and law enforcement fell short of what was required to cut out the cancer. In these circumstances, the familiar gambling cartels, and some new ones, wasted no time in moving in for the fix.

The Bangladesh Premier League had been set up in 2012, the Caribbean Premier League a year later, the Pakistan Super League in 2016. Out of that came T10 competitions. Wherever you looked on the sporting landscape pop-up events were appearing, and cricketers from all nations were offering their services. The idea of a professional committing to the same local team for his career and hoping an international call-up would follow was as dated as the notion of a batsman 'walking'. Many players – decent but not stars – now effectively lived the life of a mercenary, moving from one continent and franchise to another throughout the year.

In this carousel existence, ties of loyalty were not strong and matches could soon lose meaning. The life of a mercenary is a precarious one, and if money is on offer it usually pays to take it. In some cases, this meant the bookies' cash. Even the Indian Premier League, where the greatest names in the world were banking six-

and seven-figure cheques for six weeks' work, wasn't immune. The 2013 spot-fixing scandal involving the Chennai Super Kings was described by the country's superstar MS Dhoni, who was not even implicated, as 'the most difficult phase in my life'.

There was something else, though, about this wave of negative publicity for which cricket could not be held wholly culpable. The *News of the World*'s investigation was the fix heard around the world. It caught the attention not only of the sporting world but also of the wider media. All of a sudden, editors began to realise that sport might be fertile terrain for investigative journalism. After all, what could be nobler than fearless reporters rooting out wrongdoing that the police forces had failed to spot or tackle? And what would grab readers' attention better than their sporting idols unmasked as frauds?

An equally significant boon to this cottage industry was provided when the *Sunday Times* was globally extolled for its long and lone pursuit of doping cyclist Lance Armstrong, who finally admitted his transgressions in late 2012. But these things are easier said than done. To pursue such lines of inquiry requires time, personnel and money. None of these commodities has been in healthy supply in media organisations in recent years. Nor is there any guarantee of a 'result' at the end of it all.

Still, in December 2017, *The Sun* thought it was on to something big when a front-page splash ('We smash plot to fix cricket') reported that 'Cricket chiefs launched a probe last night after *The Sun* handed over a bombshell dossier on attempts to fix the third Ashes Test. Two bookies offered to sell us details of rigged periods of play which could be gambled on to win millions of pounds. They asked for up to £140,000 to "spot fix" markets such as the exact amount of runs scored in an over. The Indian Mr Big said: "Before match, I will tell you this over, this runs and then you have to put all the bets on that over." Asked if it was a good source he said: "Absolutely correct information."

'The pair reeled off players they say work as their "puppets". They also claimed to be working with a fixer in Australian cricket known as The Silent Man. He is said to work with former and current internationals including a World Cup-winning all-rounder.'

Despite the bold headline, there was little hard evidence of any concerted plot, as was confirmed two months later when Alex Marshall, the ICC's anti-corruption general manager, reported back on the findings of that probe: 'We have carried out an extensive global investigation with anti-corruption colleagues from member countries based on the allegations in *The Sun* and the material they shared with us. I am satisfied that there is no evidence to suggest any match has been corrupted by the individuals in the investigation, nor is there any indication that any international players, administrators or coaches have been in contact with the alleged fixers.'

In 2018 it was the turn of Al Jazeera, the major broadcasting network in the Middle East and the Arab/Muslim world, to poke around the darker corners of the game. David Harrison, an English journalist working for its investigation unit, produced documentaries in May and October that year. The usual shady individuals from Asia were filmed making grandiose claims about how deep their tentacles stretched, leading Harrison to write for the Al Jazeera website that 'the evidence, from 2011 and 2012, points to a small group of England players allegedly carrying out spot-fixes in seven matches; Australia players in five matches; Pakistan players in three, with players from other teams carrying out spot-fixes in one match. In some cases, both teams appear to have delivered a fix … Al Jazeera has obtained purported recordings of a match-fixer calling in the fixes to a notorious Indian bookmaker linked to organised crime. He is unaware that the recordings were leaked.'

The fixer at the heart of their story was Aneel Munawar, whom the BBC's *Panorama* had already tried to reel in before abandoning the project. Munawar was clearly up to no good and the suggestion that fixers were now trying to tap up groundsmen tallied with what was suspected. Yet again, however, the more outlandish claims looked tenuous, as indicated by Harrison's use of such phrases as 'points to', 'allegedly', 'appear to have', and 'purported'. Nor did the fact that the broadcaster had refused to hand over some of its tapes to the ICC help its cause.

Both these episodes merely confirmed that in this particular domain the *News of the World* story had been the gold standard – irrefutable evidence of fixing, in a Test between two major nations, at the home of cricket, with all those involved subsequently sent to jail. No one who has gone down this path since has even come close to hitting that sweet spot.

On 24 May 2019 Alex Marshall convened a press briefing at the Ken Barrington Cricket Centre at The Oval ground. The World Cup was just a week away so it seemed like the perfect time to update the media on how his ACU was going about its business. The turnout wasn't huge, probably about 15 journalists gathered in what usually would have been an indoor nets facility.

Marshall told the throng that he had identified potential corruptors of the tournament, and 'I have communicated with them which includes letters to solicitors, phone calls and WhatsApp communications. If they are seen here, at the ground, they will be thrown out. We have shared their details with the law enforcement and the police here in the UK – if our guys see them anywhere around the World Cup, they will be asked to leave.

'It's around a dozen people who have had the "disinvite" to the Cricket World Cup 2019 and who we will keep away. If any more pop up, we will be speaking to them as well. They are people who live all over the world but the majority of the corruption we deal with has its origins in the subcontinent, unregulated betting markets.' In other words, not much had changed.

A year after Marshall's speech, the former sports minister in Sri Lanka, Mahindananda Aluthgamage, accused his own team of deliberately losing the 2011 World Cup final. He produced no evidence to back up this claim but the ministry launched an inquiry and Kumar Sangakarra, the golden boy of Sri Lankan cricket who had played in the game and was President of the MCC, was asked to answer questions. To date no allegations of impropriety have been made about any fixtures at the 2019 tournament. It constitutes a victory of sorts for the ICC that this is the first time since the 2003 World Cup that it has been able to say that.

BIBLIOGRAPHY

Afridi, S., *Game Changer* (HarperCollins, 2019)

Brearley, M., *On Cricket* (Constable, 2018)

Mahmood, M., *Confessions of a Fake Sheikh* (HarperCollins, 2008)

Marqusee, M., *Anyone but England* (Two Heads Publishing, 1998)

Oborne, P., *Wounded Tiger: A History of Cricket in Pakistan* (Simon & Schuster, 2014)

Strauss, A., *Driving Ambition: My Autobiography* (Hodder & Stoughton, 2013)

Wilde, S., *Ian Botham: The Power and the Glory* (Simon & Schuster, 2011)

The following judicial reports were also of great use:

King, Justice E.L., *Commission of Inquiry into cricket match fixing and related matters* (South Africa, 2000)

Qayyum, Justice M.M ,. *Commission of Inquiry* (Pakistan, 2000)

Beloff, Hon M., Sachs, Justice A., Rao, S., *ICC v Salman Butt, Mohammad Asif and Mohammad Amir determination* (2011)

Other important sources include:
Reports on the case by ESPN Cricinfo and my colleagues in the British print media, in particular Mike Atherton's special report on Mohammad Amir in *The Times* on 20 March 2012 which draws heavily on his Sky SportS interview with the cricketer, also in March 2012

Also available at all good book stores

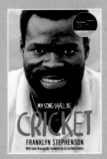

9781785316920

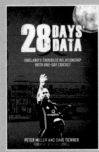

9781785315053

9781785314889

9781785314865

9781785314377

9781785311628

9781785314070

9781785315053

9781785311314